D1084785

Modern Greek Humor

Ethelyn G. Orso

Modern Greek Humor

A Collection of Jokes and Ribald Tales

INDIANA UNIVERSITY PRESS   *Bloomington & London*

Manufactured in the United States of America

Library of Congress Cataloging in Publication Data

Orso, Ethelyn, 1941—
Modern Greek humor.

Bibliography: p. 259
Includes index.
1. Greek wit and humor, Modern. I. Title.
PN6222.G707   889.71008   78-24845
ISBN 0-253-16336-6   1 2 3 4 5 83 82 81 80 79

To my parents, Carlos McLeod Orso, who traveled on ships throughout the world and who inspired me to visit those far-away places with strange-sounding names, and Ethel Touard Orso, who taught me to overcome fear, to run, and to travel.

Contents

PREFACE

Ἑκαταῖο Μιλήσιος ὧδε μυθεῖται τάδε ῥάφω, ὥς μοι δοκεῖ ἀληθέα εῖναι.
οἱ γὰρ Ἑλλήνων λόγοι τολλοί τε καί γελοῖοι, ὡς ᾽εμοί φαίνονται, ᾽ιδίν.

Hekataios the Milesian tells the story as follows: I write these things as they
seem to me to be true; for the tales of the Greeks are many and laughable, as
they appear to me.

Hekataios, *Fragment 1.*, FHG
(First half of fifth century B.C.)

From the time of Hekataios the Milesian (a Greek) to today, some
things have not changed in Greece at all. Greeks still tell many funny
stories.[1] Their persistence in doing so made my research very easy.
Finding informants who knew ten or twenty jokes was not difficult, nor
was meeting true raconteurs, individuals who could tell jokes with
great skill for hours straight, a serious problem. Indeed, the average
Greek man, woman, or child whom I met usually could tell me one or
two jokes without any effort at all.

The period of time during which this material was collected, from
June 1976 to late May 1977, was one of the happiest of my life. Possessing a great love for Greece and a year's sabbatical leave from my
teaching duties as an anthropologist and folklorist, equipped with a
good portable tape recorder, and able to speak and understand standard (informal) modern Greek, I set off on my own personal odyssey to
do field work in Greece.

Originally I had planned to do traditional anthropological field work
in the main village of an island near Piraeus. I lived for four months
there with a family of Greek-Albanian origin whose relatives in New
Orleans had arranged my stay. I was interested in producing a mono-
graph on some aspect of village life such as folk medicine or women's
folklore. I gave up that project for reasons I have described elsewhere.[2]
Basically, the problem was my inability to adapt to an acceptable role
in the community or to devise a comfortable role for myself.

In late September 1976, I visited the Social Science Research Center in Athens (as I frequently did) to allow my two colleagues in anthropology there to hear some tapes of women's bawdy lore that I had recorded in the village. Both of them encouraged me to pursue that type of material further, as it had been totally neglected in previous studies of Greek folklore.

I returned to New Orleans in early October 1976 undecided about my future research plans. American politics also had affected my situation in Greece. The Turkish invasion of Cyprus in 1974 had caused many Greeks to become strongly anti-American, particularly in regard to American foreign policy as represented by Henry Kissinger, then secretary of state. That I had experienced many unpleasant conversations simply because I was an American made me hesitant about spending another long period in Greece. I finally decided that, if Jimmy Carter won the presidential election in November 1976, I would return to Greece. As Carter had promised to replace Kissinger as secretary of state and to help solve the Cyprus question, I knew there would be a different atmosphere in Greece for Americans if he were elected.

Carter won and luckily I was right. On my first day in Crete, in late November 1976, I picked up a middle-aged woman on the road and drove her to her village. It was her belief that President Carter (whom she idolized) had been elected by the votes of the Greek-Americans, a belief I was to hear expressed repeatedly during the following six months. Thus the last period of my field work, from November 1976 to the end of May 1977, was much more pleasant and productive than the first period. The "honeymoon" with Carter was in effect during that time, and Greeks were again generally favorably disposed to Americans.

After deciding to return to Greece, I shifted the focus and scope of my research project. I decided that I would try to do with humor what Ellen Frye (1973) had done with Greek folksongs. I bought an old second-hand car and traveled about Greece. I assumed the truthful and very comfortable role of a foreign schoolteacher collecting funny stories for a book on Greek humor. I did not live with any families during this time.

During my stay in Crete, I had the invaluable help of Mikhalis Karbadakis, a friend whom I had met in 1973 in New Orleans. In 1976 Karbadakis, a native of Crete, was stationed with the Greek army near Heraklion. He agreed to help collect and interpret material from Crete. We worked together for the entire period of my last stay in Greece.

Although he does not speak English, he had lived for many years in Piraeus and spoke a more standard Greek; he thus was able to help me to understand the jokes and stories that I collected from persons who had Cretan accents unfamiliar to me. Not only did he provide a number of the jokes in this collection, but also he accompanied me on trips to many villages in Crete where we collected together. Without his help in both collecting and interpreting, my project would have been nearly impossible in Crete.

After four months in Crete, I moved to Athens for the last two months of my stay. During the first month I lived in a pension in Plaka, the old section of Athens. During the second month I resided in the dormitory of the American School of Classical Studies in Athens, where I received invaluable assistance and encouragement from Professor Colin Edmonson.

While living in Athens, I met and interviewed a wide variety of Greeks from many different regions of Greece, including Hios (Chios), Samos, the Peloponnesus, Thessaloniki, Alexandroupolis, Rhodes, and elsewhere. Also, I interviewed people of Greek origin from Cyprus and Russia. From Athens I made short field trips and weekend trips to surrounding villages to collect material there. Throughout the entire period of my research, I also visited Piraeus, Karditsa, Thiva, Ioannina, Korinthos, and the islands of Crete, Mykonos, Siros, Tinos, Paros, Salamis, and Aegina.

While engaged in my research in Greece, I employed standard anthropological techniques associated with participant observation as well as methods borrowed from American folklorists. Probably my most important tactic was to collect jokes primarily from groups rather than from solitary informants. The existence of the *paréa*,[3] a Greek social unit most easily described as an informal friendship group, facilitated that well-known technique. Although I obtained the material in this collection mainly by direct solicitation, its presentation within the *paréa* assumed a natural context. I collected from people in *paréa* setting in many types of environments: private homes, shops, offices, restaurants, coffeehouses, nightclubs, and a classroom. Unfortunately, I was unable to collect frequently in typical life-crisis situations (weddings, baptisms, funerals), but I did collect several times at name-day parties.

I collected from a wide range of informants, including peasants, shepherds, mechanics, students, teachers, professors, fishermen, shop-owners and shopkeepers, waiters, secretaries, lawyers, a judge, maids, sailors (both in commerce and in the Greek navy), soldiers, housewives, cab drivers, artists, chanters in the Greek Orthodox Church, intellectuals, construction workers, one mathematician, unmarried women with no occupations, seamstresses, hotel keepers, kiosk (*periptero*) owners and operators, clerks, butchers, errand boys, and others. Most of my informants were adults; however, I also interviewed adolescents while I taught English conversation in a night school in Heraklion, Crete, for two months. I was also able to interview several youngsters who were relatives of my informants. Probably none of my informants belongs to the "aristocratic" class, that is, the highest social stratum in Greece. Although all of my informants (numbering over one hundred) knew that I was collecting jokes for a book on Greek humor, I did not secure written permission to use their names in association with the particular jokes that they told me, and for that reason I do not include their names in this book.

I frequently went into the all-male domain of the coffeehouse (*cafenion*) to collect jokes. As a foreign woman I escaped the taboos placed on Greek women to avoid the *cafenion*. After explaining my purpose, usually to the owner, I typically was invited to join a *paréa* of Greeks sitting together in the establishment, was treated to coffee or to something stronger, and was told as many jokes as the men could remember. Those sessions frequently went on for many hours, with some men leaving and others joining the *paréa*. Since I began my intensive collecting in the winter, most of the people engaged in agriculture had little or no work and were happy to pass their time in a joke-telling session. Few tourists were around then, and the pace of life was very slow.

I tape-recorded jokes as they were being told to me only when I had permission. On many occasions, however, when I had planned to go out to do some shopping, I wound up collecting jokes instead; in those instances, when I did not have the tape recorder with me, I took notes during and after the telling of the jokes and stories. In some cases I simply had to rely on memory and write the jokes later when I returned home.

I always laughed heartily at the jokes my informants told me, whether I initally understood them or not and whether I had heard them before or not. As most joke tellers seem to dislike being interrupted during their narration to explain a word or phrase, and as asking too many questions at the end of a joke breaks the flow of a joke-telling session, I relied on my field assistant, Mikhalis Karbadakis, to explain jokes to me from the tapes that I did not initially understand. I hope that my informants will forgive that dishonesty on my part. Of course, on those occasions when I was not tape-recording the material it was necessary to have difficult jokes explained to me on the spot. Moreover, Greeks are like Americans in that Greeks also do not like to tell a person a joke if he or she has heard it before (see Legman 1968). Here also I was dishonest because I usually pretended that I had not heard a joke before in order to collect, as an important part of standard folklore research, second and third versions of the same joke.

Many persons who read the manuscript of this book were surprised that I was able to collect the ribald material. They were under the impression that airing such material in the presence of a woman, especially a single woman, would be taboo in a traditional society such as that of Greece. I found, however, that once my informants realized that they would not embarrass or offend me with their stories and jokes and that I could laugh genuinely at a good joke, dirty or not, the ice was broken and the way was open for an uninhibited joke-telling session to proceed.

Many Greek men who told me *sókin* ("dirty") jokes in the *paréa* setting, however, did not look at me while they told the jokes. In other words, they told the jokes *for* me but not *to* me. Thus, especially at those times when their words were being tape-recorded, they could give me accurate versions of the jokes and stories without any of the embarrassment that normally would have occurred had I been collecting from one informant alone or had we maintained direct eye contact. Occasionally I encountered lecherous men (of all ages) who probably took advantage of my request for jokes to tell me the very *sókin* ones that they normally would tell only to other men or to their wives (or girlfriends). Legman (1968, 1975) has suggested that a man's telling dirty jokes to a woman is a substitute sex act. Such a motivation may have been present in some instances during the course of my research, but I do not feel that one can generalize broadly about all such joke telling. Moreover, I often collected different versions of the same *sókin* jokes from women in all-female groups and in mixed groups, and those women could not be accused of telling those jokes in my presence for the reasons Legman has suggested.

In translating the material into English, I have tried to preserve some of the characteristics of spoken folklore. Thus some of the translations are repetitive; for instance, the word "well" is frequently used in pauses, as we use it or as we say "and uh" in America. Many jokes are in the form of a dialogue, and I have kept the dialogue form in the translation. To help the reader who has neither visited nor read very much about Greece understand the jokes, I have added my own explanations, analyses, or interpretations where I thought they would be useful. In offering my interpretations of the jokes vis-à-vis modern Greek culture, I like to feel that I am acting somewhat as a modern-day Hekataios, since I, too, write these things as they seem to me to be true.

I have tried to avoid Americanizing the jokes any more than was absolutely necessary. The joke that has diffused to another country behaves as do all other borrowed elements of culture: it assumes native or local characteristics. It usually undergoes some change to suit the new linguistic and cultural environments, but it remains basically the same joke. While engaged in the research and preparation of this book, I encountered a good deal of skepticism about whether the collected jokes were funny in English. Doubt stems partly from the awareness of the difficulties in translating some jokes into foreign languages, but bilingual people do so spontaneously every day, as probably has been the case throughout human history. With modern communications jokes can circle the globe in a matter of days, leaping language barriers with the ease of Olympic high-jumpers. I have tried to include the funniest jokes and tales in this collection, but some of the material probably will not seem very amusing to some readers.

I should like to express my deepest gratitude to the many Greeks who served as informants for this book and who made my research so enjoyable and entertaining. My gratitude goes also to those many others whose hospitality and help made the collection possible. They are too numerous to mention by name, however, and may even wish to remain anonymous.

I particularly would like to thank Gregory Gizelis, Deputy Director, Research Department, National Center of Social Research in Athens, a Greek-born ethnographer and folklorist of the highest caliber, whom I first met in 1974 and who initially encouraged me in 1976 to pursue the study of modern Greek humor. His counseling, advice, and constant encouragement throughout my field research were indispensable to the project.

Very special thanks go to Mikhalis Karbadakis, who told me the first joke I ever heard about Anogia, my favorite village in Crete; and to Munro Edmonson for his critical reading of the first draft.

I also wish to express my gratitude to Alan Dundes of the University of California, Berkeley, who, by his criticisms and suggestions in regard to an early draft of the manuscript, made substantial contributions to this book. His encouragement gave me the needed impetus to complete the book in its final form.

Introduction

Greek society is very complex, and life in the rural Greek villages differs greatly from that in the large urban areas. Except for a veneer of technology, life in the villages has not changed drastically for over two thousand years in regard to folklore, particularly folk religion and folk customs (see Polites 1871–74; Nilsson 1940; Lawson 1964; Kyriakides 1968). Resistance to change is due primarily to the conservatism, traditionalism, and ethnocentrism of the Greek peasant. On the other hand, Athens is very much a part of today's world and faces the same problems as do all large, modern cities. Greeks who live in Athens enjoy, if they wish, very cosmopolitan life-styles, and many women in Athens are among the most fashionably dressed in Europe.

Greeks differ considerably by physical type and by regionalism. In the 1920s the exchange of populations between Turkey and Greece brought many (twenty-five percent of Greece's total population) foreign-born individuals of Greek background into the country. Five percent of the population in Greece speaks other languages, principally Turkish, Bulgarian, Serbian, Albanian, and Romany (the language of the Gypsies). The groups represented by those languages have also influenced contemporary Greek culture.

Perhaps one of the most important factors that accounts for Greek diversity is age. Some young people in Greece, especially those who, because of limited space in the Greek universities, go abroad to study, have values and life-styles quite different from those of the older generation. Probably the majority of young people, however, follow a traditional life-style with no desire to change or to imitate foreign (European or American) models. Modern education plus living in the modern world, influenced by television and movies, may account for many of the age-related differences among Greeks.

Socioeconomic factors are also significant in creating diversity in Greece. Although Greece has had a parliamentary democracy since the overthrow of the military dictatorship that governed from 1967 to 1974, I found that Greeks are more class conscious than are Americans and that Greek society is more highly stratified than is American society. The introduction of a king into Greece in 1833 by the European "big powers" (Russia, England, and France) produced class divisions and awarenesses that can be observed today, despite Greece's democracy. Many Greeks, citing family position, prestige, and wealth, still consider themselves "aristocrats."

The two Greek languages further facilitate class consciousness. Only the well educated are able to speak *katharévusa,* the formal language; all others have great difficulty understanding it. Informal Greek, *dhimotikí,* is known by all. The "aristocrats" can communicate with the "people" in *dhimotikí,* but the "people" are unable to address the "aristocrats" in *katharévusa.* (See joke 111, which ridicules the poor villager's situation vis-à-vis *katharévusa.*)

Also, the presence of two distinct grammatical forms for second-person pronouns and verbs (found also in many other Indo-European languages such as Spanish, French, and German, but lacking in English), facilitates class consciousness. In addressing another person the speaker must choose the singular form (indicating informality) or the plural form (indicating respect). A young Greek woman whom I know once complained that an arrogant Greek had dared to address her in the "singular" (the informal). Her complaints indicated that he had failed to show the respect she thought she merited or that he tried to be "familiar," that is, to flirt with her.

Despite their complexity and diversity, however, I have dared in this book to generalize about "Greeks" in terms of their attitudes, values, and behavior patterns. I am aware of the exceptions; nevertheless, Greeks share many common elements, and those elements unite in what anthropologists call "culture."

Although I did not manage to visit as many places in Greece as I had hoped to, I feel that the collection is representative of Greek humor in general. Some jokes that I first heard in small, remote villages in the mountains of Crete I later heard in Athens from people from Macedonia. There is nothing to stop the spread of jokes within Greece, and the large amount of travel by Greeks within their own country facilitates the spread of jokes. Some avid joke tellers even call their friends long distance to tell them the "latest" jokes.

Greeks travel extensively in their own country for many reasons. The government-imposed economic restrictions on foreign travel make it difficult for the average Greek to travel abroad simply as a tourist. Most Greeks are very hardworking, and many never take extended vacations; instead, they make business trips or weekend trips on the ample holidays to visit the towns and villages of relatives and friends or to see places they have never seen before. As Greece has always been an important maritime country, the many Greek men who work on fishing boats, ferries, and cruise ships in Greek waters also get to do a lot of traveling inside Greece. Even Greek women, who spend the greater part of their lives inside their homes, are more and more often taking excursions by "pullman" bus to go sightseeing, to attend cultural events (summer drama festivals), or to make religious pilgrimages. Their excursions are composed mostly of all-female groups, with a few elderly, married men along. (I made several such excursions in the summer of 1976 for the purpose of collecting women's folklore.)

Humor is a basic part of the (internal) travel because Greeks like to "pass the time"[1] by having fun; jokes and laughter provide the necessary ingredients. For example, on my return to America in May 1977, during the ten-hour, non-stop flight from Athens to New York, I sat next to an elderly Greek couple, whom I did not know, from the Peloponnesus. These people, especially the seventy-five-year-old husband, amused me throughout the flight with funny "stories," jokes, wit, pantomine, crazy remarks, and the like, without their even knowing that I not only had a special interest in, but also had been collecting, similar material. When I began writing some of the jokes in a small notebook, they began performing even more. When, exhausted, we reached New York, they said, "We passed the trip really beautifully, didn't we? We had jokes and teasing, and we really laughed a lot! When you come to Greece the next time, be sure to come and visit us!" (Note the traditional Greek hospitality.)

Greek humor covers an extremely broad range of topics, but much of it is earthy, off-color, or bawdy. According to Richard Dorson (1972:30), the joke, particularly the off-color joke, is the major folk narrative genre in contemporary society. Dorson may have been speaking only of contemporary American society, but the same appears to me to be true of contemporary Greek society. As a subgenre of the folktale (Brunvand 1968:109), the joke has largely replaced the folktale in American humor. This is not the case in Greece, where the joke and the humorous, bawdy folktale exist side by side as the two major genres of Greek humor. Indeed, many of the folktales in this collection date to the Middle Ages, at least, when they were included in the Italian *Novella* (see Rotunda 1942).

Gershon Legman, the undisputed authority on erotic folklore, and Dorson both remarked not too long ago that there have been no accurate collections of orally collected jokes in any language (Dorson 1972:30). The present collection is one of the recent efforts to fill that gap in our understanding of humor, in Greece and elsewhere, because jokes usually have international analogues (see Legman 1968). Many in this collection probably originated in countries outside Greece. Since a number of Greeks travel regularly between Athens and New York, it is not surprising that many jokes included here are well known in America. (Note, for example, all the references in the text to Legman's two collections [1968, 1975] of jokes in English).

Until the recent past a very negative attitude toward the scholarly study and publication of bawdy folklore prevailed in the United States and in Europe.[2] A classic example of a previously unpublished work is Vance Randolph's *Pissing in the*

Snow and Other Ozark Folktales (1976).[3] Randolph had published several collections of Ozark folklore, but publishers would not print the "obscene" material in his collections, which he placed together and circulated in manuscript form for twenty years among scholars (such as Legman) interested in bawdy humor. That the material was finally published in 1976 was due in large part to the efforts of Rayna Green.[4] As Legman and Green have pointed out, one absurd aspect of the puritanical attitude toward scholarly studies of bawdy material is that at the same time such material was refused publication, pornographic books such as *Candy* were available in bookstores, drugstores, and even supermarkets all over the country.

Collections of folklore published both in the United States and in Greece have been censored to eliminate bawdy elements. Sometimes the censorship occurred in the collecting; at other times it occurred at the publisher's insistence. In most cases, however, we are totally in the dark as to who censored the "offensive" material; the absence of even a reference to omitted material leaves the false impression that it does not exist. An example of that kind of censorship occurred in the case of George Megas' *Folktales of Greece* (1970).

Megas has spent a considerable portion of his life studying Greek folklore, especially Greek folktales, of which he is the living authority. When asked to put together a collection of Greek folktales for the *Folktales of the World* series (University of Chicago Press, 1963–) Megas evidently chose only those that contained no off-color, or bawdy, elements. The collection that he presented conforms to the image that many nonfolklorists have of folklore: that it is "quaint" and "charming." I noticed only one example of his material's overlapping with mine, and that is his Tale 66, "The Honest Wife." Megas' tale is clearly a variant of my joke 264, which concerns the use of sodomy as a means of revenge. Both versions are probably variants of Tale Type 1730, The Entrapped Suitors, in the Aarne-Thompson system. I heard the tale on several occasions and in several places—in Crete, in Athens, and even in New Orleans from a Greek from Hios—and all versions contained the element of sodomy for revenge, absent from Megas' version.[5]

Thus Megas' *Folktales of Greece* and other collections in English of Greek folktales (Dawkins 1950, 1953) have given a distorted picture of the real nature of the expressive behavior of the Greek people. By keeping certain material out of print, publishers and folklorists have not eliminated it. And by collecting it and printing it, one certainly does not give it a life or an existence that it would not otherwise have. When I began my project of collecting examples of Greek humor in 1976, I decided to collect everything that I heard incidentally or was told directly. I later decided not to censor the material because I wish to give an accurate picture of Greek expressive behavior vis-à-vis humor for those who wish to understand and appreciate it. This collection may offend some people, but its doing so is certainly not my intention.

In annotating the material, I have relied on the following: (1) Gershon Legman's *Rationale of the Dirty Joke*, two volumes, which I call Legman I and Legman II. (2) Antti Aarne's *The Types of the Folktale*, translated by Stith Thompson. Tale-type numbers are preceded by AT and followed by the tale-type titles. Appendix A lists in numerical order the tale-type numbers, along with the numbers of the relevant items in this collection. (3) Stith Thompson's *Motif-Index of Folk Literature*, six volumes.[6] The motif numbers are preceded by an alphabet letter and are followed by a verbal description. Appendix B lists in numerical order the motif numbers, along with the numbers of the relevant items in this collection. (4) Frank A. Hoffmann's *An Analytical Survey of Anglo-American Traditional Erotica*, in which he proposes tale-type numbers for the gaps in Thompson's *Motif-Index* such as X700.–X799., Jokes concerning sex. Hoffmann's numbers appear in italics in appendix B and throughout the text.

The two main concerns of Greek humor appear to be erotic themes and deception. That jokes involving sexual humor occur in every chapter of the book should by itself say a lot. The list of motif numbers in appendix B demonstrates that the material is heavily weighted toward clever trickery and deception; the majority of motif numbers (from Thompson's *Motif-Index*) are in "J: The Wise and the Foolish" and "K: Deceptions."

Another element found in thirty percent of the jokes in this collection is the magical number· three. Classicists, anthropologists, and folklorists label it magical because of its constant ritualistic use in Western civilization. The three-patterning of jokes and of culture in general both in the United States (see Dundes 1968) and in Greece is one proof of the close relationship of our two cultures.[7] In both Greek and American humor, actions are usually repeated three times, with something funny occurring on the third time. In other cases, the joke involves three principals. Greek humor goes a step further by revealing that even sexual actions are three-patterned (see, for example, jokes 202, 270, and 288).[8] The three pattern is ancient in Greek culture, but one can only speculate as to its origin (see also Dundes 1968).

Greeks usually use the word *anékdota* for what we in America would call a joke. Two other words are also used in Greek for jokes: *astéia*, a silly (thing), and *historía*, a story. The word *athivolés* is used in Crete for what American folklorists usually call anecdotes. Greek jokes, many of which are actually folktales, usually begin with standard opening phrases: *Kápote* ("Sometime"), *Mia forá* ("One time"), or *Mia forá, ópos to léne* ("One time, as they tell it"). The opening phrase is followed by a distinct pause, which I indicate by a comma after the phrase.

The material in this collection is arranged as a compromise between my two academic interests: anthropology and folklore. As an anthropologist, I wanted to present the material in the native categories of my informants. This method of classification posed some unpredictable difficulties that I was unable completely to overcome. In trying to elicit native Greek categories of humor, I often asked my informants to tell me how many different kinds of jokes there are. Many said that there are only two kinds: the *sókin* ("dirty") and *elefrá* ("light," meaning nondirty). Other informants insisted that there are three kinds of jokes: *sókin*, political, and satirical.

One of my informants, who could be considered a true raconteur, suggested two broad categories: general and *sókin*. Under the heading of "general," he listed the following subcategories: satirical, political, family situation, occupational, and local. He

divided the *sókin* category into two types: very *sókin* and little
sókin. I have used a somewhat modified version of his system:
chapters one through seven contain general jokes; chapters
eight and nine contain *sókin* jokes.

The main problem in obtaining a complete classification of
Greek humor from my Greek informants was that most of them
preferred not to categorize jokes if they could avoid doing so.
Most informants ignored my question about categories and
simply told me jokes. Greeks in general seem to prefer to relate
to real things such as people and jokes instead of to abstractions
such as categories. That the verb *to categorize* in popular Greek
means "to criticize," or "to condemn," may also be significant.
Nonetheless, joke-telling sessions in Greece seem to proceed
by joke association; that is, one political joke will evoke another
political joke, one parrot joke another parrot joke, and so on.
Joke telling is usually a reciprocal exchange, although not
exactly a verbal duel; a thing or an event in a joke told by one
person will evoke an association in the mind of a listener, who
will probably tell the next joke from that association.

In classifying the material as a folklorist, I inserted chapters
that my informants did not give me and probably would not
have thought of giving me. Chapters three and four, which deal
respectively with esoteric and exoteric Greek humor, are
examples of the type of scholarly intrusion suggested by
William Hugh Jansen (1965).

Most of the chapter headings in this book are those that I
began using during the period of research. That they point to
valid categories of jokes became apparent when, for example, I
could elicit jokes from informants by asking "Do you know a
Bobos joke?" or "Do you know any jokes about priests?" Some
of my original chapters needed subdivisions, particularly chapter eight, "Very *Sókin* Jokes." These subheadings come from the
material itself, not merely from my interpretation of it. I did not
follow Legman's classification, nor do I agree with it.

Other categories of jokes, which, because I had only a few
examples of each, I did not treat in separate chapters, but where
possible placed among other categories, include Greek Army
jokes,[9] practical jokes (true stories), lie jokes, "catch" jokes,

jokes about bars and drunks, jokes about deformed people (stutterers and the deaf), historical jokes (about famous Greek heroes such as Alexander the Great and Kolokotronis), circus jokes, jokes involving poems or other material difficult to translate, jokes about cowboys in the "Old West" (presumably of the United States), and, finally, jokes called "American."

In the same way that we Americans consider English humor "dry" when we do not understand it or find it funny, Greeks have used another Hippocratic concept to describe jokes that they find difficult to understand, not very funny, or perhaps of the "shaggy dog" type: American jokes are said to be "cold." American jokes are not anti-American in the least, nor has there been any hesitation in borrowing such nonsensical American joke fads as elephant jokes. A listener simply calls a joke "American" if he or she considers it obtuse.

The categories represented in the following chapters reflect the most popular ones during the time of my research and from my own point of view. However, another collector might find other categories more popular, depending on the nature of the collector and of the informants interviewed. But I believe this collection presents an accurate picture of contemporary Greek humor, and I hope it will be of value to others who wish to investigate this interesting but neglected part of Greek culture and folklore.

Modern Greek Humor

Chapter 1
Political Jokes

Political jokes that I first began hearing in 1973 and that continue to interest many Greeks are those about the military dictatorship that from April 21, 1967 to late July 1974 ruled Greece, the homeland of democracy. During that time Athens was turned into a city of armed military occupation. Freedom of speech and freedom of the press were totally suspended. It was illegal for more than four people to assemble at the same time without securing permission from the police. (Since Greeks often live in extended families of three generations, the law was especially annoying; a family planning a large dinner had to obtain permission for the rest of the family to come to the house.) The "Junta Triumvirate"—George Papadopoulos, Stelios Paddakos, and Nicholas Makarezos—headed the government.

Following the Junta's rise to power, many celebrated Greeks went into political exile. For example, actress Melina Mercouri went to Paris, and not only was composer and musician Mikis Theodorakis in exile, but also his music was forbidden in Greece because he supposedly was a Communist. In 1967 and 1968 people were arrested for listening to Theodorakis' music, even at cocktail parties in famous hotels in Constitution Square in Athens. Indeed, by 1968 everyone in Greece knew of somebody who had been arrested and tortured by the police.

The fear of not obeying the new laws and of not keeping one's anti-Junta opinions to oneself spread throughout the country. Greek coffeehouses (*cafeníons*), which normally function as centers of news and gossip, were astonishingly quiet during the dictatorship. Men sat drinking silently. Nobody dared to discuss

1

politics. Because the few government newspapers that were available contained no news, most people did not read them.

During my first visit to Greece in the summer of 1973, the majority of Greeks that I met were extremely reluctant to answer my questions about the Junta. Most of those who did talk were uncritical of the situation for fear of reprisals should their words be reported to the police. However, many young Greeks, students, and sailors told me of their contempt for the "Colonels" and even invited me to their parties to listen to Theodorakis records and to discuss politics.

Since one of the functions of humor is to relieve tensions and anxieties, jokes ridiculing the military regime allowed the Greeks to laugh at their plight, and by laughing they could forget their fears and anxieties, for a few moments at least. In the fantasy world of the joke, the teller and listener could poke fun at the leaders, pretend that the situation was different, escape into wishful thinking. Nonetheless, many Greeks whose own relatives were tortured or murdered by the police during that time did not find the jokes funny, and even in 1977 preferred not to listen to them. Anti-Junta jokes were exchanged only between people who knew each other very well, and they were never told in public. Men would leave the *cafenion* to tell such jokes away from strangers.

After the fall of the dictatorship, Greeks spoke of little but politics for months straight. The predominance of politics as a subject of conversation was partly a function of restored freedom of speech following a seven-year period of suppression, but it also reflects the passion with which Greeks view all things political. In general men spend more time discussing and arguing politics, but an increasing number of educated Greek women take part in political discussions. Nevertheless, even today few political jokes are told to foreigners because, as many Greeks told me, "Foreigners don't understand our politics, so they wouldn't understand our jokes." Probably for that reason I was not told many jokes about current politics. The only joke that I heard repeatedly in 1977 ridiculed the president of Greece, Konstantinos Tsatsos, who is extremely short: the joke went "Short, shorter, Tsatsos!" instead of "Short, shorter, shortest." (Since the name "Tsatsos" sounds like the slang word for "pimp" [*tsátsos*], the joke also has a second meaning: "Low, lower, 'pimp.'")

Of the jokes included here, most concerning dictatorships have international analogues and would no doubt be found today in other countries ruled by dictators (see Beckmann 1969; Dundes 1971). Many are World War II jokes that originally involved Hitler, Mussolini, Göering, and Franco. (Indeed, those jokes may come from even earlier wars in Europe.) Papadopoulos, who is satirized in the majority of the jokes in this chapter, did not surface during the first two years following the military takeover, during which time the bulk of anti-Junta jokes involved Paddakos. However, jokes about Paddakos, whom many Greeks hated even more than they hated Papadopoulos because of Paddakos' connection with the secret police, still circulate.

The first anti-Junta joke that I collected in the summer of 1973, and the first to follow below, is still my favorite and continues to circulate in Greece. I do not remember the name of the simpleton who accidently revealed a surprising truth in the joke when I first heard it, but, when I heard it again in 1976 and in 1977, the main character was the precocious lad of barbed tongue and vulgar wit, Bobos, who is currently the trickster king of Greek jokelore from Crete to Macedonia. Although chapter two treats Bobos jokes as a distinct category, I include two here because they are primarily political jokes.

1 Papadopoulos used to make many trips to the rural areas of Greece to tell the people about the "New Government" and to visit the schools. In one village, when the schoolteacher heard that he was coming, she began to instruct the students as to how they must behave when Papadopoulos came.

"Children," she began, "when Papadopoulos comes and asks your name, you must reply, 'My name is the People.' And when he asks for your mother's name, you must say, 'My mother is Greece.' And when he asks you for your father's name, you must say, 'My father is the New Government.'"

Well, Papadopoulos came and everything was going fine until the dictator came to Bobos and said:

"What's your name?"

"Bobos."

"And who is your father?"

"Petros."

"And who is your mother?"

"Helene."

After Papadopoulos left the schoolteacher scolded Bobos and told him that he must write one thousand times: "I am the People, my Mother is Greece, and my Father is the Junta" as his punishment.

So Bobos went home and started writing his punish work. At dinner time his mother called him to dinner, but he said that he could not eat just then because he had so much homework.

When Bobos finally finished writing, it was very late and he was very hungry. So he went to the kitchen, but there was no food left. So he went to tell his mother that he was hungry, and he walked into his parents' bedroom and saw them making love.

"Oh, my God!" said Bobos. "The Junta is fucking Greece and the People are hungry!"

[D1273.1.1., Three as magic number; J1340., Retorts from hungry persons.]

During the dictatorship many Greek parents were horrified at the indoctrination their children received from teachers who, intimidated by the Junta, either taught the party line or risked imprisonment and torture. Evidently, numerous anti-Junta jokes told at that time involved a classroom situation, but by 1977 only a few such jokes remained in general circulation.

2 During the time of the Junta, all Greek school children were given pictures of Papadopoulos, Paddakos, and Makarezos to take home and hang in their houses.

The next day the teacher asked one boy:

"Which picture did you hang on the wall, Johnny?"

"I hung Papadopoulos' picture in our living room," said the boy.

"Which picture did you hang, Peter?"

"Paddakos," replied the boy.

"And you, Bobos?" asked the teacher.

"I didn't hang any," said Bobos.

"What do you mean, Bobos?" asked the teacher.

"Well," said the boy, "when I asked Mother which to hang, she said

to wait until Daddy came home from overseas because he wrote us saying that when he got home he was going to hang all three of them."
   [D1273.1.1., Three as magic number.]

The date of the military takeover, April 21, 1967, was displayed everywhere in Greece during the dictatorship. It was written in neon lights on buildings, painted on stone mountains, printed on billboards, stamped on coins, and so on.

3   During the Junta Paddakos went on a tour of the provinces of northern Greece. He visited one school where the school children had received "kits" the day before containing photos of the Colonels and Greek flags and other patriotic objects with which to "spontaneously" greet the leader.
   The schoolteacher begged Paddakos to stay and hear the oral examination of the class on Greek history.
   So the teacher asked the students:
   "Who achieved the glorious Revolution of April 21, 1967, in which Communism was eradicated from our homeland?"
   "Papadopoulos and Paddakos!" shouted the boys in unison.
   "And who are the two pillars of the Greek Orthodox Church?"
   "Papadopoulos and Paddakos!"
   "And who drove the hated Turks out of Greece in 1821?"
   "Papadopoulos and Paddakos!"
   At this point one small boy in the back of the room raised his hand and said:
   "It seems to me that I heard two other names in connection with the Revolution of 1821, and they were Kolokotronis and Kanaris!"
   All the other students in the classroom turned around to look at the boy and shouted:
   "Communist!"

4   One day Paddakos and Papadopoulos visited a small village to dedicate a new school.
   After they had finished the ceremony and had eaten lunch, the two men excused themselves from the group of village officials and went for a walk. It was warm and sunny, and the two men became drowsy.
   "Let's sit under that tree and take a nap," suggested one.
   The other agreed, and each sat under the tree on opposite sides of the huge trunk and dozed off.

A while later two schoolboys passed by and saw them. One boy asked the other:

"What kind of tree is that?"

"A penis tree," replied the boy.

"What? Are you crazy?" asked the first boy.

"No, I'm serious. Don't you see those two balls on each side of the trunk?"

The preceding joke was known to American soldiers during World War II, but as told then Hitler and Göering sat beneath the tree. Following are two other jokes of World War II vintage that have been reworked to suit the Junta situation.

5 Up in heaven, at the entrance, God sits on a big golden throne, and next to him sits Christ. And, when people die and go to heaven, God stands up and greets them by shaking their hands.

When Hitler got there God stood up and shook his hand. And he did the same when Mussolini went to heaven. But when Papadopoulos went to heaven, God didn't stand up to greet him. So Christ asked him why not.

"Are you stupid?" asked God. "If I get up to greet him, he'll take my place on the throne!"

[A137.15., God on throne; D1273.1.1., Three as magic number.]

During the dictatorship the standard greeting used to indicate support of the Junta was the salute "Zíto [Hurrah] Papadopoulos!" that appears in the following joke.

6 During the dictatorship Papadopoulos and Paddakos were being driven around the countryside in a limousine. Well, the driver of the limousine suddenly struck a pig that was crossing the road, and killed it.

So Papadopoulos told the driver to go over to the nearby farmhouse and to pay the owners for the loss of their pig.

The driver walked into the farmhouse with his wallet in hand and said:

"Zíto Papadopoulos! The pig is dead!"

Papadopoulos couldn't understand why the driver returned to the car bearing gifts of cheese, wine, and olives!

In July 1973 Papadopoulos held a rigged election in which the Greeks were asked to vote "Yes" in favor of his changes of the government or "No" in disapproval. Airplanes flying over Athens prior to the election dropped thousands of blue and white slips of paper with "Yes" printed on them. From a distance the pieces of paper resembled fifty-drachme bills, which are small and blue and white.[1] The following joke was told also at one time in connection with General Franco of Spain, who flew over Madrid with his wife.

7   When the Junta was in trouble in 1974, the Junta Triumvirate took a ride in an airplane to discuss how to restore their power and prestige with the Greek people.

As they were flying over Athens, Makarezos said:

"I have an idea! Let's throw 500,000 drachmes down to the people of Athens. That will make them happy."

"No," said Paddakos, "let's throw one million drachmes; that will make them happy!"

"No," said Papadopoulos, "we must throw more money, five or ten million drachmes, to make them really happy."

"Why don't you throw yourselves down?" asked the pilot. "That will *really* make the people happy!"

[D1273.1.1., Three as magic number.]

In 1973 every shop and post office in Greece prominently displayed a picture of Papadopoulos. The following jokes depict the egotism of dictators.

8   When Papadopoulos was dictator he decided that there should be new Greek postage stamps issued with his portrait. So the new stamps were printed and put into circulation, but there were many complaints about the stamps because they did not adhere to the envelopes. So one day Papadopoulos called the head of the Greek Post Office to his office and said:

"Look, there's nothing wrong with these stamps. I lick them and they stick."

The man said, "Maybe the trouble is that the people have been spitting on the wrong side of the stamps!"

9 Paddakos had an enormous portrait of himself commissioned, and hung the painting in the living room of his home. And he would talk to the portrait and hold insipid conversations with his image, such as:

"Congratulations to you for your great success!" Or, "Look at the two of us! We're just the same!"

One day, to his surprise, the portrait replied:

"No, we're not the same! One day the people will take me down to hang you up here!"

[D1610.2.1., Speaking image.]

The Greek Orthodox clergy traditionally does not cut the hair or shave. In Greece the clergy rigidly adheres to the custom (whereas in the United States many Greek Orthodox clergymen shave and wear the hair short).

10 Two years after the Colonels took power, Papadopoulos began appointing himself to all the high governmental positions, including minister of foreign affairs, minister of economic affairs, minister of labor, minister of national defense, and the like.

One day the few remaining ministers and the Archbishop of Greece were discussing Papadopoulos and his ambition to control the entire government single-handedly. Paddakos was present.

The ministers expressed their fears that they would soon be without positions. The archbishop said:

"My friends, you have reason to worry, but not me! He wouldn't try to appoint himself as archbishop."

"Don't be so sure," said Paddakos. "Papadopoulos is starting to let his hair and beard grow!"

The following joke depicts the Junta and the Church in corrupt combination.

11 To gain control of the Greek Orthodox Church, the Colonels appointed a bishop who was a noted homosexual so as to use his homosexuality for blackmail as a means of controlling the Church.

A foreigner, obviously ignorant of the bishop's reputation and of Greek customs, came to the monastery in Athens one day to have an audience at three o'clock in the afternoon.

He rang the bell, and the old housekeeper answered the door.

"I'd like to see Father Hieronymous," said the foreigner.

"He's not available now. This is the time of the day when we Greeks have a siesta."

"Oh," said the foreigner. Then, using *katharévusa* [formal] Greek and trying to save face, he said:

"Oh, I suppose that he is in the arms of Morpheus" [the god of sleep in ancient Greece and the root of the word "morphine"].

"I don't know the boy's name," said the housekeeper, "but he's a sailor of some sort!"

The following joke not only satirizes the egotism of the Greek dictator, but also reflects a popular ethnic stereotype.

12 Papadopoulos was trying to run the whole country. He appointed himself president, vice-president, minister of defense, minister of the economy, and the like.

Well, during this time the Chinese government sent a new ambassador to Greece. So the new Chinese ambassador had to meet the president, the vice-president, and then all the ministers of the various governmental departments.

After his first two days in Athens, he told his aide:

"I am really confused! They say that all Chinese look alike, but all the Greek officials that I meet here look the same to me!"

In the next joke, egotism backfires on the hated Paddakos.

13 Everywhere that Paddakos went he would encounter the same man begging for money. And the beggar would always ask Paddakos for help.

Well, finally Paddakos got fed up with seeing the man.

"I'm going to have a law passed to authorize the police to arrest and jail beggars because you are such a nuisance," said Paddakos.

"Oh, please," said the beggar. "Can't you see I'm crippled and I can't work? How will I live?"

"Okay," said Paddakos. "I'm going to give you a chance to go straight. I'll give you one request for anything you need to give you some employment so you can stop begging."

"Then just give me a big autographed photograph of yourself," said the beggar.

"Is that all you want?" asked Paddakos (incredulous but obviously flattered).

"Yes," said the beggar.

"Well, okay, but if I ever see you begging again, I'm going to have you put in jail for the rest of your life."

So he gave the beggar the autographed photograph and left.

Months passed and Paddakos did not see the beggar again. After about three months he saw the beggar riding in the back of a Mercedes limousine! So he had a policeman stop the car so that he could talk to the beggar.

"I can't believe it! How did you do it?" asked Paddakos.

"Oh, I owe it all to you and the photograph you gave me," said the beggar.

"But how?" asked Paddakos.

"Promise me that you won't tell anybody," asked the beggar.

"Okay, I promise."

"Well, I set up a shop. And I put up a sign: PISS ON THE PHOTO-GRAPH FOR ONLY 2 DRACHMES. And that's how I made my fortune!"

[X530., Jokes concerning beggars.]

Dictators often try to increase their popularity by supporting public-works projects: they build new roads, authorize new schools and libraries, and promise government aid to victims of natural disasters. Although some worthwhile public works were accomplished during the time of the Junta, the many cases of graft and corruption overshadowed the good achieved. The following jokes deal with the corruption of those in power.

14 During the dictatorship Papadopoulos went all over the country making speeches about the new government and what it would do for the people.

In one village, after he finished speaking, he asked if there were any questions.

"What about freedom of speech?" asked a little man from the back of the crowd.

Papadopoulos ignored the question.

In every village that he visited after that, when he finished his speech and asked for questions, the same little man would always appear and ask about freedom of speech. Papadopoulos always ignored the question.

Finally, in one village when he asked for questions, the little man was not present. After a few moments someone in the crowd asked:

"What happened to the little man in the back row?"

15 During the dictatorship there was a severe flood in the north of Greece. So Paddakos went to the area to visit the flood victims.

After giving a speech promising full government support, he then spoke individually to the victims.

"My house was completely destroyed," said one man.

Paddakos turned to his secretary and said, "Write one house for that man."

The next man also needed a new house.

"Write one house for that man," continued Paddakos.

After several more requests for houses, one man came forward and said, "I know this has nothing to do with the flood, but I have a request of the new government for help. During the war I was injured and I lost my balls. I'd like the new government to send me to a hospital in Europe where I can have new balls transplanted."

"Certainly, we can do that," said Paddakos. Then, turning to his secretary, he said, "Write one house for that man."

The man overheard what Paddakos said, so he came back and said, "No, not a house, I need balls."*

"Never mind," said Paddakos, "that's what all of the others are getting anyway!"

16 One night Paddakos went for a walk in the National Park in Athens by the Palace and the National Gardens. As he passed a statue, he heard:

"Psst, hey, Paddakosi, come here, I have a big complaint to give you!"

Paddakos turned around, but all he saw was a statue of a man.

"Look, Paddakosi," continued the statue, "all the other statues in the park have horses or benches or something to sit on, but I have to stand up all the time, and I've been standing here for a *long* time! Since you're such a big man these days, can't you get me a horse to sit on?"

"Of course, I can have the new government do anything I want to improve Greece. Tomorrow I'll bring you a horse."

So the next day Paddakos went to Papadopoulos' office and asked for a horse for the statue in the National Gardens who had the complaint.

"Don't try to fool me," said Papadopoulos, "statues don't talk."

"If you don't believe me, then come with me tonight to the National Gardens and you'll hear for yourself," said Paddakos.

---

* "Balls" (*arhídia*) is a commonly used vulgar expression among certain groups of Greeks. Americans wishing to use a similar expression would probably say "shit."

So that night the two men went to the park, and they stood by the statue. Five minutes passed, and nothing was heard. Then ten minutes, then half an hour. Nothing.

"You see, I told you that statues don't talk," said Papadopoulos.

"Hey, psst, Paddakosi," said the statue. "I told you a horse, not a jackass!"

[D1620.1.7., Speaking statue.]

The following joke refers prophetically to what indeed was Papadopoulos' fate. He was incarcerated in Korydallos Prison after the fall of the Junta in 1974 and reportedly is there now (1979).

17 The two major heads of the dictatorship, Papadopoulos and Paddakos, were together in the headquarters when the chief warden of Korydallos, the largest prison in Greece, came to see them.

"Sirs," he began, "the prisoners of Korydallos have several complaints and are threatening to go on a hunger strike if their demands are not met."

"What do they want?" asked Papadopoulos.

"They want to be able to have their wives with them once a week for sex," said the warden.

After thinking for a few moments, Papadopoulos agreed. But Paddakos was shocked at this leniency to the criminals.

About a week later the warden from Korydallos returned to see the two leaders.

"Sirs," he began again, "we have more trouble at the prison. This time the prisoners are demanding television in their cells and threaten to go on strike if their demand is not met."

Papadopoulos again thought for a few moments and agreed. Paddakos was appalled by this leniency, but again he said nothing.

About a month later the warden again visited headquarters.

"Sirs," he said, "the prisoners are now demanding to have weekend passes for good behavior just like the prisoners have in Denmark."

Papadopoulos agreed, but this time Paddakos could hold his silence no longer.

"What are you doing, spending all that money for the prison and the prisoners and we don't even have good schools here in Greece?"

"Look," said Papadopoulos, "when we finish up here, we may be going to jail, but we sure won't be going to school!"

From the time of the Turkish occupation of Greece, Greeks have had a very well developed informal system of communication by which rumor and gossip travel with the speed of lightning. The accuracy of rumors is often uncanny. For example, during the first five days of the Turkish invasion of Cyprus in July 1974, when the dictatorship was collapsing, word spread in Athens that the former premier, Constantinos Caramanlis, would return from exile in France to head a new government. The rumor proved to be true.

When it was in power, the dictatorship not only censored the formal news media, but also passed a law against the dissemination of rumor. The following two jokes concern that attempt to suppress the Greeks' informal means of spreading news.

18 During the Junta, when it was illegal to spread rumor, it seemed that all the rumors were originating from one obscure little man and that all his rumors about the Junta proved to be true.

Finally, the police found the obscure little man, who was then sent to Papadopoulos and Paddakos for questioning.

"If you don't tell us the truth, you will be tortured. Did you know it is illegal to spread rumors?"

"No."

"Well, ignorance of the law is no excuse. Did you start the rumor of such and such?"

"Yes."

"And did you start the rumor of such and such?"

"Yes." (He admitted all the charges against him.)

"Well, how did you know all this? Did you use electronic bugging devices? Do you work for the CIA?"

"No," said the little man.

"Then how are your rumors so accurate?"

"Well, I just pick up the daily newspaper and read all the lies and stupidities committed and repeat them to my friends. And since I'm just a dumb villager, I never make a mistake!"

19 During the dictatorship there was a man who was always telling lots of anti-Junta jokes. Finally, somebody reported him to the police, and so he was arrested and finally taken to Papadopoulos for questioning.

"I hear that you know lots of funny stories about the new government," said Papadopoulos.

"Yes," admitted the man, "I do."

"And do you know that it is illegal to criticize the new government and that our glorious regime will last one hundred years?" asked Papadopoulos.

"No," said the man, "that joke I hadn't heard!"

The following joke also relates to the loss of certain freedoms during the dictatorship. I first heard it in a small village in the mountains of Crete, but it is well known all over Greece. The setting is usually Omonia Square in Athens, but the version of the joke as I first heard it shows its adaptability to all parts of the country.

20   During the dictatorship a village couple went to Heraklion, Crete, to do some Christmas shopping.

At the main intersection, by the open-air market, the green "Walk" light came on, and the husband rushed across the street with the crowd, but his wife was confused and afraid, so she stayed on the corner waiting.

Well, the husband was across the street, and he yelled to her, "Wife! Wife! Come here!" But the woman stayed where she was.

So the light turned red, and just then the husband decided to go back and get his wife. As he started to cross the street, the policeman stopped him.

"Where are you going?"

"I'm going to get my wife. She got left behind when the light turned red."

"Tell me her name," said the policeman, "and I'll call for her to cross the street under my protection."

"Her name! Ha! Ha! Her name!" laughed the villager. "Her name is Democracy [Freedom in other versions]! Call her if you can!"

The following not only satirizes the loss of freedom of speech, but also is an example of an "on-the-bus" joke. The crowded conditions on buses and trolleys in Athens and Piraeus provide the settings for many jokes (see also chapter seven, "Transportation Jokes").

21 One time, during the Junta, the wife of a general was riding a bus in Athens. A man standing next to her farted loudly, and she turned to him in disgust and said:

"Ugh! How terrible!"

"Look, madam," said the man, "the generals may have closed our mouths, but not our asses!"

The Junta suppressed the personal freedoms of everybody in Greece—except the military, of course. The following joke relates not only to the questionable practices and privileges of the military, but also to the traditional custom in Greece of chaperoning women.[2]

22 In 1967, during the dictatorship, one time there was a beautiful young woman riding the bus in Athens. Well, when the seat next to her was vacated, a Greek army officer of high rank sat next to her. Seeing that she was very beautiful, the officer decided to take advantage of the crowded condition on the bus, and he started to "feel her up." The young woman turned to the man and slapped him loudly in the face!

As it turned out, the young woman's father and fiancé were also on the bus.

"Are you crazy?" asked the fiancé. "Why did you strike an officer? Surely you'll go to jail!"

"Because he put his hands where he had no business," she said.

So her fiancé also gave the officer a loud slap in the face.

When the girl's father saw the fiancé strike the officer (he hadn't heard the previous conversation), he said:

"Are you insane? Hitting an officer! You'll go to jail."

"But he was feeling up your daughter," said the fiancé.

So the girl's father hit the officer in the face, too.

Well, hearing all the commotion, a little man had elbowed his way forward on the crowded bus to see what was going on. Seeing the woman and the two men hitting the officer, he went forward and also hit the man in the face.

By this time there was so much commotion that the bus driver called the police, who arrested the young woman and the three men, and took them to jail.

At the hearing the judge asked the young woman why she struck the army officer since it was a crime against the State.

"Because he made indecent advances to me on the bus."

"Brávo!" said the judge. "Your action illustrates the high morality of our Greek women!" So she was acquitted.

Then the judge called her fiancé and asked him why he struck the officer.

"I did it to protect my fiancée from the improper advances of the man."

"Brávo!" said the judge. "You were doing your duty to protect the purity of our Greek women." And he was acquitted.

Next, the girl's father was called, and he was acquitted for protecting his daughter's innocence and for preserving the honor of his family.

Finally, the little man was called before the judge.

"Why did you hit the officer? Are you related to any of the first three who were accused?"

"No."

"Then what made you come and hit the officer?" asked the judge.

"Well, I saw the girl hit the officer, then I saw the first man hit the officer, then I saw the second man hit the officer. So naturally I thought that the Junta had fallen, so I took a shot at the guy too!"

The preceding joke also illustrates another common feature of Greek life: anything that happens in public is potentially anybody's business. Passengers on buses and onlookers on the streets often become verbally involved in arguments, accidents, and other problems of any kind that occur in public. Such public behavior is an informal, yet very powerful, means of social control: together with gossip and inquisitiveness, both also prevalent in Greece, it creates a type of society in which many crimes are prevented and in which criminals are rapidly apprehended. Americans, who are inclined to ignore public occurrences in which they are not directly involved, find this public aspect of Greek life very different from that of the United States, particularly in American cities. That in many ways the behavior of Greeks in public space is more like that of Arabs than like that of Europeans is another consequence of the Turkish occupation. (See also Hall 1966 in regard to culturally determined differences in public behavior.)

The next joke shares the setting of the preceding one and further illustrates the fear in which Greeks lived during the dictatorship.

23   One time during the dictatorship, a man was riding a crowded bus in downtown Athens. There was no place to sit, so he was standing. Suddenly, he turned to the man standing next to him and asked:
"Excuse me, but are you in the military?"
"No."
"Do you work for the police?"
"No."
"Do you have a government job?"
"No."
"Then you're not connected with the government at all?"
"No."
"Then would you please get your foot off of the top of mine?"

Some government officials, because of their connections with the Colonels, also enjoyed extended personal freedoms during the dictatorship. The following joke, however, simply criticizes the average Greek bureaucrat, who is believed to do nothing all day but drink coffee and read newspapers, but who will automatically stop whatever he is doing at one-thirty sharp to go home. It is also a multiethnic-slur joke since it criticizes Russian Communists, American capitalists, and bureaucrats everywhere. (The popular multiethnic-slur jokes involving a Greek who usually is the most clever of the bunch are included in chapter four, "The Clever Greeks: Esoteric Humor.")

24   A ship was sinking off the coast of Holland. On board were three men: a Russian Communist, an American capitalist, and a Greek civil servant. As the ship was going down, the Communist began a long-winded political speech in which he criticized the capitalists for causing disasters of this type by their exploitation of the working class and the like. Well, he was talking so much that he kept swallowing water, so he drowned.
The American capitalist kept quiet, but his manner of swimming, in which he kept bringing his arms toward himself in the greedy gesture of capitalists, was totally ineffective at keeping him afloat, and so he drowned, too.
The Greek civil servant was swimming beautifully toward the shore, but when he glanced down at his watch and noticed it was one-thirty, he stopped working, and so he drowned as well!
[D1273.1.1., Three as magic number.]

The following joke pairs the dictatorship with the most popular talking animal in Greek jokelore, the parrot. Other parrot jokes are included in the section devoted to animal jokes in chapter nine, "Very *Sókin* Jokes."

25 One time, there was a Greek general who had a parrot that he taught to drink brandy, and he also taught the parrot to say "*Zíto* Papadopoulos!"

Well, after the Junta fell in 1974, the general told the parrot:

"Don't say '*Zíto* Papadopoulos' any more or I'll have to put you in jail!"

Well, one night the general gave a party at his house, and during the evening some of the guests started giving brandy to the poor parrot and got him drunk! Suddenly, the drunken parrot started shrieking:

"*Zíto* Papadopoulos! *Zíto* Papadopoulos!"

So the general put the parrot in prison!

Well, inside the prison there were a lot of men. One of the men said, "I'm in here for killing a guy."

Another man said, "I'm in here for stealing."

Then the men turned to the parrot and asked, "What are *you* in here for?"

"I'm in here," said the parrot, "because of my political opinions!"

[B211.3.4., Speaking parrot; J1118.1., Clever parrot.]

The following is a popular joke-riddle that circulated during the dictatorship.

26 Question: If Papadopoulos, Paddakos, and Makarezos are together in a rowboat, and the boat sinks, who will live?

Answer: Greece.

[D1273.1.1., Three as magic number.]

An anti-Junta joke that involved a sinking boat and that circulated during the early years of the dictatorship refers to a tragedy that occurred in Greece prior to 1967. A Tipaldos Line ferryboat on its run from Heraklion, Crete, to the port of Piraeus sank, and over two hundred passengers died. The cause of the sinking was later proved to be the negligence of the crew. Thereafter most Greeks were reluctant to travel on any of the ships or boats owned by the Tipaldos Line.

27   When the Colonels seized power in 1967, they had a meeting to decide what to do with the royal family. The king would be exiled. That was no problem since he was not a powerful figure. But the real power behind the throne, the queen mother, posed a serious problem.

One of the Colonels wanted to execute her; another wanted to imprison her; another wanted to place her under house arrest; still another wanted to have her exiled with her son, the king.

Finally, one of the Colonels interrupted this conversation.

"Let's be reasonable," he said. "We must deal with her in some manner that is appropriate to her status as queen of the Hellenes. She should be given a lovely private island, like Skorpios, and also be given a cruise ship to travel about the Greek islands."

"What?" demanded the other Colonels. "Have you lost your senses? What kind of punishment is that?"

"Oh, I forgot to say," said the Colonel, "the cruise ship will be from the Tipaldos Line!"

Probably no foreign politician was more unpopular in Greece from 1974 to 1976 than Henry Kissinger. Anti-American statements that I heard during that period always mentioned Kissinger. In the summer of 1976, souvenir shops in Athens sold posters bearing a large photograph of Kissinger with the caption, WANTED: DEAD OR ALIVE FOR THE MURDER OF 3,000 GREEK CYPRIOTS. I suspect that many anti-Kissinger jokes circulated at that time, but I collected only two.

28   Kissinger went to Spain and gave a political speech in Barcelona in one of the plazas. About twenty thousand people came to hear him speak. He talked in favor of Prime Minister Adolfo Suarez and his policies.

"If you vote for Suarez," he said, "I'll make this little building (pointing to a small house) into a skyscraper!"

"*Uba! Uba!*" shouted the crowd.

"And if you vote for Suarez," he continued, "I'll make this little plaza into a great city."

"*Uba! Uba!*" shouted the crowd.

"And if you vote for Suarez," he continued, "I'll make that cow—"

"It's a bull," interrupted a Spanish official next to him.

But Kissinger ignored the man. "I'll make that cow—"

"But, Señor Kissinger, it's a bull," insisted the Spaniard.

"How do you know it's a bull?" asked Kissinger.

"Are you crazy?" asked the Spaniard. "Don't you see its *uba?*" [teller's supposed Spanish word for "balls"].

29 In 1976 Kissinger went to China. Well, he went to a tailor to have a suit custom made. But the tailor told him:

"I'm sorry, we can't make you a suit because you're such a big man that we don't have enough cloth of the same type and color for you."

So Kissinger went to Spain, and again he tried to have a tailor-made suit, but again the tailor told him that, since he was such a big man, they didn't have enough cloth.

So Kissinger tried in London, and in Paris, and in Africa, but always he received the same reply.

Well, finally, he went to Israel and went to a tailor for a suit.

"Oh yes, for *you*, Mr. Kissinger, we can make two suits!"

✒ Greece is surrounded by hostile or Communist Bloc countries. The following joke pokes fun at one of Greece's northern neighbors, Bulgaria.

30 Before Chairman Mao died, one of his aides went rushing into the chairman's office.

"Chairman Mao! Chairman Mao! Bad news! Bulgaria has declared war on China."

Mao looked at the man, then asked him:

"How many Bulgarians are there?"

"Six million!"

"And in which hotel do they stay?" asked Mao.

The final joke in this chapter deals with a theme already mentioned in connection with those jokes that ridicule the empty promises of the Junta leaders or of politicians in general. Greeks often use their cigarette boxes as notepads, and the punch line of the joke refers to the usual fate of the information written on them. The joke also introduces an element that is the subject of chapter seven: the mental hospital and mental patients.

31 Papadopoulos went to visit a mental hospital in Athens. He met one man who seemed quite normal.

"What are you in here for?" asked Papadopoulos.

"I'm not crazy at all," said the man. "My family had me put in here so that they could steal all of my inheritance."

"Oh, that's terrible," said Papadopoulos. "I'll help to get you out."

So he took out of his pocket his white box of Greek cigarettes and a pen, and said:

"Tell me your name, your address, and I'll write the information here, and then tomorrow I'll start trying to get you out of here."

"If you think I believe you, then *you* must be crazy! When you finish the cigarettes, you'll throw away the box and forget all about me!"

Chapter 2
The Bobos Joke Cycle

Greeks first began telling Bobos jokes during the mid-1960s before the Colonels' takeover. During the time of the Junta, Bobos jokes were extremely popular, but today they constitute a fad. Virtually unknown little more than a decade ago, Bobos is quickly becoming a national phenomenon of major significance, a type of picaresque, mini-culture hero. That he is used on Greek television to advertise products of appeal to the young and that Bobos dolls are available for sale in many places are only two indications of his recent rise in popularity.

A similar joke fad in the United States during the 1930s and 1940s featured the Little Moron. In a few of the Bobos jokes, Bobos does something that the Little Moron did repeatedly: he confuses the literal meaning with the metaphorical meaning. Whereas that behavior is the salient feature of the Little Moron, Bobos' predominant characteristic is his use of vulgarity.

What does Bobos look like? Most people say he is small, fat, and dumb (*hazós*, or *koutós*), with a rather large head and a stupid expression on his face.[1] In the jokes he varies in age from a six-year-old who is in the first grade to a teenager who gets married.

Bobos seems to be the functional equivalent of "Stupid John."[2] Jokes about Stupid John, or Johnny, are found in many countries of the world, and some of the same jokes are attributed to Bobos in Greece. The traditional association of the name John with stupidity is very old in Western Europe. It may even go back to the beheading of John the Baptist, who in Greece is sometimes called "Sait John-without-the Head" to distinguish him from other Saint Johns in the Orthodox faith. The Greek saying "Forty-five Johns have the intelligence of one rooster" indicates that Greeks are aware of the Stupid John concept, but I seldom heard jokes about the numbskull figure Yannis in Greece.

Why Greeks started telling Stupid John jokes by substituting the young simpleton named Bobos is a perplexing problem. Since the name Yannis connotes only stupidity in Greek culture, perhaps another name was needed to describe a traditional numbskull character turned obscene trickster in Greek jokelore: The name Bobos appears, however, to be a loan word. Records of the linguistics department of the Academy of Athens show that the word *bóbos* is found in the Ionian Islands, where it has various meanings: it is a surname; it is a word used for the stomach of a bird or of a chicken; it is a word for a bogeyman character, used to frighten children; and, finally, it is a name for a hairstyle. Linguists at the Academy conclude that *bóbos,* as it appears in the Ionian Islands, is probably an Italian or a Venetian word that diffused to the islands because of their close proximity to and long historical connection with Italy.

Moreover, the word *bóbo* means "fool" or "simpleton" in Spanish.[3] Since Greek masculine nouns usually end in *s*, the transformation from *bóbo* to *bóbos* would have been a natural one if the word was borrowed from Spanish, as it may have been.

Is Bobos really stupid? There is much ambiguity in the jokes that are told about him. In many cases he says stupid things that are true, as in joke 1, above. Basically, however, Bobos is an obscene trickster figure.

The trickster, as defined by American folklorists, is a clever character who generally outwits a more powerful adversary by deception, cunning, and guile. In many parts of the world, the trickster figure is an animal, as Coyote functioned among the North American Indians, or Brer Rabbit among American Blacks. Indeed, the trickster appears in the lore of all cultures, for stories and jokes about this character type seem to fulfill a basic human need to appreciate and to encourage the underdog. In the majority of the Bobos jokes, he challenges adult society in the form of his teacher, of his parents, or of nonrelated adults in general. Perhaps he is a symptom of the times, for, in the last ten years, many young Greeks have resisted traditional life-styles and have attempted to live as modern Europeans. Bobos "wins," as a trickster, by his stupid remarks that are true, or more often by his use of obscenity and vulgarity, both inappropriate and unexpected in a boy his age. Bobos jokes may also represent a reaction to the new emphasis in Greece on extended formal education. Perhaps there is a feeling, among certain groups of young people, that so much schooling is unnecessary, and Bobos jokes, especially those having a school setting, are a means of release from new academic pressures. I suspect that Bobos jokes are exchanged primarily in elementary and high schools, although university students also know and exchange Bobos jokes.

Although trickster stories and jokes are found universally, the frequency of their appearance and the degree of their popularity within particular cultures varies with the particular value systems. Modern Greek culture seems to emphasize the importance of the trickster, at least in the material that I collected. The emphasis may be a function of age and social class. Bobos jokes are evidently known all over Greece, but the individuals telling them are usually under the age of thirty. Bobos does not appeal generally to the older generation or to the upper class; he is the hero of the young, of the proletariat, and of Greek machismo.

In addition to the Bobos jokes is the Greek shadow theatre that features another popular trickster hero, Karaghiozis, a poor Greek who is the embodiment of cunning and slyness (*poneriá*).[4] In the plays he is usually matched against a more powerful Turk, a pasha or a vizier (during the time of the Turkish occupation of Greece), whom he always outsmarts, usually by pretending to be someone he is not. Karaghiozis is at times vulgar, but the plays do not contain obscene speech.

In the following chapters of the book, other types of Greek tricksters appear. (For example, in chapter three, "The Clever Greeks: Esoteric Humor," most of the jokes fit into the trickster genre.) "Beware of Greeks bearing gifts" is a well-known saying in America that probably has its origin in the *Iliad,* where Homer described the famous trick of the wooden horse. Ancient Greek culture included other important trickster figures such as Odysseus, Hermes, and some of the heroes of Aristophanes' comedies. In Homer's *Odyssey* Odysseus was a master trickster who constantly saved himself and his men by cunning, deception, wit, lying, and the like. Hermes, of slightly lesser antiquity, began his life as a cattle thief who, when only one day old, used magic to steal Apollo's cattle. When his father, Zeus, questioned Hermes about his deed, Hermes skillfully began a series of half-truths and lies with the statement, "You know, Father, that I can never tell a lie." (The statement is reminiscent of the folklore attached to an American culture hero, George Washington.)

One other figure of great antiquity deserves mention here because of the coincidence of her name: Baubo, or Bobo. An old woman who played an important part in the Eleusinian Mysteries, Baubo cracked dirty jokes and made obscene gestures to make the goddess Demeter laugh. Many classicists consider Baubo the "goddess of obscenity." The modern Bobos is most likely not a lineal descendant of the ancient Baubo, but he qualifies as a contemporary demigod of obscenity. (Some jokes about Bobos also include a little girl named Boba, but I have not included any in this chapter.)

In some parts of Greece, I heard jokes about another young boy, Toutos, who seems to be the equivalent of Bobos. One young informant in Salamis Island said that Bobos was stupid whereas Toutos was clever. This distinction is not widespread, however, and the majority of Toutos jokes are of the same types as the Bobos jokes.

Bobos jokes also appear in print in Greece, but those that do are the innocent, naive, Little Moron type. Many of the books containing Bobos jokes are written for children, but collections of jokes intended for adult readers also include nonobscene Bobos examples.

The classroom, usually of an elementary school, is often the setting for the Bobos jokes that I heard. The jokes reflect the preoccupation with sex and with other bodily functions that is characteristic of children and adolescents in general. Also, the jokes relate to the problems that children experience in school and to their fantasies about resolving them.

The first two jokes of this chapter, which feature Bobos in competition with other nationals of his own age, are reminiscent of many in chapter three, "The Clever Greeks: Esoteric Humor."

32   One time, the Greek Bobos and the French Bobos made a bet as to who could make the best thing.

So the French Bobos brought a huge basketful of iron scrap and announced that he would make a ship.

"And what can you make?" asked the French Bobos.

"Do you have a sister?" asked the Greek Bobos.

"Yes."

"Then bring her here," said the Greek Bobos.

So when the French Bobos brought his sister, the Greek Bobos took her hand and started to leave.

"Where are you going?" asked the French Bobos.

"I'm going to make a crew for your ship!" said the Greek Bobos.

[H500., Tests of cleverness or ability; J1113., Clever boy.]

33   Once there was a contest to see who was the smartest boy in the world. Bobos from Greece was matched against the Italian Bobos. They met in the middle of a stadium, and there was a teacher to ask them the questions.

The teacher asked the Italian Bobos:

"What is it that goes with everything?"

The Italian Bobos thought for a moment, then said:

"Oh, that's easy, it's Coca-Cola." [In Greek advertising the slogan is that Coca-Cola goes with everything.]

Then the teacher turned to the Greek Bobos and said:

"What do *you* think goes with everything?"

"His [the Italian Bobos'] mother's pussy goes with everything!"

[H500., Tests of cleverness or ability; J1113., Clever boy.]

The following jokes show Bobos in his younger days, when he was still naive and not especially vulgar. These jokes are characteristic of a large number of innocent Bobos jokes in circulation in Greece.

34 One day the milkman came to Bobos' house, and he was talking to Bobos' mother.

So Bobos went to his father and asked him for five drachmes.

"No, I'm not giving you any money," said his father.

"If you give me five drachmes, I'll tell you what the milkman just said to Mama!"

So his father gave him ten drachmes and said to Bobos:

"Tell me, quick, what did he say?"

"He said, 'How much milk do you want?'" said Bobos.

35 One night, very late, everyone was asleep at Bobos' house. Suddenly, there was a loud noise that came from Bobos' room. Bobos' mother got up to see what had happened.

"What was that noise that I heard, Bobos?" she asked.

"Nothing," he said. "Just my pajamas that fell on the floor."

"Your pajamas?" asked his mother. "But how could your pajamas make such a loud noise?"

"Because I was wearing them!"

36 One day at school, Bobos' teacher asked him:

"Bobos, how much are four and three?"

Bobos began counting on his fingers, one, two, three . . . seven!"

Since Bobos' teacher saw him counting on his fingers, she said:

"Bobos, you must not count on your fingers! Now, put your hands in your pocket and tell me, how much are five and five?"

So Bobos was silent for a long time, and finally he said:

"Eleven."

"Bobos, when you go home this evening, be sure to tell your mother to sew up the hole in your pocket!" said his teacher.

The following is an appropriate joke in a society where men must protect their reputations and avoid being cuckolded for fear of public ridicule. (See also the introductory comments for jokes 150–52 and the introduction to chapter eight, "Very *Sókin* Jokes.")

37 Bobos was on his way to school one day, and he found a perfectly good cigarette on the street. So he took the cigarette and went into a narrow side street and started smoking it. Well, a lady passed by and saw him smoking.

"Bobos!" she said. "Does your father know you are smoking?"

"Mrs. Papas," said Bobos, "Does your husband know you are talking to another man on the street?"

38 For about a week Bobos' teacher was sick, so they sent a substitute teacher every day. The children didn't like the substitute, and the second day, when she came a little late in the morning, she found that someone had urinated on the blackboard and on her desk.

This continued for several days, so one morning the substitute said:

"We all know that somebody in this class is being very naughty. I don't want to punish the whole class because of one guilty person, so this is what we'll do: We'll all close our eyes and put our heads down on our desks, and whoever knows the name of the guilty person will come forward and write the name of the guilty person on the blackboard."

So they all closed their eyes and put their heads down on their desks, and after a few moments Bobos got up and went to the board. After he had finished, he sat down.

When the teacher said, "Eyes open," she saw that somebody had again pissed on the blackboard and next to it was written:

THE PISSING COMPANY STRIKES AGAIN!

[Legman I:70.]

39 One day at school the teacher asked the children if they knew where babies come from. But nobody knew. So she gave the class the homework assignment of finding out where babies come from.

When Bobos got home he went to find his mother. She was in the kitchen peeling potatoes.

"Mama, where do babies come from?" he asked.

"Can't you see that I'm busy? Ask me later," said his mother.

Ten minutes later he went back into the kitchen and said:

"Mama, where do babies come from?"

To get rid of him she said, "From a potato!"

So Bobos took one of the potatoes and put it in his pocket and left the kitchen, satisfied with her answer.

The next day in class, the teacher asked one boy:

"Johnny, where did your parents say that you came from?"

"From the stork," said the boy.

"Bobby, where did your parents say that you came from?"

"From under a cabbage leaf," said the boy.

"Bobos, where did your parents say that you came from?"

"Wait a minute, I'll show you," said Bobos reaching in his pocket.

The teacher, thinking that Bobos had learned the truth of where babies come from, quickly changed the subject. [In another version Bobos, reaching into his pocket, asks her, "Want me to show it to you?"]

The two preceding jokes are "catch" jokes because they trick the listener into drawing the wrong, usually vulgar, conclusion. Other examples of Greek catch jokes are jokes 275, 281, and 282.

The following are two Little Moron jokes that illustrate his habit of confusing literal and metaphorical meanings.

40 "Why did the Little Moron cross the bridge and never, never again return?"

"Because he didn't want to be a double-crosser!"

41 "Why did the Little Moron cut a hole in the rug?"

"Because he wanted to see a floor show!"

I collected only three examples of Bobos' mistaking the literal for the metaphorical, but I suspect that there are many more.

42 One day at school the teacher told the children to write something containing the words of the common Greek proverb "There is only one mother" because it was going to be Mother's Day the next week.

After about ten minutes she had the children read their compositions aloud.

The first boy said:

"Yesterday I had a fever and my mother stayed up all night nursing me because 'There is only one mother.'"

The second boy said:

"The other day it was raining and my mother walked me to school with an umbrella over my head because 'There is only one mother.'"

Bobos said:

"Yesterday two ladies came to visit us and Mother sent me to the kitchen to bring them two pieces of cake, but I couldn't because I had eaten one piece, so I said, 'There is only *one*, Mother!'"

[D1273.1.1., Three as magic number; J2450., Literal fool.]

43   One day, the teacher asked the students to write an essay about the proverb "A friend in need is a friend indeed."*

So all the students wrote essays and turned them in to the teacher.

When Bobos got home from school, his mother asked him how he passed his day at school.

‚"I wrote an essay about the proverb 'The friend, in the need appears.'"

"What did you write?" asked his mother.

"I wrote, 'Last Sunday, I was walking through the park. Suddenly, I saw a pile of green-colored shit! That must have been Costas who did that, I thought, because Costas is always eating spinach. Then later I saw a pile of black-colored shit. That must have been Johnny, I thought, because he is always eating blackberries. Then I walked right past a pile of red-colored shit. And I thought, that must have been Peter because he is always eating strawberries.

And I knew all this because "A friend appears in the need"!'"

[J401.0.1., "Friend is known in need"; J2450., Literal fool; J2470., Metaphor literally interpreted.]

44   It was carnival time in Greece, so the teacher told the students to come to class the following week dressed in costumes that illustrated Greek folklore.

Well, Bobos showed up the next week completely naked and covering his penis with his hands!

"Bobos!" shouted the teacher. "What do you mean coming to school like that?"

"I'm dressed like a Greek proverb," anounced Bobos.

"What proverb?" asked the teacher.

"A bird in the hand is worth two in the bush!" [In Greek the proverb is literally "Better three in the hand than ten in the ambush."]

[J2450., Literal fool; J2470., Metaphor literally interpreted.]

In a variant (44a) of the preceding joke, Bobos, completely naked and holding a toothpick in his teeth, arrives in the class.

*Literally "The friend, in the need appears." The expression "in the need" has come to be used also for the need to defecate. In polite speech one says, "I have need," meaning "I must go to the toilet to defecate." So the second literal meaning of the Greek proverb is "A friend appears in the shit," or "We can tell a friend by his shit."

When the teacher asks him what he. represents, he says, "An appetizer!"

In the following jokes Bobos displays his greatest skill: the ability to use vulgar words and to say vulgar things, sometimes apparently without realizing what he is saying. Young children who also demonstrate that ability are known to schoolteachers and parents everywhere, although the particular age at which children go through that "phase" varies from culture to culture.

45   When Bobos was about ten, he started learning bad words on the street from other kids. When he had learned a lot of them, he asked his father one day what the words meant. His father was too embarrassed to tell the truth, so he made up other answers, to his later dismay.

"Daddy, what's a whorehouse?" asked Bobos.

"Uh, ah, er, that's a very nice house, like ours."

"What's a queer?"

"Er, that's a nice gentleman."

"And what's a prostitute?"

"Uh, um, that's a very elegant lady."

"And what are panties?"

"Oh, those are overcoats."

"And what are balls?"

"Uh, um, balls are the coatracks where people hang their coats."

"And what's a penis?"

"Oh, er, that's an armchair."

"And what's pubic hair?"

"Well, er, that's like *kataifi* [a Greek pastry resembling shredded wheat]."

"And what's fucking?"

"Oh, er, that's when somebody is cooking."

Well, one evening Bobos' mother had gone to the hospital to visit her sister. While she was out Bobos' father was in the kitchen when the doorbell rang. So he asked Bobos to go to the door to see who it was. It was friends of the family, Mr. and Mrs. Pappas, who had come for an unexpected visit. So Bobos welcomed them into the parlor, saying:

"Welcome prostitutes and queers to our whorehouse! Please take off your panties and hang them on those balls, and please be seated on those penises! My father is in the kitchen fucking, but in a minute he'll come and bring us some pubic hair to eat!"

[Legman II:731; a variant of AT1562A, The Barn Is Burning.]

46 One day at school the principal visited Bobos' class to see what the students were learning. The teacher asked the class:

"Who will tell us about Einstein?"

All the students slouched down in their desks, and Bobos started to raise his hand, but changed his mind and quickly put his arm down. Unfortunately, the teacher saw him and said:

"Speak up, Bobos my boy, who was Einstein?"

"Einstein was the world's greatest mathematician," said Bobos.

"*Brávo*, Bobos! But what else is it that we must remember about Einstein?"

Bobos thought a minute, then said:

"Oh, I remember, he had the biggest balls in the world!"

[F547.7., Enormous testicles; X712.3.2., Large testicles.]

47 One day at school the teacher told the children to write a word on a piece of paper and to hand them in.

One child had written "apple," another had written, "cat," another had written "chair," but Bobos had written "pussy [*mouní*]."

The teacher was horrified and said to Bobos:

"Bobos, aren't you ashamed? Couldn't you have thought of a decent word to write?"

As punishment she made him stay after school and write the bad word fifty times on the blackboard. Then she made him erase the blackboard with his tongue!

When Bobos finally got home from school, two hours late, covered with chalk dust, and with his tongue thick and hanging out of his mouth, his father screamed:

"Look at you, you bad boy! Filthy dirty and two hours late! What explanation do you have?"

"If your teacher made *you* eat fifty pussies, how do you think *you* would look?" asked Bobos.

48 One day at school Bobos' teacher asked the class:

"Students, who can give me a word that begins with *M*?"

Bobos immediately raised his hand, but the teacher was afraid that he would say *mouní* [pussy], so she called on another student.

"Mama," said the boy.

"*Brávo!* Now, who can give me a word that begins with *Psi* [Ψ]?"

Immediately, Bobos raised his hand. But the teacher was afraid that he would say *psolí* [penis], so she called on another student.

"*Psomí* [bread]," said the student.

"*Brávo!* Now, who can give me a word that starts with *N*?" asked the teacher.

Only Bobos raised his hand this time, so the teacher reluctantly called on him.

"*Nános* [dwarf]," said Bobos.

"*Brávo*, Bobos!" said the teacher.

"Yes, dwarf, but look at the [huge] balls he had!" said Bobos.*

[D1273.1.1., Three as magic number; F547.7., Enormous testicles; X712.3.2., Large testicles.]

49 One day at school the teacher asked the children to name different kinds of fruit.

So the children said, "Apples, peaches, bananas, grapes, pineapple," and the like.

When it was Bobos' turn to name a fruit, he said:

"Lamp!"

"But, Bobos, a lamp is not a fruit to eat," said the teacher.

"But," protested Bobos, "every night I hear my father tell my mother, 'Turn off the lamp and I'll eat.'"†

50 One day at school Bobos' teacher came to class wearing a very low-cut blouse, and a rose was placed between her ample breasts.

"Today, children," she began, "we will learn all about the horticulture of roses. First, will one of the students explain what it is that makes the roses grow?"

One child raised his hand and said:

"Roses need lots of water to grow big."

"That's right," said the teacher, "but what else is it that makes the roses grow so big?"

Another boy raised his hand and said:

"Roses need lots of manure to grow big."

At that moment Bobos raised his hand. "I don't understand," he said.

---

*In Greek: *Nay, nános, alla na ti arhídia pou éihe!* giving at the same time the gesture used to indicate large testicles; see appendix C.

A widespread folk belief in Greece is that dwarves have exceptionally large testicles.

†The verb *to eat* has many different usages in modern Greek. To eat a cold bath is to be disappointed; to eat wood is to receive punishment; to eat money is to spend money extravagantly; in vulgar usage to eat means to fuck and does not imply oragenital sex. So Bobos' father was really saying, "Turn off the lamp and I'll screw you."

"If roses need manure, why are you feeding your rose milk instead of putting it up your ass so it can get the manure?"

[X350., Jokes on teachers.]

51   One day at school the teacher asked the students to tell what was the first thing they did when they were born.

"I cried," said Johnny.

"I went to sleep," said Costas.

"While I was being born," said Bobos, "I grabbed a mirror to look at myself in my fur coat!"

[Legman I:586; X1014.1.* Lie: remarkable memory; J1772.4.2., Child takes mother's pubic hair to be a fur cap; X721., Humor concerning birth.]

52   One day Bobos asked his mother:

"Mother, why is it that we make the sign of the cross?"

"Because," said his mother, "Christ was crucified on a cross."

"Then, if Christ was crucified on a spit [*soúvla*], would we do this ['sidewinder' gesture of copulation; see appendix C] instead?"

53   One day when Bobos was walking home from school, he was passing under a balcony and something landed on his head. It was a used rubber!

So he went to the door of the house with the balcony and rang the bell. An old woman came to the door.

"What do you want?" she asked.

"I want to know who lives upstairs," said Bobos.

"Just my daughter and my son-in-law," said the old woman.

"Well, then, here's your grandson!" said Bobos, handing her the rubber.

[Legman I:434.]

Implicit in the punch line of the preceding joke is the prevalent Greek view of the main purpose of marriage: to produce male progeny. As the Greek word for child (*to paidí*) refers only to a male child and is usually not used to refer to a female child, the joke could probably never end with "Here's your granddaughter!" Daughters are desired only after sons have been produced.[5]

54 One day at school Bobos' teacher held up a white cloth in one hand and a red cloth in the other hand. She asked the children to tell her what they thought of when they saw the two pieces of cloth.

Helenitsa said the white cloth reminded her of new snow, and the red cloth, of apples.

Takis said that the white cloth reminded him of the clean towels and sheets that his mother washed every week, and the red cloth reminded him of a bullfighter.

Bobos kept waving his hand in the air, so the teacher finally called on him with great reluctance.

"When I see the two pieces of cloth, I think of pussy!"

"But, Bobos," said the teacher, "why in the world would you make that association?"

"Whatever I see, I think of pussy!" said Bobos.

[D1273.1.1., Three as magic number; X350., Jokes on teachers.]

All of us inevitably grow up, and so does Bobos. He progresses from a simpleton to a foulmouthed boy to a sexually sly lad. In the following jokes Bobos is sexually active, or at least he knows what it is all about.

The theme of the sexually innocent female who demands more and more sex once she has experienced it, a theme present in the first joke below, is a common feature of the jokes in one section of chapter eight, "Very *Sókin* Jokes."

55 Bobos liked a girl named Helenitsa, and this girl was young and still a virgin.

Helenitsa's mother was always warning her to be careful when she went out, not to "break it."* But Helenitsa was a little dumb, so she didn't really understand what her mother meant.

One night Bobos took Helenitsa to the movies. Before she left home, all dressed up, her mother said to her:

"Now Helenitsa, be careful, don't let Bobos break it!"

So Bobos and Helenitsa went to the movies. On the way home Bobos had a clever idea. He took Helenitsa home down a dark, narrow street. Suddenly, he ran ahead and hid himself. Helenitsa followed, and, when she got near him, he jumped out and frightened her. She

*The reference is to the maidenhead, the proof of a girl's virginity. I heard this admonition quite often from older women who would tease the younger girls on the group excursions I joined in the summer of 1976.

screamed and shrieked in fear. Just at that moment he ripped a piece of
cloth that he had in his pocket before. Then he said:

"Now you've done it! You've broken it!"

"Oh, what will I do? What will I do?" cried Helenitsa. "If I go home
and my mother finds out that it's broken, she'll beat me!"

"Don't worry," said Bobos. "I can fix it so that she won't know.
Down here in my pants, I have a special needle and thread, and I'll
sew it back up. Just take off your panties and lie down."

So he fucked her once, then twice, then three times, then four. Finally, he was too tired to continue, so he said:

"That's enough sewing. It's fixed now."

But Helenitsa said:

"No, I think it needs some more stitches to be really fixed."

"Well, I can't do it, because I'm out of thread," said Bobos.

So, Helenitsa reached down and grabbed his balls and said:

"That's a lie! You still have two spools of thread left!"

[AT 1542**, The Maiden's Honor; J86., Needle and thread symbolize
sex; K1315.2.3., Seduction by sham process of repairing vagina; K1363.,
Seduction through ignorance of sex; X735.9.5., No more yarn.]

In the next joke Bobos is old enough to get married, but we
see him reverting to his earlier demonstrated stupidity.

56 When Bobos grew up he married Helenitsa. After the wedding
night Bobos went to visit his father the next morning.

"Well, son, how was it last night?"

"Oh, it was fine," said Bobos.

"Tell me what happened?" asked his father. "What did you do first?"

"First, I put Helenitsa on the bed."

"*Brávo! Brávo!* Then what did you do?"

"Then I took off her dress."

"*Brávo! Brávo!* Then what did you do?"

"Then I took off her slip."

"*Brávo!* Then what did you do?"

"Then I took off her brassiere."

"*Brávo,* my boy! Then what did you do?"

"Then I took off her panties."

"Great! Terrific! Congratulations, my boy! Then what?"

"Then I took the elastic out of her panties and shot a spit ball at
her!" [In another version he says, "I killed a fly that was on the bed!"]

[Legman I:162.]

57   One day at school Bobos' teacher announced that it was her birthday.

"Since today is my birthday," she said, "I've decided to let each of you do whatever you want to do, just for today."

Johnny decided that he wanted to go and visit with the other fifth-grade class. Peter wanted to have all *A*'s for the day. Maria wanted to draw pictures on the blackboard. When it was Bobos' turn to make his request, he said that he wanted to put his finger in the teacher's navel!

"But, Bobos," protested the teacher, "we can't do that in class."

"But you promised," whined Bobos.

"Okay," said the teacher, "come to my office during recess."

So during recess Bobos went to the teacher's office.

"Close your eyes," said Bobos, and he proceeded to undress the teacher. When he had all her clothes off, he started to do his "work" with her.

"Wait a minute, Bobos," said the teacher. "That's not my navel."

"I know," said Bobos. "And that's not my finger, either."

[Inversion of K1399.5., Teacher seduces pupil; X350., Jokes on teachers.]

58   One day at school the teacher said:

"Boys, I want you to move all the desks to the back of the room. Then I want all the right-handed boys to go stand against the right wall, and I want all the left-handed boys to go stand against the left wall."

So the boys moved the desks to the back of the room, and then some of them went to the right side of the room, and the others went to the left side of the room.

All except Bobos. He was standing all alone in the middle of the room.

"Why are you standing in the middle of the room, Bobos?" asked the teacher.

"I don't use either hand [implying masturbation]. I have a woman [*gómena*]!"*

---

*The word *gómena* denotes a woman as sex object. Women who are "used" primarily for sex or who wear sexy clothes are called *gómenas*. *Ginéka*, the standard word that means both woman and wife, has no direct sexual association. In another version of the joke, Bobos says, "Because I masturbate with both hands!"

The next joke, one of the most popular among those I collected about Bobos, involves incest. I suspect that this joke, in one form or another, is widespread throughout the world. The joke also alludes to patrilocal residence, a common practice in many of the agricultural villages in Greece, but not necessarily a feature of urban life. In many cases, however, in Athens and in other urban areas, a couple lives next to the bride's parents.

59 One day Bobos asked his father for some money to go to a whorehouse because some other boys in his class had done it, and he wanted to know what it was all about. So his father gave him two hundred drachmes.

As Bobos left his house, he passed his grandmother's house next door.

"Where are you going, Bobos?" she asked.

"I'm going to a whorehouse!" he said.

"And where did you get the money for that?" she asked.

"From my father," said Bobos. "He gave me two hundred drachmes."

"Come on, Bobos," she said. "Are you going to waste all that money on a whore? Come on inside and I'll let you do it to me for free and you can keep the money!"

So Bobos agreed, and after about half an hour he went back home.

"Home so soon?" asked his father.

"I didn't go to the whorehouse after all," said Bobos. "Instead, I fucked Grandmother!"

"Oh, my God! You stupid jerk! You mean that you fucked my mother!"

"Don't get so excited," said Bobos. "After all, look how many years you've been fucking *my* mother!"

[Legman I:96; Legman II:198–99; N825.3.3., Help from grandmother; Inversion of T423., Youth attempts to seduce his grandmother.]

The preceding joke exists in many versions. In some cases the grandmother takes the money, which varies from five drachmes in one version to five hundred drachmes in others. In some versions it is Bobos' father's sister instead of his grandmother.

60 One day in school the teacher asked the children to tell her what they did every day before they came to school.

All of the children listed a series: "I woke up, I washed my face, I ate my breakfast, I kissed my mother goodbye, and I walked to school."

When it was Bobos' turn, the teacher was surprised by what he said:

"I get up, I get bathed, I eat breakfast, I jump on our *veránda* two or three times, then I come to school."*

The teacher was very upset when she heard this because she thought that Bobos must have some problem at home to behave in this manner.

So one day she paid a visit to Bobos' house to talk with his mother about his problem.

"Hello, I'm Bobos' teacher," she said at the door.

"Oh, do come in and welcome to our house. Please sit down. I'm so glad to meet you. But first, let me offer you something. A sweet, perhaps? Or some coffee?" asked Bobos' mother.

"I'll have some coffee," said the teacher.

"Veranda," called Bobos' mother to the maid, "please bring us a coffee for Bobos' teacher!"

61 One day after school Bobos went to his teacher's house. After a while he said:

"I'll give you two hundred drachmes if you let me see your tits!"

"Shame on you, Bobos! What do you think I am?"

Finally, after thinking it over, she changed her mind and took off her blouse and her brassiere. So Bobos gave her the money.

After a few minutes of looking at her, he said:

"I'll give you five hundred drachmes if you let me see your pussy!"

"Bobos! Shame on you! What do you think?"

But after thinking it over, and needing the money, she changed her mind. So she took off her skirt, her slip, and her panties, and Bobos gave her the money.

After looking at her pussy for a while, he said:

"If you let me fuck you, I'll give you one thousand drachmes!"

After a long consideration the teacher agreed. So she took the money and let him do it to her.

After they finished she was going to the bathroom when the telephone rang. It was the school principal. He asked her:

"Did Bobos get to your house yet with your salary?"

[K1361.2., Progressive purchase of favors; Inversion of K1399.5., Teacher seduces pupil.]

The following is an old joke, easily adapted for Bobos.[6] The setting for the joke as told here also points out a widespread

---

. *"To jump" [*pidów*] is slang for "to fuck." *Veránda* usually refers to a type of porch, but it can also be a woman's name, albeit a most uncommon one.

social custom in Greece. Greeks drink what is often called "Turkish" coffee: the coffee is ground to a powder, boiled in a small pot (*bríki*) with water and sugar, and poured into a small cup. The coffee sediment in the cup is used for divination purposes: patterns in the sediment suggest figures, letters, doors, numbers, and so on. Greek women often get together in the afternoon at one of the women's houses to drink coffee and to tell fortunes.

62 One day Bobos' mother saw two of her maiden aunts at the grocery store. She invited them to come to her house for coffee, but they refused, saying:

"Not because of you. It's Bobos and all the bad language that he uses. It's really shocking!"

"But Bobos won't be home from school for an hour, so we have plenty of time," said Bobos' mother.

So the three women went to Bobos' house and drank coffee, read each other's coffee cups to learn their fortunes, and then got carried away with the latest gossip. Suddenly, Bobos walked in!

"Good afternoon," said Bobos. (It was amazing! He didn't curse at all; he just said "Good afternoon"!)

Thinking that perhaps Bobos had had a change of character, one of his aunts ventured a question:

"What grade did you get today, Bobos?"

"A ten [an A]," said Bobos, again without any profanity.

Encouraged by his seeming politeness, the other aunt also asked:

"What did your teacher tell you today, Bobos?"

"She said that there was an American ship coming to Piraeus with men who have big pricks and that they're looking for women!"

"I knew we shouldn't have come here, Katharine," said one of the aunts to the other. "Let's go," she said, and they got up to leave.

"What's the hurry?" asked Bobos. "The ship isn't arriving until day after tomorrow!"

[Legman I:235.]

63 One day Bobos went to visit the three spinsters who lived next door. While he was there they gave him three pieces of bread, butter, and honey to eat.

Well, he sat and talked, and he licked the honey off the first piece of bread, then he licked the honey off the second piece of bread. When the ladies realized what he was doing, they scolded him and said:

"Shame on you, Bobos! Now you must eat the last piece of bread and not just lick the honey off as on the first two!"

When Bobos returned home his father asked him what he had been doing all that time next door.

"Oh, I licked two and I ate [fucked] one!" said Bobos.

[D1273.1.1., Three as magic number.]

64 One day at school the teacher asked the students:

"Students, who can tell me the different ways that people have sex?"

Immediately, Bobos raised his hand and started shouting:

"Forty! Forty!"

Since the teacher was tired of Bobos' pranks, instead she called on Helenitsa, who knew three.

"The first," said Helenitsa, "is the man on top of the woman."

Bobos raised his hand again and shouted:

"Forty-one!"

[Legman I:545.]

In all Greek movie houses, a five- to fifteen-minute break, the intermission, occurs between the first and the second reels of film. Long movies have two intermissions; evidently each movie house has only one projector. During intermission people usually go to the lobby to smoke, and a peddler carrying a tray of candies, nuts, soft drinks, pumpkin seeds,[7] and the like, sells refreshments inside.

65 One evening Bobos' father wanted to have sex with Bobos' mother, so he said to Bobos:

"Take this money and go to the movies."

"I don't want to go to the movies," said Bobos.

"I don't care," said his father. "Take the money and go so that I can be alone with your mother."

Well, Bobos was curious, so he pretended to leave, but instead he went and hid in the wardrobe of his parents' bedroom.

Later his parents came in and they made love, and Bobos was peeking through the keyhole of the wardrobe.

After they finished the husband smoked a cigarette.

"What's this, the intermission?" asked Bobos' mother.

"Yes," said Bobos' father.

So Bobos came out of the wardrobe and said:

"Peanuts, soft drinks, chocolates!"

Chapter 3
The Clever Greeks: Esoteric Humor

Cleverness and intelligence are appreciated all over the world, and this chapter contains a selection of jokes in which Greeks pride themselves on having those qualities.

Anthropologists in America have shown that all groups of people in the world are ethnocentric (from Greek: *éthnos* meaning tribe or nation, and *kéntron* meaning center). Ethnocentrism is the universal tendency for all people to believe that their way of life is superior, their religion the true one, their music the best, their language the most difficult and the most precise, and so on. However, not all groups of people are equally ethnocentric. Some, like the Bushmen of South Africa, are only mildly ethnocentric. Others, like the German Nazis, were so ethnocentric that they excused genocide for the sake of their own racial "superiority." The modern Greeks fall somewhere between those two extremes of ethnocentrism. However, most Greeks are known the world over as proud people, perhaps a bit "clannish," but also extremely hospitable, funloving, and hardworking.

Greek *philótimo* ("honor," "pride," "self-esteem") is in large part responsible for Greek ethnocentrism, and thus, by extension, one could say that *philótimo* is also the basis of the jokes that emphasize Greek cleverness. Every Greek has his or her *philótimo*, as an individual, as a member of a family, and, most important, as a Greek. On this quality rests Greek individualism, because it is sheer *being*, apart from position and achievement, that is respected.

Greek democracy and concepts of equality derive from

42

philótimo: everyone, both as a person and as a Greek, is equal to everyone else, neither superior nor inferior. This does not mean that Greek society is not class structured or that Greeks have no class awareness, but it means that each person derives merit from his or her *philótimo*; inferiority comes only with the forfeiting of the *philótimo* (see Lee 1953). Greek nationalism also derives from *philótimo*. All Greeks share a common and glorious past, and, if the nation is threatened, it is the right and privilege of rich and poor alike to fight together for Greek freedom.

Greek *philótimo* is easily bruised, however, and one cannot have good relations with Greeks unless one is aware of Greek *philótimo*. That it is important to pay tribute to it and to avoid offending it was most apparent to me when on several occasions my role as a social scientist, striving to overcome my own ethnocentrisms in order to view another culture relative to its own values, conflicted with Greek resentment of being addressed or described in purely objective terms.

The American folklorist William Hugh Jansen (1965) developed a theory of folklore in which he discussed the esoteric-exoteric factor. In their esoteric humor Greeks reveal what they think of themselves and what they suppose other nationals think of them. In their exoteric humor, usually in the form of stereotyping humor, Greeks reveal what they think of other nationals. Greek esoteric humor is based on many factors. Greeks were isolated by religion and language for hundreds of years under Turkish domination. The great achievements of the ancient Greeks, and the manner in which Western scholars turn to ancient Greece as the source of wisdom and knowledge, justify, in the modern Greek mind, a feeling of superiority. The use of the Greek language for scientific and scholarly purposes (for example, the words *ethnocentric, esoteric*, and *exoteric* all derive from Greek) justifies the modern Greek view that the Greek language is the richest and the most logical in the world.

Because of the misfortunes of history and environment, Greece today is an economically struggling country that perhaps only in shipping has managed to surpass the glories of its past. As Greece endeavors to take its place among the nations of modern Europe, the Greek government faces many difficult problems, particularly with the economy. Probably for reasons such as these, Greek esoteric humor emphasizes cleverness as the trait in which Greeks outshine other nationals. And it is *Elliniki poneriá* (Greek "craftiness," or "slyness," "cunning," "knavery"), described in connection with the Bobos cycle, that is applauded. *Poneriá* is not a quality universally admired by Greeks, nor is it universally possessed by them. However, foreigners are often warned to beware of it when visiting Greece, and many Greeks also complain of the characteristic in their fellow citizens. And most Greeks admit to the widespread belief that "it takes two Jews to beat a Greek, but it takes two Greeks to beat an Armenian." (I never heard, however, any funny stories about Armenians.)

The first jokes in this chapter involve the Greek language. Modern Greek exists in two forms: the "popular," *dhimotikí*; and the "formal," *katharévusa*. *Dhimotikí* is the everyday language of the people and contains loan words from other languages that have been incorporated into the Greek language in the course of recent Greek history. *Dhimotikí* is primarily a spoken language, that of Greek songs and ballads, and does not have a fixed orthography. It is, however, largely used by modern writers of poetry and of fiction. *Katharévusa*, a conscious and artificial return to older Greek, is taught in schools, adopted for official purposes, and used in a more or less "pure" form by newspapers.

Foreigners wishing to communicate with Greeks usually study *dhimotikí*. It is a difficult language, especially for a native English speaker, because of its complex system of grammar. Most Greeks are astounded to hear a foreigner speaking their language and usually assume that the foreigner is of Greek descent. When the foreigner complains of the difficulty of the language, he or she often will be told a story that illustrates the impossibility of thoroughly learning modern Greek.

Many different people in Greece told me the following joke, but always in the context of my struggling with the language. The joke relies also on another aspect of communication, which linguists call kinesics (popularly known as body language).

Greeks, and other peoples in the Mediterranean region, have a complex system of kinesic communication that involves parts of the face, the hands, and even other parts of the body.

66 An American wanted his son to learn Greek, so he sent him to Greece for a year to study the language.

When the young man arrived, he found a language teacher and began taking daily lessons. At the end of the year, the young man thought that he knew Greek. So he bought his ticket to return to New York by passenger ship.

When he arrived at the harbor in Piraeus, he didn't see the ship. So he asked a Greek standing on the wharf:

"Did the ship for New York leave yet?"

The Greek whistled and waved his right hand around in circles [meaning that the ship had left *long* before].

The American didn't understand, so he went up to another Greek man standing on the wharf and asked:

"Did the ship for New York leave yet?"

The Greek replied:

"Now [again implying that the man was late]?"

Finally, the American went up to another Greek on the wharf and again asked if the ship had left for New York. The man replied:

"*Now*, that *you* came?"

So the American went to his teacher's house and complained that he had not done a good job of teaching him the language because he hadn't understood what the three men in Piraeus had told him.

"Don't feel bad," said his teacher. "After all, not everybody can learn all there is to learn in Greek!"

[AT1699, Misunderstanding Because of Ignorance of a Foreign Language.]

The following is another widespread joke that involves a kinesic gesture known and used in Mediterranean countries.

67 Way up in the mountains of Greece, there were two shepherds that were tending their flocks. They were atop two peaks that were separated by a ravine about five hundred meters wide.

One shepherd shouted to the other:

"Hey, Vasili, have you seen my donkey by any chance?"

The other shepherd tilted his head backwards once and clicked his tongue [meaning "no," but how could the first shepherd see and hear the second's reply?]!

[AT924, Discussion by Sign Language.]

The last joke concerning the Greek language has a very distant setting: Korea.

68   During the Korean War these two Greeks volunteered and went to Korea to help fight with the Americans.

When they got there the one from Thessaloniki asked the other one from Athens:

*"Sen san rou re Jian?"**

"Ti ípes [What did you say]?" asked the Athenian.

An American soldier overheard them talking and said to his friend:

"Listen to that! Those guys just got here and *already* they are speaking Chinese!"

In recent years Greeks have undergone a change of attitude toward America and Americans. Anti-American sentiment results from the American military presence in Greece, now widely unpopular. Many Greeks of all political parties want the American military to leave Greece; its presence undoubtedly reminds them of former military occupations by the Turks, the Italians, and the Germans. Most Greeks resent particularly the special privileges enjoyed by the American military personnel in Greece. The following three jokes involve direct competition between Greeks and Americans, but I suspect that the last two originally involved conflict with Turks and have been reworked recently to feature Americans.

69   There were two liars, an American liar and a Greek liar.

So the American liar said:

"In America, everything is so big! You can't imagine! Why, in New York City there is a building with ten thousand floors!"

---

*In imitation of the way some macho Greeks (*mánges*) pronounce *Sou édossan roúha re Yánni?* ("Did they give you clothes, re Johnny?"). Greeks commonly use *moré, re,* and *vre* as terms of address although they are not polite expressions, having a meaning similar to "stupid." Of the three, *vre* is the most impolite.

"Are you sure that it's *really* that tall?" asked the Greek liar.

"Well, maybe not. It's probably a handspan below that," said the American liar.

"Well, in Greece we too have fabulous things. For instance, in Greece the women give birth to children from their navels!"

"Oh, come on now," said the American liar. "Who would believe that women give birth through their navels?"

"Well, maybe not," said the Greek liar. "Maybe it's a handspan below that that they give birth!"

[AT1920, Contest in Lying; X904., The teller reduces the size of his lie; X1030.1., Lie: the great building.]

70   There were two liars, a Black American and a Greek.

The Black American said:

"Since in America we have so many different people, white, black, red, we decided to make Mohammed our God. Well, once I was on a ship in the Caribbean Sea. And there was a huge hurricane, and so we prayed to Mohammed. So Mohammed shat, and shat, and shat, and from the shit an island was made next to the ship and we were saved."

So the Greek said:

"Well, once I was on a ship, and it was sinking in the same sea. And we made our [Orthodox sign of the] cross and prayed to God. So God put his penis down, and it was like a bridge, and we walked across it to the dry land!"

"Oh, really?" said the Black American liar. "Your God has *such* a big penis?"

"Yes, since your Mohammed has such a big asshole to make so much shit, *that's* why our God has such a big penis!"

[AT1920, Contest in Lying; D469., Transformation: Miscellaneous object to other objects; D480., Size of object transformed; R138., Rescue from shipwreck; T615., Supernatural growth; X900., Humor of lies and exaggeration.]

In another version (70a) of the preceding joke, the version I believe to be the original, a Greek and a Turk were on a ship going from Piraeus to Crete, a voyage that in the past took three days. During the trip a severe storm took place, and the ship was taking on water. As the passengers were screaming hysterically, the Turk calmly told a Greek how he had been saved once before in a similar storm by praying to Mohammed. From that point on the two stories are the same.

In the last joke involving Greek-American hostilities, again sodomy is used in one-upmanship.

71 Here in Heraklion two men were fishing from the harbor. One was a Black American soldier, from the air base, and the other was a man from Heraklion.

So they caught a big fish at the same time. (The fish had taken both of their hooks.) And so they both tried to get the fish, and they started fighting.

"It's my fish!" shouted the Cretan.

"No, it's my fish!" shouted the American.

"Let's make a bet," said the Cretan. "Let's fuck each other, and whoever screams with pain first loses the fish."

"Okay," said the American.

So the Cretan fucked the American, and the American kept quiet so that he wouldn't lose the bet.

When it was the American's turn to fuck the Cretan, the Cretan said:

"Never mind, you take the fish! We really shouldn't fight over just a fish!"

[N93., Wagers dealing with sex.]

The next five jokes resemble the multi-ethnic-slur jokes in that each involves several different nationals. In the typical multi-ethnic-slur joke, no one nation comes away unscathed; in the following jokes, however, the clever Greek always comes out ahead.

72 One time, three liars were talking: an American, a Russian, and a Greek.

"In Russia," said the Russian, "our doctors performed a stupendous operation where they transplanted a leg from one person to another!"

"Did the patient live?" asked the other two.

"Yes," replied the Russian.

"That's nothing! In America," said the American, "our doctors removed the heart of a patient and replaced it with a battery!"

"Did the patient live?" asked the other two.

"Yes," replied the American.

"That's nothing," said the Greek. "In Greece our doctors removed the brain of a patient and replaced it with shit!"

"Did the patient live?" asked the other two.

"Yes, he lived and he ruled!"*

[D1273.1.1., Three as magic number; F668.1., Skillful surgeon removes and replaces vital organs.]

The emphasis on Greek sexual superiority in the following joke and in many others in this chapter is a function of the high value of machismo in Greek society.

73 Sometime, there were four men: a Greek, a German, a Frenchman, and a Persian.

They were having an argument about whose country was the best and what were the best things made in their countries.

The German said:

"In Germany we make the best cars with the best transmissions."

The Persian said:

"In Persia we make the most beautiful rugs in the world."

The Frenchman said:

"In France we have the most beautiful girls in the world."

So, finally, the Greek said:

"In Greece we have the best cocks to fuck the French girls on top of Persian carpets inside German automobiles!"

74 Sometime, there were three men together in the same compartment of a train: a Greek, a German, and a Persian.

Suddenly the train stopped and the devil appeared. He told them that, unless they could challenge him to do something that he could *not* do, he would take them to hell. Otherwise, he would let them go.

So the German said:

"In Germany we make the best transmissions for automobiles. Can you make a better transmission?"

---

*Presumably, this joke is from the time that Greece was ruled by kings. Also, the joke plays on a common Greek expression, Zo kai vasilévo ("I live and I rule," or "I'm on top of the world!"), used in response to someone asking, "You're still alive? I hadn't seen you so long I thought you were dead." Another interpretation is that, even with shit for brains, any Greek can outsmart Russians and Americans.

But the devil could make very good transmissions, so he sent the German to hell.

The Persian brought out a magic carpet that could fly, but the devil had one that flew even faster, so he sent the Persian to hell.

So the Greek thought and thought: What to do? What to do?

Finally, he stood up, raised one leg, and farted loudly!

"Sketch that!" he shouted to the devil.

Well, since the devil couldn't sketch a fart, he let the Greek go.

[AT1176, Catching a Man's Broken Wind; D1155., Magic carpet; D1273.1.1., Three as magic number.]

75 Sometime, there were three men in an airplane: an Englishman, a German, and a Greek. Well, the plane's engines caught on fire, and so the three men had to bail out in parachutes.

They all landed on a small island, but to their surprise the island had no houses, no bushes, no trees, only penises everywhere! Thousands of penises!

Well, the German got hungry. So he took a can of food out of his sack, but when he sat down to eat his food, a penis fucked him!

The Englishman suffered the same fate when he sat down to eat his food.

But the Greek was more clever. First, he masturbated five or six of the penises, and so they fell down, limp. Then he sat down and ate his food without getting screwed!

[D1273.1.1., Three as magic number; F730., Extraordinary islands.]

The following joke reflects the anti-American sentiment that was so prevalent in 1976 because of universal dislike of the American secretary of state, Henry Kissinger.

76 One time, on an airplane going from Greece to England, there were three men: an American, a Russian, and a Greek.

During the flight the pilot told them that he was having severe engine trouble and that the plane was too heavy. Somebody had to get out of the plane!

So the Russian opened the door and said:

"Long live Russia!" And he jumped out of the plane.

A while later the pilot announced that the plane was still too heavy. The Greek and the American started arguing about who was going to jump out, so finally the British pilot, in exasperation, said:

"Long live England!" And he jumped out of the plane!

Well, the Greek was smart, so he quickly went to fly the airplane. But the plane continued to lose altitude, so the Greek said:

"One of us has to go! Who will it be?"

Well, they kept arguing, and finally the Greek stood up, opened the door, and said:

"Long live Greece!"

But, instead of jumping out, as the American *thought* he would do, the Greek grabbed the American and threw *him* out of the plane!

[D1273.1.1., Three as magic number.]

In another version (76a) of the preceding joke, the last two men on board the airplane are a Greek and a Turk. In trying to push each other out of the aircraft, they both fall out, but each manages to grab a rope dangling from the plane. While they are suspended from the rope, the Greek whistles a belly-dance (*tsiftetéle*) tune. The Turk begins to clap to the music and falls. The Greek then climbs back up to the plane and is saved. (J2133.13., Fool hanging by hands, claps, then falls.)

In the group of jokes to follow, cleverness and *poneriá* are emphasized *per se*. The jokes illustrate the different types of tricksters in Greek folklore. In some examples other nationals are involved in the situation, but their presence is not a prerequisite.

77 A shopowner had a young boy working for him as an errand boy. One day he told the boy to take a very big and heavy box to the other side of the town.

The boy was struggling to carry the box, and a man finally stopped him and offered to help him.

Along the way the man said:

"You know, your boss shouldn't make you carry such a heavy and big box so far."

"Yes," said the boy. "I told him that before I left. But he said that I would meet some stupid person along the way who would help me carry it!"

The next joke illustrates the widespread, but incorrect, view of the male's role in determining the sex of the children. Men who have sons are viewed as supermasculine, whereas those who have only daughters are seen as less potent. That folk attitude is not restricted to Greece, but it places its heaviest burden on males in a society (such as that in Greece) that emphasizes virility and machismo.

78   There was a man who had five daughters. One day he met another man who had ten sons.

"Ten sons! How did you do it? Do you have some secret?"

"Yes, I have a secret, but because I like you I will tell you. First, paint your bed blue. Then, dye all of your sheets, pillowcases, and blankets blue. Next, paint your bathroom blue."

"Then what should I do?" asked the man without sons.

"Do you have an ikon over your bed?"

"Yes, of the Virgin Mary."

"Well, get one of Christ and put it over the bed."

"Then what should I do?"

"Buy blue pajamas for yourself and a blue nightgown for your wife."

"Then what should I do?"

"Then—well, you must take a bath together with your wife. Then put on the blue pajamas and have her put on the blue nightgown."

"Yes? Then what?"

"Then call me and I'll finish the job and you'll have a son!"

[Legman I:789; K115.1.4., Pseudo-magic charm for engendering offspring; T3.1., Blue fortunate in love matters.]

79   A Greek sailor on the deck of a ship in the harbor at Piraeus saw a man selling canaries on the dock.

"How much are the canaries?" he shouted.

"Twenty drachmes each," said the vendor.

"Twenty drachmes?" asked the sailor. "That's too much. I'll give you ten."

"Twenty or nothing," said the vendor.

"Okay," said the sailor, "I'll take one."

So the vendor put a bird in a little paper sack and gave it to a small boy to deliver to the sailor.

When the sailor got the bird, he threw the coins down to the vendor.

As the ship was leaving, the sailor called out:

"Hey, vendor, if those twenty drachmes are good at the bank, call me!" (He had given old money from 1944 to 1954 that was no longer in circulation.)

"Hey, sailor," said the vendor. "And if that yellow-painted sparrow sings, you call *me*!"

[K130., Sale of worthless animal.]

80   A bank employee had a friend who couldn't understand how the bank employee had so much. So he asked him:

"How do you do it on your salary? You have a car, a villa, good clothes, everything! But you only make eight thousand drachmes a month."

"I'll show you," said the bank employee. "Tomorrow come to the bank at eleven in the morning and watch what I do."

So the next morning, at eleven o'clock, the bank employee went to the bank manager and said:

"Want to make a bet?"

"Okay," said the manager. "What is it?"

"I bet you one hundred thousand drachmes that you don't have a penis!"

"That's a steal," said the bank manager in great confidence, beginning to unbutton his trousers.

"Wait just a minute," said the bank employee, and he left the office.

Then the bank employee went to all the other employees and said:

"I'll bet you two hundred thousand drachmes that the bank manager will take down his pants and show me his balls!"

"Impossible!" said the other employees, and they made the bet.

Then the man went back to the manager's office, and the other employees peeped in the door that was left slightly ajar.

The manager took down his pants and said, touching himself:

"There, you see! Now pay me the one hundred thousand drachmes!"

So the man paid the manager, and then he went outside and collected two hundred thousand drachmes from the other employees. So he had gained one hundred thousand drachmes!

So then his friend understood how he got the money for the car, the villa, and the clothes!

[Legman I:107; Legman II:543.]

81   A Greek businessman went to Germany to visit a trade fair. The Germans were displaying all the latest marvels of modern technology. At one exhibit a German showed the Greek the newest machine for butchering and preparing pork.

"At this end," said the German, "we put the pig in. Then it gets bathed, shaved, killed, butchered, all automatically. Then, at the other end, sausages come out, ready to cook."

"I see," said the Greek. "First you put in the pig and then you take out the sausages! Well, in Greece we're not so underdeveloped after all, because we have an even *better* system. First, we put in the sausage, and then later we take out the pig!"

[Legman II:559.]

82 Two Greeks went to Cuba. Well, their first night there they went out to dinner in a fine restaurant.

Well, inside the restaurant there were three Cubans with full beards sitting and eating. When the men finished they called the waiter who brought them the bill. Well, they all stood up and said loudly:

"*Viva* Castro!"

And they tore up the bill and left without paying.

So the Greeks called the waiter and asked him who the bearded men were.

"Oh, they're Castro's police," he said.

So the Greeks finished their meal, paid the bill and left. But they decided that the next night they would also get a free meal.

So the next night they went to an even better restaurant, and they ordered all the best food and the best wine. When they had finished eating, they called the waiter, and he brought them the bill.

So they stood up and shouted:

"*Viva* Castro!"

Then they tore up the bill and started to leave.

"What do you think you're doing?" asked the waiter.

"We're Castro's police," the Greeks said.

"But Castro's police all have beards," insisted the waiter.

So the Greeks took down their trousers and pointed to their pubic hair and said:

"We're the secret police!"

[AT1526A, Supper Won by a Trick: Another Person to Pay; K305.3., Youths clever thieves.]

83 One time, there were two Greek friends who wanted to take a trip.

"Let's go to France," said one.

"But we don't speak French," said the other.

"Let's go to England," said the first.

"But we don't know English," said the second.

"I know," said the first. "We can go to Russia because I know a little Russian."

So they went to Russia, and they went to a restaurant to eat.

"I know how to order in Russian," said the first friend. "Don't worry about a thing."

When the waiter came the Greek told him:

"Ruski waiter! Please bring us macaronófski, soupófski, breadófski, and wineófski."

So the waiter brought them macaroni, soup, bread, and wine.

"See how good my Russian is?" bragged the first friend.

After they finished eating the man called the waiter and said:

"Ruski waiter, bring us the billófski."

So the waiter brought the bill.

"See how good my Russian is?" asked the first friend.

"Listen," said the waiter, "if I wasn't a Greekófski, you'd have eaten ballófskis!"

84   There were two Greeks in Germany without money and without jobs. All they talked about was how they could make some money.

Finally, one of them said:

"I've got an idea how we could make lots of money. We'll stage a play, 'How the Greeks Steal,' and we'll sell lots of tickets!"

So they got a sheet, a table, a chair, and a bowl. They set up a stage in a corner of the main town square, against the stone walls. Then they set up the sheet in front, across the corner, like a curtain.

Then they put up a sign on the curtain: "Theatre Tonight! HOW THE GREEKS STEAL. Acclaimed cast. Tickets: five marks."

So the Germans in the village were curious, and the two Greeks sold lots of tickets.

That night all the people gathered in the square to see the play. They waited and waited, but nothing happened.

Finally, somebody got impatient and pulled the sheet back. There, on the table, propped up against the bowl was another sign:

"*That's* how the Greeks steal!"

[K305.3., Youths clever thieves.]

85   When the Americans were sending astronauts into space, they needed a third astronaut to go to the moon with the two American astronauts.

Well, the Americans opened an office in Athens to recruit an astronaut to go to the moon. The Americans hired a Greek man to be the director of the agency.

First, he interviewed a German:

"I want one million dollars to go to the moon," said the German.

Next, came an Englishman:

"I want two million to go to the moon," he said.

Finally, a Greek came and said:

"I want five million dollars to go to the moon."

"Five million dollars! Why so much money?" asked the director.

"Two million for me, two million for you, and one million for the German, and we'll send *him* to the moon."

The last part of this chapter includes some examples of jokes told in Crete about people from the village of Anogia. Situated high in the mountains about twenty-two miles southwest of Heraklion, Anogia has a population of about four thousand people. During World War II most of the village was destroyed by the Germans. The present prosperity of the village is due in part to the fine quality and great beauty of the handmade textiles produced by the village women. During vacation periods many tour buses visit the village daily, and tourists invade the shops and houses for souvenirs.

Anogia has become famous because of its popularization in the folklore of Crete. The men of Anogia were traditionally considered to be sheep thieves in Crete. Today, however, Cretan folklore depicts them as verbal tricksters whose cleverness and wit are universally admired.

Anogians are proud of their village and their heritage. The village has produced, in addition to fine woolen textiles, several well-known artists and musicians, among them the musician Nikos Ksilouris, whose own fame probably has helped spread the fame of his village outside Crete. Anogians living in Athens and abroad subscribe to a monthly newspaper, *The Voice of the Anogian,* which always includes a selection of *athivolés,* or anecdotes, about actual events and people in Anogia. The newspaper contains also some of the jokes that are in wide circulation in Crete and in Athens (among Cretans) about the clever Anogian who usually has the last word.

Figuring in the first joke to follow is the *períptero,* or kiosk, practically a Greek institution and ubiquitous throughout the country. In downtown Athens *perípteros,* sometimes three or more to a block, line the streets at the edge of the sidewalks.

They are tiny wooden structures with one door, windows on all sides, and an attendant seated inside. *Períptero* attendants, usually disabled veterans, war widows, or relatives of victims of World War II, receive government permits for their jobs.

The *períptero* is the typical Greek male's first morning stop, for the purchase of a newspaper and cigarettes (sold only at the kiosks). Around the newspapers and cigarettes are crowded candy, gum, souvenirs, postcards, toys, "worry beads," key chains, soap, toothpaste, shaving cream, watchbands, combs, and other items. Many *peripteros* also have paperback books, maps, dictionaries, and occasionally a telephone that can be used for one-and-a-half or two drachmes.

86 (In some small villages in Greece, people have accounts at the baker's, the butcher's, the general store, and the *períptero*, where they buy cigarettes and newspapers. So when they buy something, the amount is written on their account, and they pay at the end of the week or the month.)

Well, one time an Anogian went to Athens, and he needed some cigarettes. So he went to a *períptero* and asked for a pack of Ace cigarettes.

When he got the cigarettes, he started to leave.

"Wait," said the man in the *períptero*, "you haven't paid for those cigarettes."

"Write it [on my account]!" said the Anogian.

"Here in Athens," said the man in the *períptero*, "we don't write accounts."

"So, you have *such* good memories here in Athens that you don't have to write?" asked the Anogian as he left.

87 A man from Anogia went to Athens and was hungry. He didn't have any money, but, believing that the Athenians are stupid people, he went into a restaurant with a plan to get a free meal.

He sat at a table, and when the waiter came he said:

"I want to make a bet with you. I bet you that after I eat and drink I'll sing you some *mandinádes* [Cretan song-poems] so beautiful that you'll pay for my dinner! And if you don't like them, then I'll pay."

The waiter agreed to the bet.

So the Anogian ate and drank, and then the waiter came over and sat down to hear the *mandinádes*.

The Anogian sang a *mandináda,* but the waiter said that he didn't like it. So the Anogian sang another, and another, and another, but the waiter still didn't like them. So finally the Anogian sang:

"I ate your delicious food, and I drank your delicious wine, and now I'll pay and leave, so you can finish your work on time."

"Do you like that?" asked the Anogian.

"Yes, *that* [one] I like," said the waiter.

"Then you've lost the bet and you must pay for the meal!" said the Anogian as he got up to leave.

[AT1526A, Supper Won by a Trick: Another Person to Pay; J1578.*, Penniless guest makes an agreement with his host . . . (Rotunda 1942).]

88   A man from Anogia went to Heraklion to sell a ram. He had the ram tied on a rope, and he walked all the way. Just outside Heraklion two thieves saw him, and one went ahead to distract the Anogian while the other went behind and cut the rope and stole the ram. When the man finally noticed that his ram was gone, he had reached the gates of Heraklion. He looked everywhere, but he couldn't find his ram.

It was late and there were no buses back to Anogia, so he had to take a room in a hotel for the night.

The desk clerk gave him a room with two beds, and he went upstairs to the room. Since he was very dirty, and his clothes were full of mud, he decided to sleep under the bed.

Very late in the night, a man and his girlfriend came to the hotel to find a room. The clerk told them that there was only one empty bed in the whole hotel, and it was in the same room where the Anogian was sleeping.

"Never mind," said the young man, "we'll only stay for one hour."

So they went to the room, and when they looked inside they didn't see anybody.

"That's better," said the young man, "the room's empty."

So they undressed and started to make love. While they were really enjoying themselves, the young man shouted to his girl friend:

"Quick, cover yourself, the whole world is looking!"

The Anogian stood up and said:

"If the whole world is looking, maybe it can see where my ram is?"

[AT1355B, Adulteress Tells Her Lover: "I Can See the Whole World." Hidden Shepherd Asks, "Can You See My Lost Calves?"]

In another version (88a) the young man says to his girlfriend, "When I look in your eyes I can see all over the world." Then the Anogian stands up and says, "Maybe you can see where my ram is?"

89   Two shepherds from the mountains close to Anogia decided to visit Heraklion. It was the first time that either of them had been to the "big city."

"What will we do in Heraklion?" asked the first one as they were walking to the town.

"We'll go to a movie," said the second one.

When they got to Heraklion, they didn't know where the theatres were. They walked and walked. Finally, they approached a big, new apartment building with lots of bright lights downstairs.

The second shepherd said:

"That's a movie house. Let's go in."

So they walked in, but there was nothing in the lobby but stairs. So they walked up one, two, three flights of stairs. Finally, they got to the rooftop.

On the roof was a cot, and there was a couple making love!

"Oh, it's a sex movie!" said the first shepherd.

So they sat down to watch. After about fifteen minutes the couple stopped, and the man smoked a cigarette.

"What's that?" asked the first shepherd.

"That's the intermission," said the second shepherd.

After the man finished smoking, they started making love again. Once, twice, three times, four times.

Finally, the second shepherd said to his friend:

"Let's go, this is where we came in. You don't want to see the whole movie over again, do you?"

[Legman I:128.]

90   Two shepherds tending their flock outside of Anogia went to the well to get water one night. One looked down into the well and saw the reflection of the moon on the top of the water.

"Come here, *kumbáre!*"* said the first shepherd. "The moon has fallen into the well!"

Kumbáre, kumbára are terms of address for men and women who are the godparents of one's child or who are one's wedding sponsors. In Crete, however, they are used often without the literal meaning as warm terms of address and friendship among people from the same village or from the same region. *Kumbáre* is also sometimes used informally to address a waiter or a cab driver.

So the other came and looked and said:

"We must get a rope and a hook, and then we can pull it out!"

So they got a rope and a hook, and they threw the hook down into the well. When they started pulling, the hook got caught in a rock on the side of the well and got stuck.

So they pulled harder and harder, and finally the rock gave way and they both fell down.

When they were flat on the ground, they looked up and saw the moon high up in the sky.

The first shepherd said:

"Well, it *was* hard work, eh, *kumbáre,* but look how far up in the sky we threw the moon!"

[AT1335A, Rescuing the Moon.]

91 A man from Anogia went to Athens for the first time. He was wearing typical Cretan clothes: a black fringed scarf [*saríki*] wrapped around his head, a black shirt and vest, and baggy, wide-legged pants [*vrákes*] tucked into knee-high black leather boots.

When he got off the boat in Piraeus, he passed by a group of young men who started to heckle him about his strange clothing:

"Hey, old man, why do you wear those baggy pants?"

But the Anogian said nothing; he just scratched his head.

"Hey, grandpa, where did you get those antique boots?"

Again the Anogian said nothing; he only scratched his head.

"Hey, grandpa," said another youth, "when you scratch your head, why don't you take off that funny black scarf?"

Finally, the Anogian responded:

"And I suppose that *you* take your pants off when you scratch your ass?"

[AT1337, Peasant Visits the City.]

92 A man from Anogia was taken to trial in the court in Heraklion for stealing a goat. Several witnesses testified against him, and he had been brought to court many times before. Finally, the judge asked him:

Athenians use the term to try to establish rapport with villagers. The compadre relationship, a pattern found throughout Mediterranean Europe and Latin America, is very important in Greece. Through the compadre relationship even more individuals are incorporated into the large, extended family, because the compadres become fictive kinsmen. In Greece the Church extends incest taboos to include the *kumbáros* and his family (Friedl 1962:72).

"Did you steal the goat?"

"No, I didn't steal it."

The judge asked the district attorney if he had any questions to ask the accused So the district attorney asked:

"Did you steal the goat?"

"No, no, I didn't do it!"

Exasperated with the Anogian, the district attorney said:

"Go, get out of here so I won't have to see you anymore!"

"Why?" asked the Anogian. "Are you getting a transfer?"

[K550., Escape by false plea.]

93 A man from Anogia went to Heraklion. While he was there he decided to visit a bordello.

Well, he went with one of the prostitutes to her room. When she was getting undressed, he noticed a large picture hanging above the bed.

"Who's that?" asked the Anogian.

"Who's *that?*" asked the prostitute incredulously. "That's the Virgin Mary."

"Uh-*hum!*" said the Anogian.

Well, when they had finished the Anogian got dressed and left the bordello. As he was crossing the street, a policeman grabbed him and took him to the court.

The judge asked him:

"Did you steal a sheep from the suburb of Saint John?"

"Yes," admitted the Anogian, "because I was hungry and had nothing to eat."

"Five months in jail!" said the judge.

As he was leaving the courtroom with two policemen who were escorting him to the jail, the Anogian saw a picture hanging above the door.

"Who's that?" asked the Anogian.

"Who's *that?*" asked the policeman incredulously. "*That's* Jesus Christ, the son of the Holy Virgin."

"Ah, *so!* The same family!" said the Anogian. "The mother's with the whores and the son's in the courthouse!"

[J1162., Plea by admitting accusations.]

94 Sometime, an Anogian went down to the seashore for the first time. Well, he found a crab. He had never seen a crab before, and it frightened him. But he took courage, grabbed his backpack from his shoulder, and threw it on top of the crab and caught it.

"I'll take this wild beast to the mayor of Anogia," he thought to himself. "He'll know what it is!"

So he went back up the mountains to the village of Anogia, and,
telling people that he had caught a terrible wild beast, he went to the
mayor's house. When he got inside the house, he opened the bag and
dropped the crab onto the floor. (The mayor had never seen a crab
before, either, but he didn't say so.)

The crab began to walk forward, so the Anogian put a piece of wood
in its way, and then the crab backed up. Then he put the piece of wood
behind the crab, and it started forward again.

Just then somebody came into the mayor's house and said:

"I want to see the wild beast that the whole village is talking about.
What's it called?"

"It's a *pígen-e-élla* [a go-and-come, or a round trip]," announced the
mayor of Anogia!

95 One time, in one of the coffeehouses of Anogia, during the grape
harvest of August, some men were talking:

"I can carry one hamper of grapes," said one man.

"I can carry two," said another.

A young boy, about sixteen, named Johnny, said:

"Bah! That's nothing! I can carry five hampers!"

"You shouldn't talk, Johnny," said an old man in the coffeehouse.
"You should bray like a donkey!"

[D1273.1.1., Three as magic number.]

96 An Anogian went to the sea for the first time. So he decided to go
swimming. But he didn't know how to swim, so he sank to the bottom!

Luckily, some tourists saw him go down in the sea, so they rescued
him and gave him artificial respiration. When he came to and got up,
half an hour later, he stood up, went to the edge of the water and,
shaking his fist at the sea, said:

"Cursed [*anáthema*] sea! You can float entire ships, so why can't you
carry one poor, old Anogian?"

[AT1293*, Learn to Swim.]

97 One time, there were two shepherds who lived up in the mountains outside Anogia. They did their own cooking, but they only had
beans, or rice, or fava beans [*koukiá*] to eat. One evening one shepherd
had cooked the beans, but there were very few beans and not enough
for the two men. So the shepherd was planning to eat them all himself
and not give any to the other. When they sat down to eat, the first

shepherd, who had cooked, put the pot of beans in the middle of the table, but he didn't serve any. Then he asked the second shepherd:

"Tell me the story of how your father died." (He knew that it was a long story, because he had heard it before.)

So the second shepherd started to tell the long story of his father's lengthy sickness, how it started in Heraklion with fever, how the doctors had sent him to Athens, and so on.

In the meantime the first shepherd ate all the beans while the other was talking.

When the second shepherd started to eat, the first told him:

"What's all that commotion that the sheep are making? Better go and check."

So the two men went to check the sheep, and so the second shepherd didn't eat that night.

The next night the first shepherd cooked rice, but there was very little rice.

When they sat down to eat, the first shepherd said to the second:

"Last night you didn't finish telling me how your father died."

So the second shepherd continued about how his father had stayed in the hospital in Athens and then returned to Crete, where he immediately got pneumonia, and again continued telling the long story.

In the meantime the first shepherd had eaten all the rice.

So the second shepherd finally realized what was going on and said:

"Yesterday you asked how my father died and ate all the beans. Today you asked how my father died and ate all the rice. So tomorrow I'm going to ask you to tell the story of how *your* father died so *I* can eat all the food!"

The next night they were eating fava beans, and the second shepherd asked the first:

"So now tell me, how did *your* father die?"

The first shepherd said:

"He had a heart attack and dropped dead!" And he kept on eating the fava beans!

[J1115.9., Clever shepherd; K364., Partner misappropriates common goods; K2296., Treacherous partner; X12., Man interrupted each time he tries to eat.]

98 Sometime, an Anogian borrowed a lot of money from the Agricultural Bank in Heraklion to increase his flock of sheep. Well, he was supposed to repay the money in monthly installments, but after a few months he stopped paying on his loan.

So the bank started sending him letters for him to come into the bank and make his payments. But he ignored the letters; he couldn't read. After a while the bank was sending him a letter every five days.

Finally, after several months, the Anogian went to Heraklion and he went to the Agricultural Bank. When he went to the teller and gave his name, all the bank employees stopped working and stared in disbelief that the man had finally come to pay on his account.

So the Anogian pounded his fist on the counter and asked:

"How much do I owe the bank?"

"Twenty-eight thousand, one hundred and forty-five drachmes," said the teller.

"Does that include interest?"

"No. With interest and late-payment fines, the total is thirty-one thousand, seven hundred and forty-three drachmes."

One of the bank employees came over and began to dust off the Anogian's clothes. The man was so happy that the Anogian was going to pay out his account that he wanted to give him special treatment.

Well, the Anogian banged his fist on the counter again and said:

"That's the kind of man I am! I like to know what I owe!" And he left the bank without paying anything!

99 Sometime, two *kumbároi* from Anogia went to a wedding in Heraklion, where they ate and drank and drank and ate and ate and drank in typical Cretan fashion. After the feast was over, they started staggering toward the bus. One of the men was too drunk to continue, so he slept by the road. The other managed to reach the bus, but was too late to get a seat and had to stand up.

His moustache was full of food from the wedding feast, and a fly kept buzzing around his face and landing on his moustache. After several swats at the fly, the Anogian finally caught the fly in his fist. He yelled to the ticket taker:

"Come here and open the window!"

"What for? It's winter and everyone will get cold!"

"Never mind," said the Anogian, "just open the window!"

So the ticket taker finally opened the window and the Anogian addressed the fly in his fist in the following way:

"You didn't *like* riding the bus to Anogia, eh? So now you can walk there!"

And he pitched the fly out of the window and closed it!

[T133., Travel to wedding.]

100 An Anogian went to Heraklion to do some shopping. He saw a

shop that had some dried and salted fish [*bakaláos*] in the window. So he went inside and asked:

"How much are those shoe soles?"

"They're not shoe soles," said the grocer, laughing. "They're *bakaláos*, dried fish, and very good."

"Give me five of them," said the Anogian.

When the grocer went to wrap up the fish, the Anogian told him not to bother, and he took the dried fish and stuck his pointed walking stick through the fish and carried them on his shoulder. Before he left the store, he asked the grocer:

"Do me a favor and write down how to cook these fish so my wife will know."

So the grocer wrote a recipe and the Anogian put the piece of paper in his shirt pocket.

On the way back to the village, the Anogian had to urinate, so he put all his packages down and the walking stick with the *bakaláos* on it next to them and went behind a tree. While he was busy a dog came along and sniffed the *bakaláos* and took them in his mouth and started to leave. The Anogian saw him and shouted:

"What are you doing, taking the *bakaláos*? Well, you won't know how to eat them, because *I* have the recipe here, in my shirt pocket!"

[AT1684B, The Recipe Is Saved.]

101 One time, an Athenian who had heard about the cleverness of the Anogians came to Crete with his car [by ferryboat] and went to visit the village of Anogia. As he approached the village, he saw an Anogian riding his donkey into the village. So the Athenian stopped his car and got out and said to the Anogian:

"Eh, *kumbáre*, what a beautiful donkey you have! I'll give you five thousand drachmes for it!"

"*Moré kumbáre*," said the Anogian, "an entire automobile you're driving and you want my donkey?"

"Come on, *kumbáre*," said the Athenian, "how much do you want? Ten, fifteen, twenty thousand? Whatever you want, I'll pay, just sell me that donkey."

"Look, *moré kumbáre*," said the Anogian, "I can't sell you my donkey because I need it for my work. But if the saddle fits you, I'll *give* you the donkey!" [In other words, the Anogian was making a jackass out of the Athenian.]

The next joke in this section deals with a common theme in

Greek culture: the cuckold. Most of the jokes about cuckolds are in chapter eight, "Very *Sókin* Jokes." However, in the following joke we see that even the clever Anogian can be outsmarted by a magic table and tricked by an unfaithful wife.

102 One time, three men from Anogia went to Athens. They were hungry, so they went to find a restaurant.

Inside the restaurant the waiter asked them if they would like the "magic table." They didn't know what he meant, so he told them that it could answer any question involving numbers by knocking on the floor.

So the Anogians sat at the magic table, and, after they had finished their meal, the first one said:

"Eh, magic table, can you tell me how many sheep I have?"

And the table tapped forty times on the floor!

"This table really is magic!" said the first Anogian.

The second Anogian asked the table:

"Eh, magic table, can you tell me how many teeth I have?"

And the table rocked back and forth and tapped eleven times.

"The table really knows everything!" said the second man.

The third Anogian, thinking that he would ask a question that the table couldn't answer, said:

"Eh, magic table, can you tell me what my wife is doing right now?"

And the table rocked back and forth and shuddered, and finally it flipped over and landed upside down on the floor with its legs up in the air, and the tablecloth fell on top, and the drawers started opening and closing!

The third Anogian called for the waiter.

"What's going on?" he asked. "I asked the table a question, and, instead of answering, it flipped over!"

"What did you ask it?" asked the waiter.

"What my wife is doing now," said the Anogian.

"Well," said the waiter, "it's clear to me that the table is telling you that your wife is flat on her back with her legs up in the air and rocking around in bed with somebody else!"

[Legman II:217; D1153., Magic table; D1273.1.1., Three as magic number; X749.3.1., Rapping and action of table indicate that missing woman is enjoying intercourse.]

The old part of Heraklion is surrounded by a stone wall built, beginning in 1212 A.D., by the Venetians to fortify the city. The *Hanióporta*, one of the three original gates, opens to the western part of Crete. The following joke, as do many others about Anogians, mentions that historic gate since it is the entrance to Heraklion that Anogians must use.

103 One time, as they say, an Anogian loaded his donkey with cheeses and went down to Heraklion to sell them. As he passed inside the *Hanióporta*, he saw a *manávis* [a vendor of fresh produce] who had some big watermelons for sale.

"Eh, *kumbáre*," asked the Anogian, "what are those things?"

"Those are *poularomána* [donkey eggs]!"

"How much do they cost?" asked the Anogian.

"So much," said the *manávis*.

So the Anogian traded his cheeses for a watermelon and tied it to the top of the donkey and started back up the mountains to Anogia.

On the way the Anogian stopped to relieve himself. While he was busy the donkey moved around a bit looking for something to nibble on, and the watermelon fell off the saddle! It landed on the top of a bush under which a hare was sleeping, and, as the watermelon hit the ground and broke, the hare darted out from under the bush and ran away!

When the Anogian returned home, his wife asked:

"What's the matter with you? You look so worried!"

"I bought a mare's egg, and on the way home the egg broke, and the colt ran away and I couldn't catch him!"

"Never mind," said the wife, "you can buy another one."

"Yes, but this one ran as fast as a bullet. I'll never get another as fast as that one!"

[AT1319, Pumpkin Sold As Ass's Egg.]

104 One time, a long time ago in Anogia, an Anogian went to see the doctor because he had a strong pain in his eye.

Well, in those days we only had *praktikói* [empirical doctors] in the village, not real medical doctors.

So the *praktikós* told the man to fast for two or three days [not to eat oil], and then his eye would get better.

So the man went home and told his wife not to put oil in his food for two or three days.

"Why?" asked his wife.

"Because that is what the *praktikós* told me to do to cure my eye!"

"Bah!" said the wife. "Do you have to close the door [stomach] to fix the window [eye]?"

[Inversion of X372.3., Eyedrops prescribed for stomach ache so that patient can see what he eats.]

The following joke mentions *rakí*, or *tsikoudiá*, the national drink in Crete. Made by distilling grape squeezings, it is clear white and very potent. I finally was able to acquire a taste for it, since I was constantly offered some in the Cretan coffeehouses. Greek women usually do not drink in public, but as a foreigner I was expected to do so.

105 A man from Anogia went to Heraklion to sell some cheeses. But first he went to a coffeehouse and had a *rakí*. He saw a man from Heraklion in the coffeehouse, and so he had a plan to make some money from him.

So the Anogian said:

"I've got ten cheeses in the sack. But if you can guess how many cheeses there are, I'll give you half. If not, you must give me three thousand drachmes." (He didn't realize that he had already said there were ten cheeses!)

So the man from Heraklion said:

"Let's see: five is not enough, fifteen is too many. I'll guess there are ten!"

Well, the Anogian opened the sack, and, since there were ten cheeses, he had to give the man five of them.

Then the Anogian went and sold the remaining five cheeses, but he was short of money since he had lost the other five cheeses in his bet. So he made another plan to get some money. On the street he grabbed a tomcat and put him in the sack. Then he went back to the coffeehouse, and the same man was inside who had taken his five cheeses in the first bet.

So the Anogian said:

"If you can guess what's in the sack, I'll pay you three thousand drachmes. But if you lose you must pay me the three thousand."

"It's a bet," said the man from Heraklion, because just as the Anogian had stopped talking, something in the sack moved and a "meow" came forth.

"It's a [female] cat!" said the man from Heraklion.

"Wrong," said the Anogian, opening the sack and letting the tomcat out. "It's a tomcat, and you owe me three thousand drachmes!"

[AT1346A*, Guess How Many Eggs I Have and You Shall Get All Seven.]

Many jokes, similar to ones told about Anogians, are told simply about villagers from villages whose names are not specified. Jokes about Greek villagers are also a part of esoteric folklore, but evident in the jokes is an ambivalence toward the villagers: are they clever or are they dumb? Probably, they are both.

As industrialization in Greece increases, people continue to abandon farms, the countryside, and even the islands, and to flock to Athens to find work or to study. Many foreigners do not realize that Athens was a small village in 1833 when the Turks were defeated and when the first Greek king, Otho of Bavaria, decided to place the modern capital of the Hellenes on the site of the ancient city-state. The population of Athens (including adjacent areas such as Piraeus) jumped from perhaps one thousand in 1833 to three million in 1977. The greatest increase has occurred in the last twenty-five years. Villagers who move to Athens often try to become urbanites overnight and frequently will not admit having come from elsewhere. They insist that they are Athenians; they try to assume sophisticated manners, and sometimes they even ridicule "dumb" villagers.

On the other hand, native Athenians generally love to go to the villages every time a holiday permits them a few days off. At Easter Athens becomes almost a ghost city; almost everyone returns to the patriarchal village to visit relatives and to roast lamb outdoors, if possible. Greeks face a terrible dilemma: they want the comforts of Athens and the opportunities for business and employment, but they also yearn for the tranquility and satisfaction of village life with its simple pleasures and joys. One can sympathize deeply with their mixed feelings, for the high population density in Athens has reduced tremendously the quality of life there for everyone. The city chokes on air pollution and suffers from overcrowding and noise pollution, as well.

In modernizing and in joining the European Common Market, Greeks have had to give up much that was traditional. For example, they may have to end the traditional Mediterranean siesta, the afternoon break that affects almost everyone, native and foreign. During siesta shops normally close for several hours, as does practically everything except some restaurants, *tavérnes*, and coffeehouses. People go home to eat and to rest before returning to their jobs in the late afternoon. People work later than we do in America; often they go out after work and eat dinner at an hour that seems very late by our standards. In the spring of 1977 Athens went off the siesta for about a month on a trial basis. Old habits die hard, however, and not everybody observed the new eight-to-five schedule. It is rumored that entering the Common Market will force the Greeks to abandon the siesta entirely. It would be only one change among many.

The jokes told about villagers reflect the ambivalent feelings most Athenians have toward their way of life. Some jokes depict villagers as very clever; others, as very dumb. Anogians are singled out for admiration because of their "cleverness," which all Greeks admire. Many other jokes (see chapter eight) depict shepherds as incredibly stupid. (That they do is in itself amazing in a country where practically everybody's grandfather kept sheep.) The majority of the following jokes depict villagers as stupid. I do not know whether that is statistically relevant or not. Interestingly enough, many of the jokes about dumb villagers were told to me by villagers or peasants.

106 One summer a man from a village met a woman tourist from Germany. They had a nice romance, then she left to return to her country. About a month after she left, the villager received a letter from her, but it was written in German, and so he couldn't read it.

So he took the letter and went to the large town nearby to find somebody to read the letter to him.

He really didn't know where to go, but he walked up and down looking for somebody who looked well educated.

Finally, he saw a man sitting in an office, and he was very well dressed with a nice suit and a tie and a fine hat. So the villager thought, "Surely that man can read my letter!"

So he went in the office, and asked the man, "Can you read?"

"Of course I can read!" said the man.

"Will you read this letter to me, please?" asked the villager.

So the well-dressed man took the letter, and when he saw it he said, "This letter's written in German and I can't read German."

"But," protested the villager, "surely a man like you with a fine suit and hat and tie ought to be able to read foreign languages!"

"Is that so?" asked the well-dressed man. "In that case, I'll lend you my suit and hat and tie, and then *you* read the letter yourself!"

[Surely a variant of AT1331*, Learning to Read, and of AT1331A*, Buying Spectacles.]

107 Two men from a small village in the mountains of Greece were traveling together by plane for the first time.

There was a lot of turbulence, and the plane started going up and down suddenly. The men were worried, but they tried to appear calm and nonchalant because they didn't want anybody sitting close to them to know that it was their first plane trip!

More turbulence occurred, and the plane started losing altitude rapidly.

The villager sitting by the window looked down and announced loudly:

"My Virgin! The plane is falling down!"

The other villager, still wanting to appear sophisticated, replied in a loud voice:

"What do you care? Is it *your* plane? Is it *my* plane?"

108 A villager had some work to do, so he borrowed some donkeys from his neighbors. As he was getting ready to leave, he asked his son to count the donkeys.

"One, two, three . . . ten," said the boy.

So the man got his donkey saddled, climbed on top, and decided to check his son's arithmetic.

So he counted the donkeys, but there were only nine!

"Son!" he screamed. "You can't count! You told me there were ten donkeys, but there are only nine!"

"But you're sitting on top of the tenth donkey," said the boy.

[AT1288A, Numbskull Cannot Find Ass He Is Sitting On; J2030., Absurd inability to count.]

109 A Greek sailor sent his mother a portable radio from America while his ship was there, as a name-day present.

Well, the woman lived in a small village in Crete, and she had never had a radio before. So, naturally, she didn't know how to operate it.

After much fumbling she finally managed to turn it on. Well, it was tuned to a local station that only had news and lots of advertising with little or no music. Only talking and talking!

Well, the old woman didn't know how to turn the dial to get another station, so she left it as it was. After a few days, however, she got tired of hearing so much talking, so she put the radio away.

About a week later she passed a small store where the shopkeeper had a radio playing Cretan music.

"Now *that's* a good radio!" said the old woman. "It plays Cretan music, not like the no-good radio that my son sent me that only talks and talks!"

[J1705.1., Stupid peasant.]

110   A man from a village went to Heraklion to take driving lessons so that he could get a driver's license.

So the teacher and the man got inside the car, with the teacher at the wheel. The teacher began the lesson:

"Here is the ignition, here is the gas, here is the brake, there is the clutch, that is the horn, and that is the 'flash.'"

"The 'flash'?" said the man. "What's a 'flash'?"

"It's for you to signal what you are going to do," said the teacher. But still the villager didn't understand.

"If you are going to turn left, you push it down. If you are going to turn right, you push it up." But still the villager didn't understand.

"Look, I'll turn the flash on, and you stick your head out the window and tell me if you see it," said the teacher. "Now—do you see it?"

"Yes—no—yes—no!" said the villager.

[J1705.1., Stupid peasant.]

The next joke describes a problem that many villagers in Crete have. The inhabitants speak a regional variation of *dhimotikí* that is in many ways almost a dialect. They must know standard *dhimotikí* and some *katharévusa* as well. Thus they must be proficient in almost three different languages whose main element in common is the alphabet. Moreover, many of the older villagers are illiterate.

111   Sometime, a villager went to the town of Hania for the first time.

Since he had never eaten meat, he was determined to go to a restaurant and eat meat. In his village he ate only beans.

So he went to a nice restaurant. But since he didn't know the word for meat (in *katharévusa*), he waited until the finely dressed gentleman at the next table had ordered to hear what he would say. "Surely," thought the villager, "such a fine gentleman will eat meat!"

The gentleman ordered:

"Giants [*gígantes:* literally "giants," but used for large beans similar to lima beans]!"

When the waiter came the villager repeated:

"Giants!"

So the villager got a plate of lima beans!

After he finished he heard the gentleman say to the waiter (in *katharévusa*, which the villager didn't understand):

"Another!"

The villager thought, *"That* must be the word for meat!" So he called the waiter and repeated what the gentleman had said. And so he got *another* plate of lima beans!

Later the gentleman said (again in *katharévusa*) to the waiter:

"A little more!"

Thinking that the gentleman was *finally* ordering meat, the villager called the waiter and again repeated what the gentleman had said. So he got *a little more* lima beans!

Well, when he returned to his village, his friends asked him:

"How was the trip to Hania? Did you eat meat?"

"No, but for a change I ate giants, and more giants, and a little more giants!"

[D1273.1.1., Three as magic number; J1705.1., Stupid peasant.]

The following jokes depict villagers as having common sense or as being clever.

112 (In the villages of Crete, the people have simple but comfortable homes, many of which have roofs of reeds or wood with earth spread on the top. And many villagers use cow manure to fill in the chinks between the wood, to keep the rain out.)

One villager had sent his son to Athens to study in the high school, and then in the university. When the young man came home for a visit, he noticed the patched places on the the ceiling and asked:

"What's that?"

His father told him:

"That's cow shit!"

"And how did the cow get on the roof?" asked the son.

"No more university for you!" said the father.

[Legman II:919; AT1225A, How Did the Cow Get on the Pole?]

The next joke depicts a common feature of the poor or of peasants the world over: their generosity with food. In Greece, however, politeness requires that food be refused the first time it is offered; some Greeks must be invited three times before they will accept something. Hospitality is one of the highest virtues in Greece, but today it is practiced mainly in rural areas and in small villages.

113 A *kumbáros* went to visit a family that he was related to through godparenthood in a small village in Greece. As it happened, he arrived just at mealtime.

"Welcome, *kumbáre*," they all said. "Come and sit with us and eat!"

"Oh, no, thank you very much," said the man. "I've just eaten and I'm full up to here [pointing to throat]."

But as is traditional in the Greek home, the family insisted on offering hospitality to the man. So they repeated:

"Come on, sit down with us and eat!"

"No, really," said the *kumbáros*, "I'm very full; I just ate. I'm full up to here [pointing to throat]!"

"Never mind," they insisted, "come and keep us company at the table."

So the *kumbáros* sat down and ate and ate and ate. Well, after the meal was finished, and the *kumbáros* had departed, one of the children in the family asked:

"Mother, how much food can the *kumbáros* hold between his throat and the top of his head?"

[P320., Hospitality.]

114 Early one morning a man went to visit his *kumbáros*. In the village where the *kumbáros* lived, the people don't eat breakfast of coffee, toast, butter and jelly, and the like. They eat what is left over from the evening meal. Or if nothing is left over, they eat bread and olives.

So when he got to his *kumbáros'* house, he was greeted and invited to sit down at the table. And the *kumbáros* put a round, hard cheese and some olives for the guest to eat on the table.

Since the man didn't have a knife with him, he couldn't eat the cheese, as it was very hard. So he ate only olives.

"Eat some cheese, *kumbáre*," the host told the guest.

"I see the cheese, but the olives are good."

So he finished, and he left and went home.

About a month later the same man again visited his *kumbáros*. And the *kumbáros* again brought a cheese, bigger and more expensive than the last time, and some olives for the guest to eat.

So the guest brought out his own knife and cut a big chunk of cheese and ate it. Then another chunk. And another.

Finally, the *kumbáros* said:

"Hey, *kumbáre*, eat some olives, they are good!"

"I see the olives, but the cheese is better," said the man.

[AT1449*, The Stingy Hostess at the Inn; J1561., Inhospitality repaid.]

115   Sometime, a man had a donkey to sell, so he went to the weekly street market [*bazáari* in Crete] in his village and took the donkey with him.

A man came up to him and said:

"Are you selling the donkey? How much?"

"So much," responded the man.

"But the donkey's tail is not in good condition," said the customer.

So the man took his donkey and left that place. After a while another man came and asked:

"Are you selling that donkey?"

"Yes."

"How much?"

"So much."

"But his tail isn't very good!" said the man.

So the owner of the donkey got angry and cut off the donkey's tail and put it into his pocket.

After a while another man asked him:

"Are you selling that donkey? How much?"

"That much," said the man.

"But the donkey doesn't have a tail!"

So the man reached in his pocket, took out the tail, and said:

"Here's the tail! Now, do you want the donkey or not?"

116   There was a couple in a village and the wife was always contrary to her husband. If he wanted wine, she wanted water. If he said it was hot, she said it was cold.

One time, in winter, it had been raining a lot, and the couple went to gather their olives. Well, they had to cross a river that was rather high from all the rain. Well, they forded the stream because there was no bridge, and the man went first. Then he heard his wife screaming for help! She had fallen into the river and was swept away by the current!

So the man went to look for his wife. A little way off he saw a friend.

"Hey, *kumbáre,* what are you doing?" asked the friend.

"I'm looking for my wife. She fell into the river and it carried her off," said the man.

"But are you crazy?" asked the friend. "You must go downstream to look for her!"

"But my wife is so contrary, she always goes against everything! So that's why I'm looking for her up here," said the man.

[AT1365A, The Obstinate Wife: Wife Falls into a Stream.]

117   One day a rich man was getting dressed, and, when he was ready to put on his shoes, he noticed they were covered with mud. So he called his servant:

"What is this?" he asked. "Why haven't you cleaned my shoes?"

"It seems silly to me to clean those shoes every day," said the servant, "because you just get them full of mud all over again!"

Well, in the evening the servant went to the kitchen to eat his dinner, but he found his plate empty.

So he called his master.

"Why is there no food for me?" he asked.

"It's stupid to feed you every night," said the master, "because the next day you just get hungry all over again!"

After that the servant cleaned his master's shoes every day and was fed every night.

Some Greeks still tell stories of a very special villager, whom they call "Hodjas."[1] Evidently the Greeks borrowed stories of Hodjas from the Turks;[2] indeed, the name itself bears close resemblance to the title given in the past to the Moslem religious men who read the Koran. Hodjas is a villager who is very human, wise and foolish by turn—sometimes a trickster, sometimes the tricked. There is some evidence that his stories were used in the past as a means of illustrating basic values or commonsense truths.

A shopkeeper in Heraklion told me many of the following

stories of Hodjas. He remembered being told the stories as a child and is fond of repeating them to his children. Villagers told me most of the remaining stories, and I would not be surprised to learn that Athenians only read stories of Hodjas to their children from children's books. In other words, I think that perhaps Hodjas is passing from the world of oral storytelling to that of the printed page.

118 When Hodjas was a young man, he was a real "night owl." Night after night he would go out with his friends, drinking and dancing, and would return home just before daybreak.

His father was very unhappy with this behavior and was always lecturing the boy:

"What you need to do is get married to a nice girl and settle down and make a family," he would say day after day. Or: "You're wasting your money and ruining your health! Why don't you get married? How about Maria? She would make a good wife."

"Leave me alone," Hodjas would always say. "I'm not ready to get married yet!"

But finally Hodjas gave in and agreed to get married. Well, after he was married four or five months, he had lost about twenty pounds, and he was completely run down from making love with his wife all the time!

One afternoon he was taking a nap in the garden, and a fly landed on his forehead and awakened him. And the fly kept bothering him, and he couldn't go back to sleep!

"Go away, leave me alone," said Hodjas. "Otherwise as a punishment I'll go tell my father to get you a wife and marry you off. Then you'll know how it feels to be so tired and to be bothered when you're trying to sleep!"

119 One evening a friend of Hodjas came to visit. He brought a rabbit, and so Hodjas' wife fixed a soup with the rabbit and they had dinner together.

The next night a man came to Hodjas' house who said he was a friend of the friend who had been the night before and brought the rabbit. He didn't bring anything to eat, so Hodjas' wife served rabbit soup again with some water added.

Well, the next night another man came to the house who was a friend of the friend of Hodjas' friend. He didn't bring anything, so Hodjas put more water in the soup, and they had dinner together.

Finally, on the next night another man came who was the friend of the friend of the friend of Hodjas' friend. So Hodjas put more water in the soup, and they sat down to eat.

The man looked at his bowl that was full of hot water and said: "What's that?"

"That's the soup of the soup of the soup of the soup of the rabbit that my friend brought me five days ago!" said Hodjas.

[AT1552*, The Hare of the Third Remove.]

120 Hodjas was always dressed in rags because he was poor and he didn't care how he looked.

But when there were weddings or baptisms, the people wouldn't let him into the party because his clothes were so old and torn and dirty.

So one time, when he learned that there was going to be a big wedding in his village just after Christmas, he decided to buy some new clothes.

So he went to the wedding party all dressed up, and immediately everybody was very nice to him.

"Greetings, Hodjas," said one man. "You really look fine in those new clothes! Come and sit by my side and have some wine!"

"Hello, Hodjas," said the groom's mother. "Welcome to our wedding feast! Have some meat and bread and cheese," as she served him a heaping plate of food.

So Hodjas started eating, and he surprised everybody by putting some meat in one pocket, and some salad in another pocket, and some potatoes in still another pocket, and then by pouring some wine on his trousers!

"What are you doing?" asked the man sitting by his side. "Are you crazy?"

"I can't sit here and eat without giving some food and wine to my new clothes! After all, they got me into the feast in the first place!"

[AT1558, Welcome to the Clothes.]

121 One day Hodjas was returning home from the fields. In one hand he held his son's hand; in the other, the reins of the donkey.

So he passed a man from his village, who said:

"Eh, Hodjas! Aren't you ashamed to be walking next to a donkey! The animal should be carrying you!"

So Hodjas got on top of the donkey and continued to his village.

Later another man passed him on the road and said:

"Eh, Hodjas! Aren't you ashamed to ride the donkey and make your little boy walk?"

So Hodjas put his son on the donkey with him and continued toward the village.

Later he passed another man, who said:

"Eh, Hodjas! Aren't you ashamed? The poor donkey carrying two people! What do you think it is, a truck?"

So Hodjas tied the donkey's legs together, front to front and back to back, and put a pole through the legs, and then he and his son carried the donkey into the village!

[AT1215, The Miller, His Son, and the Ass: Trying to Please Everyone.]

122 Hodjas decided that he would become a baker, so he started to build an oven. Of course, several of the village men were playing "sidewalk superintendents" and giving him unwanted advice and instructions.

When he started to make the oven door, one man said:

"Don't put the door on that side! In the winter the wind always blows from that direction, and it'll put out your fire!"

So Hodjas went to the opposite side and started to build the oven door. But another man said:

"That's a big mistake! In the summer the *meltémi* winds come from that direction, and you'll never get the oven started!"

So Hodjas went to another side and started to make the oven door, but another man said the winds in the spring would cause him trouble.

Well, Hodjas got very exasperated, and he left his work. In half an hour he returned with a wagon, and he started building the oven on top of the wagon!

"What are you doing now?" asked the men.

"I'm building a portable oven so I can always move it around so that the winds won't put out the fire inside!"

[AT1325A, The Fireplace Gives Too Much Heat: Decide to Move It.]

123 One time, Hodjas went onto his balcony and prayed for God to send him a thousand *líres*,* but no less than one thousand.

Well, the neighbor who lived upstairs heard him and decided to tease him. So he dropped a sack with nine hundred and ninety-nine *líres* on Hodjas' balcony.

So when Hodjas opened the sack and counted the money and saw it

*A *líre* is a gold coin, usually of British origin (the sovereign), that in 1977 was worth about nine hundred drachmes.

was only nine hundred and ninety-nine, he said in the direction of the sky:

"If you really want me to have only nine hundred and ninety-nine, God, then it's okay with me!" So he went into his house and kept the money!

So the neighbor brought charges against Hodjas to return the money. And Hodjas received a summons to appear in court.

Well, Hodjas went upstairs to his neighbor's house and said:

"You want me to go to court, but I can't go because I don't have a suit to wear!"

So the neighbor gave Hodjas a nice suit to wear.

"And how can I go to court if I have no shoes to wear?"

So the neighbor gave Hodjas a good pair of shoes to wear.

"And how can I go to court if I have to walk?"

So the neighbor gave him a car to use to go to court.

Well, when Hodjas appeared before the judge for possessing property that belonged to another, the judge acquitted him, saying:

"Why would such a well-dressed man, with a good suit and a car, need to take what doesn't belong to him?"

[AT1543, Not One Penny Less; J1473.1., 999 gold pieces.]

Chapter 4
Ethnic-Slur Jokes:
Greek Exoteric Humor

Ethnic insults usually attribute certain characteristics to social groups, or they give a popular account of the national character of other countries. Folklorists refer to those jokes that characterize specific peoples or places as "ethnic-slur" jokes. Generally, ethnic-slur jokes are derogatory, and they strengthen the awareness of divisions between groups. In Greek folklore, as in that of all other places in the world, ethnic-slur jokes exist in two forms: intragroup jokes, told about particular kinds of Greeks; and intergroup jokes, told about people from other countries (Dundes 1965:43).

Intragroup ethnic-slur jokes in Greece include, for example, those about the *Hiótes*, the people from the island of Hios in the eastern Aegean Sea, close to the Turkish mainland.[1] *Hiótes* are characterized as stingy, dumb, and peculiar in the jokes told about them by other Greeks.[2] Greeks also tell jokes about Greek-Americans. Some jokes refer to Greeks who emigrated to America; others are about Americans of Greek descent. Most of the jokes about Greek-Americans make fun of their inability to speak modern Greek (*dhimotikí*) properly or of the tendency of Greek-Americans to "play the big shot" when visiting Greece.

Intergroup ethnic-slur jokes in Greece characterize other nationals in unflattering terms. To my surprise, however, I seldom heard jokes ridiculing Turks, although according to reliable sources until recently many such jokes circulated. I certainly heard a lot of anti-Turkish sentiment expressed, but maybe the Greeks feel too strongly about the Turks to joke about them anymore. (Since 1974 many Greeks have been anticipating an-

other war with Turkey.) Indeed, none of the ethnic-slur jokes
that I heard dealt with any of the countries bordering on
Greece. The only groups specified in the material that I col-
lected were Scots and Mexicans.[3] Possibly many other ethnic
groups are satirized in this type of humor, but I cannot be sure.
Certainly Greeks have stereotypes concerning Blacks and
Chinese, which are revealed in chapter eight, "Very *Sókin*
Jokes."

INTRAGROUP JOKES

The Hiótes

124 During the war [World War II], the Germans launched an invasion of the island of Hios, and they soon had captured all of the major
villages.

Then they sent out search parties to capture any men who were hiding in the countryside.

The Germans would walk for a kilometer, then call:

"Is there anybody else whom we haven't captured?"

"Only me!" some stupid *Hiótis* would reply, and the Germans would
go and grab him.

This happened over and over again. Finally, a smart *Hiótis* heard the
Germans calling:

"Is there anybody else that we haven't captured?"

And the smart Hiótis *said:*

[*Egó pou ého mialó, then tha miló!*]

"I who have brains will not speak!"

But of course he said it out loud, and of course the Germans heard
him and captured him too.

[AT1341B*, Escaped Slave's Talkativeness Brings About His Recap-
ture; X680., Jokes concerning various cities; X681., Blason populaire;
J2136., Numbskull brings about his own capture.]

125 Two captain's wives from Hios had been with their husbands on
their ships to America, so they pretended that they knew how to speak
English well.

One day the two women saw each other on the street, so they tried to
show off their English:

"How are you, *Kiría* [Mrs.] Katiko?"

"Fine," said the other woman. "Can you tell me what óra [hour] it is?"

"Yes. It is six kai pénde [and five, meaning five after six]." (The two women were too stupid to realize that they were not really speaking English!)

[X680., Jokes concerning various cities; X681., Blason populaire.]

126 Many years ago there was a captain from Hios who was always cheating the crew when he paid them since they didn't know arithmetic. He paid the crew every three weeks.

So when the steward went to be paid, the captain said:

"Three times fifty is ninety and ten from the captain is one hundred."

"Okay," said the steward and took the hundred drachmes.

Next a seaman went to be paid. So the captain said:

"Three times fifty is one hundred and fifty and ten is one hundred."

"No! Three times fifty is one hundred and fifty and ten is one hundred and sixty," said the seaman.

"No," said the captain, "one hundred."

"No, one hundred and sixty," said the seaman.

"Well, since you know so much arithmetic, we'll dock you in the next port so that you won't teach arithmetic to the rest of the crew."

[K256., Deceptive wages; W151., Greed; W152., Stinginess; X680., Jokes concerning various cities; X681., Blason populaire.]

127 One time, there was a stingy captain from Hios who liked to trick the crew out of money. So he had two money bags: one filled with coins and the other filled with paper money.

When it was payday he called Manolios [standard name for the dumbest member of the crew] to get his money.

"Manolios," began the captain, "you're smart. So which money do you prefer? Coins or paper money?"

"Give me the coins," said the sailor, "because they're heavier!"*

[J1249., Clever dividing, miscellaneous; K256., Deceptive wages; W151., Greed; X680., Jokes concerning various cities; X681., Blason populaire.]

128 One time, on a ship from Hios, the captain, who was always trying to get more work out of the crew, told Manolios:

---

*"Heaviness" is a quality admired by supermasculine (mánges) Greek men; in the joke Manolios equates weight with value.

"If you work harder you'll get one extra egg every day, but don't tell anybody."

So, naturally, Manolios told all the rest of the crew about the captain's offer.

The next day the entire crew ate one extra egg apiece at breakfast.

After breakfast the captain came on the loudspeaker and said:

"Attention! All of you who ate the extra egg, now you must all work harder!"

[Inversion of J1341.13., Servant who receives only one egg for breakfast does half as much work ... ; X680., Jokes concerning various cities; X681., Blason populaire.]

The Americanized Greeks

129 There was this Greek who had lived many years in America. Well, he came back to Greece without a dime, and he went to a village in Crete and pretended to be very, very rich. He played the big shot. He always talked about sending for his money from his bank in America to build a new school, or a new church, or to fix the roads. But he really had no money at all in America.

Not realizing that the man was lying, the villagers got together and decided that they had better get the man married in the village so that he wouldn't leave.

So they married him with a woman whom nobody else would marry, and so he stayed.

Well, he was always "waiting" for his money to come from the bank, but it never did, of course.

Well, he got sick and he died. So the villagers went to his house to find his will. Well, they found a will, and this is what it said:

"To God I leave my soul. To my wife I leave my penis. To the village I leave my balls."

And at the bottom was also written:

"This will written without a lawyer or witness, and whoever doesn't like it can write his name on my balls." [See the discussion of this expression on p. 186.]

[X681., Blason populaire.]

The following jokes criticize Americans of Greek descent who speak the Greek language liberally interspersed with English words that they either do not know in Greek or think are the same in Greek. Many times they make devastating linguistic blunders.

130 One time, a Greek-American girl came to Athens for a vacation. One evening she was with some cousins and their friends in a *tavérna*.

"Let's go to the beach!" she said.

So to please her they drove to the beach. Since nobody had bathing suits, they just sat on the beach and drank wine.

The Greek-American girl stretched out on the sand to observe the beauty of the sky with the stars and moon shining brightly.

After the wine was finished, the group was ready to leave.

"Come on, Helene," they called to her. "Let's go."

"Oh, not yet, let's stay longer," she pleaded.

"Come on, you aren't sun bathing, you know," they said.

"No, but I'm pussy bathing," she said.*

[X681., Blason populaire.]

131 One summer a rich Greek-American girl came to Greece for her vacation. Well, she had a big, fully equipped Cadillac with her to travel around with.

Well, she met a Greek boy, and so they decided to go for a drive in her Cadillac.

When they got inside the car, the boy started to open the window since it was like an oven inside the car, which had been left in the sun.

"Don't open the window," said the girl. "I'll turn on the little bear."†

[X681., Blason populaire.]

132 One time, a Greek-American came to Greece on a vacation. Well, his cousin, a native Athenian, was showing him the sights.

One day the Greek-American called his cousin and said:

"Since it's such a beautiful day, why don't we go on a picnic?"

The Athenian didn't understand the word "picnic," but he agreed to the suggestion.

"What should I do?" he asked.

"Find two girls to come with us," said the Greek-American, "and I'll take care of the rest."

So the Athenian called a girlfriend, Maria, to invite her and her best friend to go on a "picnic."

---

*Káno héliotherapía means literally "I make sun therapy," but the Greek-American girl said Káno múni-therapía, thinking she was saying "I'm moon bathing." She did not realize that múni ("moon") sounds like mouní ("pussy"), and her friends understood her to say, "I'm pussy bathing."

†"Air condition," given a Greek pronunciation, sounds like arkoudítsa ("little bear").

"Okay," said Maria, "but what should I wear on a 'picnic'?"

"How should I know?" said the boy. "Just wipe your ass well and wear anything you like!"

[X681., Blason populaire.]

Whereas the jokes above make fun of Greek-Americans who go to 'Greece and make mistakes, the following jokes reverse the situation and ridicule Greeks in America.

133 One time, an old man went to America to visit his two sons who had migrated there.

Well, one evening the three men went out together. So they went to a bar.

When the bartender came to take their order, the first son said:

"Give me a Coca-Cola."

The second son said:

"Give me a Pepsi-Cola."

Well, the old man wondered and wondered. What to order? Finally, he said:

"Give me a *hondró kóla* [fat ass]."

[X681., Blason populaire.]

134 One time, a Greek family saved money for years so as to send one of their sons to America. He was to serve as a kind of a beachhead for the rest of the family to come.

When he got to New York, he was very disappointed because the streets were not paved in gold as he had heard.

He wandered around the East River area and desperately needed to go to the toilet, but didn't know where to find one. It was early in the morning, and the streets were deserted. Finally, spotting a policeman, he made gestures to communicate his problem. The policeman pointed to one of the brownstone apartment houses across the street.

The Greek crossed the street and went downstairs, where he encountered a hall with four locked doors.

Finally, in desperation, he knocked on one of the doors. After a minute the door opened, and a hand holding an empty milk bottle appeared.

"What a strange country," thought the Greek as he took the bottle and proceeded to fill it up with urine.

When he returned the bottle to the waiting hand, he was handed three dollars, and then the door closed.

The Greek rushed to the nearest telegraph office and sent a telegram to his brother:

COME IMMEDIATELY! YOU'RE PISSING AWAY A FORTUNE!

[Legman II:940; X681., Blason populaire.]

135   One time, a Greek and his sister went to live in America. After two years the Greek returned to his village, and his sister was to return later.

On the first evening of his return, he went to the village coffeehouse. All the village was there waiting to hear stories about life in America.

"In America," started the Greek, "you can go to the best restaurants and eat as much as you like and not have to pay!"

The crowd murmured in astonishment.

"In America you can live in a beautiful apartment and not have to pay the rent!"

Again a murmur of disbelief from the crowd.

"In America you can even get spending money without any effort!"

"Come on now, Costa," said one of the men in the crowd. "Did all that really happen to you?"

"Well, no," said Costa, "but it did to my *sister!*"

[Legman I:251; Legman II:203; X681., Blason populaire.]

INTERGROUP JOKES

The Scots

Jokes about Scotsmen are usually preceded by a remark such as "This is a joke about a Scotsman. You know, the Scots are very stingy."

136   One time, a Scotsman went into a hotel and asked about a room. He put his suitcase down by the desk and said:

"What's the price for a single room?"

So the desk clerk said:

"On the second floor the single rooms are twenty dollars a night; on the third floor the single rooms are fifteen dollars a night; on the fourth floor the single rooms are ten dollars a night—"

"Wait a minute!" said the Scotsman, and he went outside to look at the hotel from the street.

Then he went back into the lobby, picked up his suitcase, and said to the clerk:

"Never mind, this hotel's not tall enough for me!"

[X650., Jokes concerning other races or nations; X681., Blason populaire.]

137 One time, a Scotsman ran to catch a bus, but he missed it. So when he got home, he told his father:

"Father, I won six pence today!"

"How?" asked his father.

"Because I missed the bus and I ran home."

"So why didn't you miss a cab and win three pounds?"

[X650., Jokes concerning other races or nations; X681., Blason populaire.]

138 The following advertisement appeared in a Scottish newspaper in the classified section in the "Want Ads":

"A war veteran missing his right foot wishes to meet a war veteran missing his left foot. Purpose: to share a pair of new shoes, size forty-two."

[X650., Jokes concerning other races or nations; X681., Blason populaire.]

The Mexicans

Ethnic-slur jokes about Mexicans are usually preceded by a remark such as "This is a joke about a Mexican. You know, the Mexicans are very lazy."

139 One time, in Mexico, there were these three Mexicans sitting in the shade, on the ground, leaning against a house, just dozing.

Well, a horse went racing past them!

A year later the first Mexican said:

"That was really a fine white horse!"

After another year had passed, the second Mexican said:

"That horse wasn't white! It was brown!"

After another year the third Mexican said:

"If you two don't stop that stupid conversation, I'm leaving!"

[AT1948, Too Much Talk; D1273.1.1., Three as magic number; X650., Jokes concerning other races or nations; X681., Blason populaire.]

140 Sometime, in Mexico, there was a lazy Mexican sitting on the ground, wearing a big sombrero, leaning against a house in a small village, sound asleep. Next to him a bull was standing, but the bull was also sleeping.

Well, a tourist came to the village, and his watch stopped. So he saw the Mexican, and he went over and shook him and said:

"Excuse me, but could you tell me the time?"

Well, the Mexican reached over, took the bull's balls in his hand, lifted them one time and then said:

"Uh, it's about twelve o'clock."

Well, the tourist fixed his watch and thanked the Mexican and left. But later he thought:

"What a system of telling the time—from the weight of the bull's balls! Incredible! I can't believe it!"

So the tourist went back and shook the Mexican again and said:

"Excuse me, but what time is it?"

So again the Mexican took the bull's balls in his hand, raised them one time, and said:

"It's about ten after twelve."

So the tourist thanked him and walked off, really curious. How could the Mexican be so accurate? His own watch said twelve-ten! So he walked a bit, then deciding really to put the Mexican to the final test, he went back and shook him again and asked for the third time.

Again the Mexican lifted the bull's balls once and said:

"It's about twenty past twelve."

Well, the tourist looked at his watch, and it was exactly twelve-twenty! So he said:

"How incredible! What a system! But you must tell me your secret. How can you tell what time it is by lifting the bull's balls?"

"I lift the balls so I can see the clock in the church tower over there!"

[Legman II:489; X650., Jokes concerning other races or nations; X681., Blason populaire.]

The preceding joke depicts also the stupidity of tourists. Other examples of jokes about tourists that I heard mentioned only female tourists, not as being stupid, however, but rather as being oversexed (see chapter eight, "Very *Sókin* Jokes"), as, according to the stereotype, are all women, Greek and foreign.

Chapter 5
Humor Directed at the Church and the Clergy

Every visitor to Greece quickly becomes aware of the omnipresence of the Greek Orthodox Church. In the cities, in the villages, even in deserted fields and on faraway mountainsides, small, rectangular churches topped with cupolas catch the eye. At one time on the small barren island of Mykonos, today a jet-setter's paradise, were three hundred and sixty-five churches, one for every day of the year; now the number of churches on Mykonos is closer to four hundred. Along Greek highways, roads, and country paths stand miniature churches and tiny whitewashed shrines, which are lit at night by flickering oil lamps and which contain ikons of the saints, the Virgin, or Christ. The shrines have been built, for the most part, by devout Greeks whose lives were spared in accidents while traveling. In Greece today church and state are combined in partnership for the good of the Hellenes. And the Greek layman, devout or blasphemous, finds his life regulated by the sacraments of the Church, just as the rhythm of national life is regulated by the Church calendar.

One frequently sees on Greek streets priests wearing long, black, flowing robes, similar to the academic gowns worn at commencement exercises in Europe and in America. The Greek priests, like holy men in the Far East, do not cut their hair or beards. On top of the bulky buns of their hair, they wear flat-top black hats that resemble short stovepipes.

Since the days of Chaucer at least, Europeans have satirized and ridiculed priests and monks. The theme usually is that of men with unusual sexual appetites who hide behind the clerical gowns and who use their roles as holy men to deceive and seduce the innocent. Many of the stories that I collected about these rascally individuals probably date to the time of Chaucer. Other stories are reminiscent of themes found in the *Decameron* and in other Italian *novelle* dating to the Middle Ages (see Rotunda 1942.)

The Greek priest is especially suitable as the object of humor because he is a paradox, an anomaly. He is both a holy man and an earthly man. Wearing his black robes and never cutting his hair and beard, he gives all the appearance of an ascetic; in most cases, however, he is also a married man, the father of a family, and a small businessman or farmer. Although no member of the higher clergy may marry, deacons and priests may do so when they are ordained. They may not, however, remarry should the wife die. Should a married priest wish to rise in rank, his wife must retire to a nunnery.

The human mind, particularly if it has been influenced by the principles of Aristotelian logic (as is the case in the Western world) dislikes the anomaly. The mind prefers to have things fit neatly into the categories language provides for reality. Things fitting simultaneously into two or more logical categories of exclusion—that is, paradoxes—are often the concerns of ritual, superstition, and folklore. And, indeed, superstitious Greeks observe rituals in regard to priests. When they see a priest on the street, Greeks often spit (magic number) three times in a ritual that protects the superstitious individual both by the holy number three and by the common means (spitting) of avoiding the "evil eye" or any other harm possibly emanating from the anomalous priest. If a person leaving on a journey encounters three priests on the road, the superstitious traveler must immediately return home or risk grave misfortune on the trip. The Greek writer Nikos Kazantzakis (1958, 1965) has described those rituals of protection, and I observed that they are still practiced in present-day Greece.

Although much of the material in this chapter points to strong anticlerical sentiment in Greece and although many individuals are openly scornful of the Greek clergy, no strong movement away from the Greek Orthodox Church is apparent. Less than five percent of the population belong to other religious groups. Many persons never attend church services, but they almost always turn to the Church for the life-crisis rituals of baptism, marriage, and funerals. Greeks consider themselves Orthodox Christians above all else.

As religious as Greeks appear to be generally, it is interesting that the most commonly used oath in Greece is "Fuck the [his, her, their, or your] Virgin [*Gammóti panaghía (tou, tis, tous, sou)*]!" This oath, normally used by men, may be heard repeatedly during an average day spent in Greece. Women, if swearing, usually prefer the "Fuck the [your, his, her, or their] Cross" (*Gammóto stavró [sou, tou, tis, tous]*). The following is a well-known joke concerning the former oath.

141 One day a group of farmers went to visit the priest at the famous church of the Virgin Mary in the island of Tinos. They asked to borrow the miraculous ikon of the Virgin for a few days to take her to their nearby island, where the crops were dying as a result of a long drought.

"I'm sorry," said the priest, "but the Virgin cannot travel at the moment because she is indisposed."

"What do you mean?" asked the farmers. "Is she sick?"

"No," said the priest, "but after all you men have been saying 'Fuck the Virgin' for so long, she finally got pregnant!"

[V268.5., Image of Virgin Mary works miracles.]

Many of the jokes in this chapter describe sexual acts, but, as their main purpose seems to be to ridicule the clergy or to express anticlerical attitudes, I have included them here rather than among the *sókin* jokes in chapter eight.

VERY *SÓKIN* JOKES ABOUT HETEROSEXUAL ACTS OF PRIESTS

142 A Greek captain who had his own ship decided that he wanted to get married. So he asked his family to find him a nice girl. Well, they did, and so he got married.

On the day after their wedding, the captain received notice that he must sail immediately for Italy. Well, he left his new bride with great sadness and promised to return as soon as possible.

After a month the girl noticed that she was pregnant. One day, when she was at confession, she told the priest of her condition.

"Oh, that's very bad! To get pregnant from only one night of sex is very dangerous. Surely the baby will be born deformed, without arms or legs! It needs more sex to finish the job!"

"But my husband is gone, and so what can I do?"

"Don't worry," said the priest, "as my religious duty I'll fix the baby."

So the priest fucked the captain's wife eight or ten different times; then he told her that the baby would be born normal.

Well, the woman wrote her husband and told him that they were going to have a baby and not to worry that they had made the baby only from the wedding night because the priest had finished the job!

When the captain came back to Greece, he was determined to get some satisfaction or revenge.

So he learned who the priest was and that he was going to pass the harbor on the next day on the way to a church outside of the town.

So the captain had his crew ready, and, when the priest passed by the ship, the crew threw rocks and sacks of dust on him, saying:

"This is from St. John! This is from St. Paul! This is from St. Nikolas!"

When the priest finally got away and arrived at the church, the sexton said:

"So you finally got here!"

"Yes, and what have you been doing?" asked the priest.

"Just dusting the ikons," said the sexton.

"Don't mention that word to me!" said the priest.

So the captain had revenge because he got even with the priest in the end.

[AT1424, Friar Adds Missing Nose to Unborn Child; J652.3., Priest seduces man's wife.]

In the next two stories, a trickster figure appears in the form of the cuckolded husband.

143   A soldier was away from home for five years, and while he was gone the priest was enjoying the soldier's wife.

When the soldier got home, he learned about it from his friends. So he swore to get revenge.

The night before a big religious celebration at a church twenty kilometers outside of town, the soldier went sneaking into the priest's house and woke up the priest's wife and daughter. Imitating the priest's voice in the dark room, the soldier said:

"Wake up! It's time to get started on our journey to the church for the celebration."

So the wife and daughter got ready, and they left.

After they had walked about fifteen kilometers, the soldier said, again imitating the priest's voice:

"It's still early, and I'm very sleepy. Let's sleep by the side of the road for an hour."

So when the two women were sleeping, the soldier stole all of their jewelry!

When they woke up they saw that they were alone and that all of their jewelry was missing! They started crying.

So the soldier came up to them and asked what the problem was.

"We've been robbed," said the woman. "My ring and gold chain were stolen, and my daughter's gold cross and chain."

The soldier said to her:

"I know where your jewelry has gone. You have a magnet in your pussy. That's what happened. The ring and chain were pulled inside your pussy. But I have a special hook, and I can fish them out for you."

"Oh, please, yes," said the priest's wife. "Fish out the ring and the chain." And she raised her skirts.

So he fucked the priest's wife, and when she wasn't looking he dropped the ring and chain onto the ground by her legs.

"There are your things," he said.

And he did the same to the priest's daughter, and then he dropped the gold cross and chain onto the ground.

So the two women were very happy, and they went on to the church.

When they got there the priest was very upset.

"Where have you been?" he asked.

"We slept by the road, and, since our pussies were like magnets and we didn't know it, all our jewelry went inside them! But a good man came along who had a fish hook, and he found them."

"Oh, then maybe the man can help me, because I've lost the silver incense burner."

So the priest's wife went to the soldier and said:

"Can you try and find the priest's incense burner? Maybe it's gone up into my pussy, too."

So he fucked her again, but since he didn't have the incense burner, he told her:

"It's up in there, but I can't get it out! It's completely round and has no corners where the hook can catch it."

And so the priest's wife went and told the priest what had happened. And when the priest realized what the soldier had done, he couldn't do anything because he had already screwed the soldier's wife!

[Legman I:378–79; J652.3., Priest seduces man's wife; K1315.2.2., Seduction by alleged retrieving of lost gem; 1424A, Priest seduces man's wife. Husband, upon returning, serves priest's wife in same manner under pretense of searching for her lost earrings.]

144   A soldier was away for five years, and while he was gone, the village priest was enjoying his wife.

When the soldier got home, he found out, and he was determined to get revenge.

So he went to the priest, who was a rich farmer, and said:

"I've been gone for five years, and I don't have any money. Could you give me some work on your farm?"

So the priest said yes because he had a guilty conscience.

About a month later the priest said to the soldier:

"Go to my house and get the yoke and the two oxen ready."

So the soldier went to the priest's house, and he said to the priest's wife:

"The priest told me to come here and for you to let me fuck you and your daughter."

So the wife said:

"If that's what he said, then it's okay with me."

So the soldier fucked her and her daughter!

And then, as the priest was approaching the house, he called to the soldier:

"Did you take both of them?"

"Yes," said the soldier, "I took both of them!"

When the priest learned what had happened, he couldn't do anything because he had fucked the soldier's wife!

[Legman I:262; AT1563, "Both?"; J652.3., Priest seduces man's wife; K1354., Seduction by bearing false order from father or husband.]

145   There was a priest who was always chasing women. Well, he was making eyes at one woman in church one day, and, after the service was over, she went to him and said:

"If you come by my house this afternoon, my husband will be away."

So the priest went to her house early in the afternoon. She lived in an apartment above a carpentry shop.

So the priest went upstairs, and he and the woman were having a good time, when suddenly the woman stopped and said:

"Oh, my Virgin, I hear my husband coming in the front door! Quick, get out of here somehow!"

So the priest, who was naked, grabbed his robes and went out on the balcony, hoping to find a fire escape. But there was none. So he jumped down, landing in a pile of lumber!

When they heard the noise, the carpenters rushed outside. What a surprise to see a naked priest holding his robes!

"Don't be afraid," said the priest. "God sent me down from heaven to find some nails, about *this* size" (pointing to his penis)!

[J652.3., Priest seduces man's wife; K1273.1., Priest surprised in intrigue flees in haste; X52., Ridiculous nakedness.]

The next joke involves confession. That apparently many jokes about the clergy relate an incident taking place in the confessional is noteworthy because many Greeks take communion only once a year, at Easter. Such stories may be very old, harkening back to a time when taking communion was more common, or they may have diffused from Roman Catholic countries where confession and communion are at present more widely practiced.

146　A woman went to confession and said to the priest:

"Father, I have sinned. I went with a man."

"What? What did you do?"

"First, he took off my dress."

So the priest took off her dress.

"Then what did he do?"

"Then he took off my slip."

So the priest took off her slip.

"Then he took off my bra and panties."

So the priest was really excited, and he took off her bra and her panties.

"Then what did he do?"

"Then he fucked me!"

So the priest fucked her.

"Oh, my priest, that's the biggest sin!"

"Which?" asked the priest.

"He had syphilis!" she said.

"And now, you old whore, *now* you tell me that?" asked the priest.

[Legman I:419; K1339.6., Seduction by priest during confession; Q240., Sexual sins punished; *K1399.6.2.*, "That and a great deal more ...", *X724.10.2.*, Seducer receives case of venereal disease.]

147 In a village there was a widow who was always going to church. So one day the priest decided he would go to her house and seduce her.

So that evening he went to her house, and he fucked her!

Well, after that the widow didn't come back to church because the priest had not satisfied her.

Finally, at Easter, she came to church again. When the priest passed close to her, she made the sign of the cross and said, while crossing herself:

First, touching her forehead, she said, "You who have no brains—"

Then, touching her pussy, "for this—"

Then, touching her right breast, "or this—"

Then, touching her left breast, "or *this*—"

"Go to the devil!"

[Legman II:575–76.]

Greek churches have no statuary and are decorated only with paintings, either frescoes or ikons, of Christ, the Virgin, the saints, angels, or other religious subjects. The following joke (as well as jokes 158 and 159) indicates that ignorant and superstitious Greek peasants think of the ikons as real, living persons.[1]

148 One time, a woman went to confession. After she confessed to a lot of trivia, the priest told her:

"To save your soul you must go and pray to the ikon of Christ and hope for divine guidance."

So the woman went over to the large ikon and began her prayers. In the meantime the priest slipped behind the wall where the ikon was affixed and told the woman in a deep voice:

"The only way to save yourself is to have intercourse with the priest!"

So then the woman went back to the priest and told him what "Christ" had told her.

"Probably you didn't understand correctly. Go pray again and hope for divine guidance."

So she returned to the ikon and the priest again went behind the ikon and repeated what he had told her before.

So she returned to the priest and told him that "Christ" had told her the same thing.

So the priest looked up to the dome of the church and said:

"Oh, my Christ! Why do you place all these difficult tasks upon *me?*"

[AT1324*, The Man Behind the Crucifix.]

THE CORRUPTION OF PRIESTS

149 Sometime, a farmer had a sow that he kept in the fields in the back of his house.

Well, one day when he went to fetch the sow, he saw that she had rooted up a box containing a fortune in golden *líres*.

So suddenly the man became very rich.

As the years passed by, the old sow died.

So the man went to the village priest and said:

"My sow has died and I want you to give her a Christian burial!"

"But, my son," protested the priest, "we can only do that for people."

So the man reached in his pocket and gave the priest ten golden *líres*.

So of course the priest agreed to give the sow a very fine burial.

Well, somebody in the village went to the bishop and told him what the priest had done. So the bishop called the priest to come and see him.

"What's this I hear that you gave the funeral rites to a sow?"

"Before the pig died," began the priest, "she left a will saying that she wanted a Christian burial, and she left ten *líres* for her funeral expenses. So I only followed the instructions of the will."

"Well," said the bishop, "for that I'm going to have you brought to court, and have your beard shaved and have your hair cut, and have you disrobed as a priest!"

So the priest returned to the village, and he went to the house of the man who owned the sow and told him all his problems.

"Don't worry," said the man, "I'll fix everything."

So the man went to see the bishop and he told him:

"I have good news for you! In my sow's will she wrote to give the bishop of our district fifty golden *líres!* So here is your money!"

The bishop looked at the money and said:

"Oh, the poor, good, sow! She even remembered me at the end!"
[AT1842, The Testament of the Dog; B562.1.1., Hogs root up gold treasure; N511., Treasure in ground.]

THE "PRIESTWIFE"

The next three jokes deal with the "priestwife" (*papadiá*), who is depicted as cuckolding her husband, the priest. Cuckoldry is the worst possible insult to a Greek man. The cuckold (*keratás*) is said to "wear horns," and the wife's putting the "horns" on her husband is an ironical allusion to the sexual potency that he does not possess. The "horns" may also indicate the social ridicule that a wife's adultery brings to her husband.

150 Sometime, there was a village priest whose wife was expecting a baby.

One day somebody asked the priest how many months pregnant his wife was.

"How should I know?" said the priest. "Ask the mayor or ask the chantor [similar to the cantor in the Jewish religion]!"

151 During the war [unnamed], a priest was transferred from one village to another. So the priest and his wife packed up their belongings and loaded them onto their donkeys and began their trip.

On the way they came across a place where there had been some terrible fighting. And there were about five decapitated corpses in the road.

"Oh, my God!" said the priest. "I wonder who those poor men were? But there's no way to tell since the heads are missing."

A bit farther along the road, they passed a place where there were decapitated corpses, and the murderers had cut off the victims' penises as well!

"No way to tell who they were," said the priest, and they continued on their journey.

A bit farther they passed a place where they saw about ten heads on the road! But, since the murderers had gouged out the eyes, they still couldn't recognize the victims.

A bit farther they passed a place in the road where they saw about ten or twelve penises.

"Oh look," said the priestwife, "there's Costas, there's Johnny, there's George, there's Peter, et cetera, et cetera."

[Legman II:482; H57., Recognition by missing member; S176., Mutilation: sex organs cut off.]

152 Sometime, in a village, there was an old priest whose wife was fooling around with other men. Well, the priest found out, and so he decided to catch his wife and her lovers. So he pretended that he had to go on a trip. He had his wife fix his suitcase, and he saddled his donkey. And as he was leaving, he told her:

"Now, don't let any other man come into my house while I'm away on my trip."

"Oh, what do you mean?" said his wife. "I wouldn't think of doing such a thing!"

So the priest rode off. As soon as he was gone, his wife called:

"Psst, psst, George, come on over quick, the priest is gone."

So George went over to her house and, just as they started fucking, there was a knock on the door.

"Oh, it's the priest! Quick, hide!" said the priestwife.

So George got up on top of the wardrobe. When the priest came inside, he looked around and said:

"It smells of people and sin in here!"

"No, no, there's nobody here but me!" said his wife.

And the priest replied:

"Well, my God who is up on high—(George said, "No, no, it's only me up here.")—will burn you for your sins!"

"But I didn't do anything!" said the priestwife.

So the priest left again for his journey, and again his wife called:

"Psst, psst, Costa, come quick, the priest is gone!"

So Costa came, and, just as they started fucking, there was a knock on the door.

"Oh, it's the priest! Quick, hide!" said the priestwife.

So Costa went and hid under the wardrobe. When the priest came in, he said:

"It smells of people and sin in here!"

"Nobody's here but me," insisted his wife.

"Never mind. The sinners down below—(Costa said, "No, no, priest, it's only me down here.")—will roast in hell for their sins."

So the priest left again, and again his wife called:

"Psst, psst, Mitsara, come quick! The priest is gone!"

So Mitsara came, and, as soon as they started fucking, there was a knock on the door!

"Quick, go hide!" said the priestwife. "It's the priest!"

So Mitsara went and hid inside the wardrobe. When the priest came in, he said:

"It smells of people and sin in here!"

"But I'm all alone," said the wife.

"Never mind," said the priest. "Only when we are locked inside the grave—(Mitsara said, "It's only me; open the door!")—do we know the truth!"

So then the priest went to the wardrobe and dragged the three men out. He told them that, as their punishment, they must go to the fields and each return with some fruit.

The first man came back with an apricot. The priest took it and shoved it up the man's ass as punishment. The man screamed in pain.

The second man came with a cucumber. So the priest shoved it up his ass as punishment. The man was screaming in pain, but suddenly he started laughing.

"What's so funny?" asked the priest.

"Look! Here comes Mitsara with a watermelon!"

[Legman II:157, 967; AT1689, "Thank God They Weren't Peaches"; AT1355A, The Lord Above; the Lord Below; D1273.1.1., Three as magic number; H466.1., Feigned absence to test wife's faithfulness.]

For a full appreciation of the preceding joke, it is useful to know that in ancient Greece one of the punishments faced by a young man who committed adultery with a married woman was to have a radish forced up his anus by the offended husband. This act converted the adulterer to a "wide-arse," a slur term used for passive homosexuals (Dover 1978:105–06, 140).

MONKS AND MONASTERIES

I suspect that there were more stories and jokes about the monks in circulation in the past than is the case today. Before 1925 religious orders and monasteries owned extensive land in Greece. Religious orders still own areas such as Mount Athos, a peninsula southeast of Thessaloniki; women and female animals are not permitted to set foot on Mount Athos. But the monastic orders have come to the end of an era. They have lost the wealth, patronage, and power that they once commanded.

In 1925, to accommodate the influx of Greeks fleeing Asia Minor, the government expropriated ecclesiastical lands for the landless refugees. Many of the once-magnificent monasteries at Athos are now abandoned and in a state of collapse.

153 A bishop went to visit all the monasteries of his district. They were all doing well, and finally he went to the last monastery.

When he got there the place was deserted and nobody came to greet him! He looked in all the rooms, but he couldn't find a soul!

Finally, he went to the basement, and there he saw all the monks, naked!

"What are you doing like that down here?" demanded the bishop.

"We're playing a game," said one of the monks.

"What game?" asked the bishop.

"We wait to see if a fly lands on somebody's penis. Then, if it does, that monk gets to fuck all the others!"

"And why do you have that poor monk tied up by his hands and feet?" asked the bishop.

"Oh. That monk put honey on his penis so that lots of flies would land on it. So we're punishing him!"

[B152.2., Fly indicates successful suitor; Q464., Covering with honey and exposing to flies; V465.1.1., Incontinent monk (priest); X457., Jokes on monks.]

154 A man went to confession. But, since he had so many sins, the priest told him that to be saved he must go to a monastery for the rest of his life.

So he went to a monastery. He knocked on the door, but nobody answered. So he went inside.

As he passed the first room, he saw a monk masturbating!

As he passed the second room, he saw two monks engaging in sodomy!

As he passed the third room, he saw there were three monks in a row, and each one was fucking the one in front of him!

When he passed the fourth room, he saw the abbot. The abbot asked him why he had come, and he told him.

"But, after what I have seen, I don't want to become a monk," said the man.

"But you must have patience," said the abbot. "After three years *you'll* get to be the man in the middle in the third room!"

[T463., Sodomy; V20., Confession of sins; V465.1.1., Incontinent monk (priest); X457., Jokes on monks.]

HOMOSEXUAL PRIESTS

155 Two homosexual priests went to Athens for Easter. They arrived two days early, by boat.

When they were walking in Piraeus, they passed a handsome young sailor on the street.

"Oh, what a sweet boy," said one of the priests. "I'd just love to eat him!"

"Aren't you ashamed to talk like that? Don't you realize that it's Lent and meat is forbidden now?"

"Yes," said the first priest, "meat is forbidden, but seafood is okay!"

THE OVERSTRICT PRIEST

156 A shepherd went to the village one time to go to confession and take communion. After he made his confession, he told the priest:

"Forgive me, Father, but, since I had to get up so early today and had such a long walk to come here, I drank a little milk this morning."

"Never mind, my son," said the priest.

So the priest gave him a glass of vinegar instead of wine, and, instead of the communion bread, the priest took a piece of wood and knocked him on the head!

As the shepherd was leaving the church, a woman carrying a child was entering the church.

"Where are you going?" asked the shepherd.

"I'm taking Johnny to communion," said the woman.

"Well," he said, "I guess he can take the vinegar, but the blow on the head will kill him for sure!"

[Q223.9., Neglect to fast punished; X448.*, Bishop is over-zealous in administering the sacrament. Strikes the parishioner (Rotunda 1942).]

SACRILEGIOUS LAY PERSONS

157 Two men went fishing and took their lunch because they wanted to stay all day. They went to a river, and they separated to fish, but they agreed to meet at lunchtime close to a small church.

At noon one man had a sack full of fish, but his companion hadn't caught even one fish!

"I must have back luck," said the fisherman without any fish. "But I'll do something to change my luck."

"What? Use different bait?"

"No, something else. You'll see."

So after lunch they separated, and the unlucky man went into the small church and prayed to the ikon of the Blessed Virgin.

"Blessed Virgin, if you help me to catch a fish, I'll give you a big can of oil to light all the lamps of this church."

So he returned to his spot on the river and started fishing. After a little while he had a big strike, a *huge* fish. It took him about ten minutes to bring it in, and, just as he was ready to grab the fish, he said:

"Now that I've got the fish, my luck's come back, and I don't have to give the oil to the church!"

Just as he said that, the fish jumped off the hook and flipped back into the water!

The man looked up to heaven and said:

"Don't you like even *one* little joke?"

[AT1718*, God Can't Take a Joke; K231.3., Refusal to make sacrifice after need is past.]

158 A shepherd was guarding his flock in the mountains when it suddenly started to rain. Spotting a small church nearby, he ran to the church to take shelter during the rainstorm.

Inside the church he saw a lamp full of [olive] oil. He was hungry, so he took some bread out of his backpack and dipped it in the oil and ate and ate.

After the rain stopped he put his staff across his shoulders, with his arms on top, and started to leave the church. But his staff was longer than the door was wide, so naturally he couldn't get out of the door. Not understanding that it was his staff that was keeping him from leaving the church, and thinking that God was angry with him for taking the oil, he said:

"Okay, Christ, I'm sorry that I took the oil. Let me go and I'll bring you another bottle of oil."

But still he couldn't get out of the door.

"Okay, I'll bring you two bottles of oil!"

Still he couldn't pass.

"Okay, I'll bring you three bottles of oil!"

But still the shepherd was unable to pass through the door!

So he got very angry and went back in the church and smashed the candelabra and struck the ikons with his stick! Then he walked out of the church, this time with his stick in his hand.

When he got outside, free at last, he said:

"So! The saints wanted excitement and the Virgin wanted a good beating to let me leave the church!"

[A variant of AT1643, The Broken Image.]

159 A thief went into a church and stood in front of the ikon of the Blessed Virgin. He addressed the ikon:

"My Virgin, I'm so poor, may I take one drachme [from the offering box]?"

Then, using a woman's voice, the thief answered himself, pretending to be the Virgin Mary:

"Take it, my son."

"May I take five drachmes?"

"Take it, my son," said the thief, again using a woman's voice.

"May I take ten drachmes?"

"Take it, my son."

"May I take one hundred?"

"Take it, my son."

So the thief took one hundred drachmes and left, but the old man who cleaned the church heard what the thief had said and saw him take the money.

Well, the next day the thief returned. But the old man saw him coming and went and hid in back of the ikon.

Again the thief came and stood in front of the ikon of the Virgin and said:

"My dear Virgin, I'm really in trouble. May I take another one hundred drachmes?"

"Don't take it!" said the old man in a masculine voice.

"Shut up, you little bastard! I'm talking to your mother!"

[AT1476*, Prayer to Christ Child's Mother.]

JOKES ABOUT PRIESTS' VIRTUES

160 Two priests were eating in a restaurant. One was married and the other was single. The married one was telling the single one that he should get married.

The single priest said that he didn't want to marry because women were so bad.

"No, no!" said the married priest. "They're not *all* bad. A woman is like a barrel that's filled half with honey and the other half with shit. When you're first married you have lots of honey. And only after a long time do you get to the shit."

A man was sitting at the next table and he overheard the two priests talking. Finally, he said:

"I must have opened my wife's barrel upside down because with her it's been nothing but shit from the beginning!"

161 Sometime, there was a village priest who had been in the same village for twenty years.

Well, the women in that village, when they went to confession, would use unusual words. Instead of saying that they had committed adultery, they would say that they had slipped! But there was no problem because the old priest understood them.

Well, the priest got a letter from the archbishop telling him he was being sent to another village and that a new priest would be coming to take over.

So he waited and waited for the new priest to come, but it was winter and there was lots of bad weather, so the new priest was delayed. So the evening before he left the village, the old priest told the mayor of the village all the instructions for the new priest. And he said:

"Oh, before I forget! Tell the new priest that in confession, when the women say 'I slipped,' it means that they committed adultery."

Well, a few days later the new priest arrived. So the mayor gave him all of the old priest's instructions, but he forgot to tell him what "I slipped" meant.

So the first day that the new priest heard confession, a woman came in and told him:

"Forgive me, Father, I slipped."

Well, the priest didn't understand, but he saw the woman was wearing very high-heeled shoes, so he said:

"It was probably just your high heels, but never mind, be careful in the future."

The next woman who came also said that she "slipped." But the priest saw that she wasn't wearing high heels, so he warned her to be careful where she walked.

When the third woman came and also told him that she "slipped," the priest concluded that the roads in the village must be the fault. So he told her to be careful when she walked on the road.

Well, that evening the priest saw the mayor in the coffeehouse, and he told him:

"We have a big problem in this village! The roads are so bad that the women are always slipping! You must do something quick to fix the roads!"

Well, the mayor remembered what the old priest had told him, and so he started laughing:

"The roads! Ha, ha, ha!"

"What's so funny?" asked the priest.

"I forgot to tell you, ha, ha! The old priest said to tell you that, in confession, if the women say 'I slipped,' it really means 'I committed adultery.' Ha, ha!"

"If I were you, I wouldn't laugh so hard," said the priest. "Your wife told me that she slipped five times last week alone!"

[V20., Confession of sins; X410., Jokes on parsons.]

162   One day a priest was walking down the road and he passed a man who had a little bell tied to his leg.

"Tell me, my son," asked the priest, "why do you have that bell tied on your leg?"

"To warn the little animals, the ants, the caterpillars, the worms, the insects, that I am coming so that I won't accidentally kill them," said the man.

"Oh, what a saint!" thought the priest. "Tell me, my son, have you ever committed a sin?"

"Well, once I made love with my sister-in-law because she's very pretty."

"Shame, shame!" said the priest. "Is that the only time that you sinned?"

"Well, my mother-in-law is also very beautiful, so one time I screwed her!"

"Oh! Shame, shame," said the priest. "Is that all?"

"No, I also fucked my father-in-law one time because he is very handsome," said the man.

"I have some advice for you," said the priest. "In the future you should wear that little bell on your penis, not on your leg!"

[U11.1.1.2., Penitent in confession worries about little sins and be-littles the big ones; V222.6., Bell sounds at approach of saint.]

HEAVEN AND HELL

163 One time, a man died of a cold. So he went to heaven, but, since he was so *very* cold, they decided to send him to hell for a while to warm him up.

So when he got to hell, the devil said:

"Where can we put him to warm him up?"

So they put him in a big oven. After a few minutes they opened the door, but the man said:

"I'm still freezing cold!"

So they put him inside and in the back of an even bigger and hotter oven.

Well, the devil who was watching the oven door dozed off and slept for a year before he woke up! When he woke up he said:

"Oh! Probably that man has burned to a crisp!"

So he opened the door, and the man said:

"Close the door, you're making a draft!"

[A671.3.1., Coldness in hell.]

164 Sometime, Satan came down to earth and found a man in a village to help him. The man always told the devil who was bad and who to take to hell. So Satan promised the man that when he died he would remember him and do him a favor.

So the man died and went to hell. When Satan saw him he remembered him right away.

"Oh, it's you, my friend! Well, because you helped me I'm going to let you choose any place here that you want to stay."

So the man looked around. In one place people were being boiled in oil; in another place people were being roasted on a spit! In another place people were standing in a pool of shit and urine up to their shoulders and drinking something that looked like coffee.

"I want to go to the pool!" said the man.

So he went and got into the pool filled with filth, and just then one of the devils came over and said:

"Okay, coffeebreak is over! Put your heads back in the water!"

[Legman II:945; E755.2.7., Devils tormenting sinners in hell.]

165 A man died and went to heaven. He knocked at the door, but Saint Peter didn't open.

"Open the door!" screamed the man in agitation.

Still Saint Peter didn't open the door.

"Fuck your Virgin, open the door!"

Christ heard the man and said to Saint Peter:

"Open up the door fast, Peter, it's one of my mother's customers!"

[A661.0.1., Gate of heaven; A661.0.1.2., St. Peter as porter of heaven.]

166   One time, a famous soccer player died and went to heaven. He got to the pearly gates and knocked, but Saint Peter told him:

"Not now, we're very busy!"

So he waited and waited, but nothing happened. So he knocked again.

"I told you that we're really busy; wait a while!"

So again the man waited and waited, and again he knocked.

"Oh, it's you again," said Saint Peter. "Tell me, what job did you do before you died?"

"I was defense for the Olympic Soccer Team."

"Come on in then, quick! We're losing two to nothing to hell!"

[A661.0.1., Gate of heaven; A661.0.1.2., St. Peter as porter of heaven.]

THE CONFESSIONAL

167   One time, a woman went to confession. Well, she told the priest that she had masturbated several times since her last confession.

"Which hand did you do that with?" asked the priest.

"With my right hand."

"Then the only way to cleanse your sin is for you to go to the Jordan River and wash your right hand in its waters."

So the woman traveled all the way to the Jordan River. When she got there and began to wash her hand in the river, she saw a woman from her village who was at the river gargling!

[Legman II:134; A1549.4., Penance for sins.]

168   A young man went to confession:

"Forgive me, Father, for I have sinned. I told lies, and I used bad words, and I masturbated twenty times!"

"Twenty times!" said the priest. "Then you must say the prayers twenty times in front of the Virgin's ikon to be forgiven."

Later another young man went to the priest and made his confession:

"Forgive me, Father, for I have sinned. I used bad words, I cursed, and I masturbated thirty times!"

"Thirty times!" said the priest. "Then go and say the prayers thirty times in front of the ikon of Christ."

Later another young man came and said:

"Forgive me, Father, I have sinned. I masturbated twenty-seven times!"

"Twenty-seven times!" said the priest. "Then go stand in front of the ikon of the Virgin and masturbate three more times, then go to the ikon of Christ and say the prayers thirty times!"

[D1273.1.1., Three as magic number.]

169 A priest was hearing confession when a young man came in. The priest asked him:

"Did you curse?"

"Yes," said the boy, "I curse every day!"

"Then I can't give you communion," said the priest.

"To my balls!" said the boy [also gesture given; see below, pp. 186–87 and appendix C].

Well, the priest felt sorry for the boy, so he tried again:

"Did you fight?" asked the priest.

"Sure, I fight every day!" said the boy.

"Then I can't give you communion," said the priest.

"To my balls!" said the boy.

Finally, in exasperation, the priest said:

"The only way that I can give you communion is if you go up to the top of the bell tower and jump down."

"If I jump and don't get killed, then you'll give me communion?" asked the boy.

"If you jump and don't get killed, then to *my* balls!" said the priest.

FUNNY INCIDENTS IN CHURCH

The following jokes have as their common subject funny incidents that happened in church, a subject I believe to be the most prevalent among those jokes about the Church that circulate in Greece. Although some are clearly fantasy, many of the jokes probably have their origins in real events. The first joke below adds yet another element—that animal trickster, the parrot.

170   A village priest had a parrot in the church. The parrot sat on a small swing, and on each leg was attached a small string.

One day the archbishop came to visit the church.

The priest told him:

"We have trained a parrot to talk."

"Really?" asked the archbishop. "What does he say?"

"If you pull the string on his right leg, he recites the Lord's Prayer. If you pull the string on his left leg, he recites the Credo," said the priest.

"What happens if you pull both the strings at the same time?" asked the archbishop.

"I'll fall off my perch, you dumb queer!" said the parrot.

[Legman I:202; B211.3.4., Speaking parrot; J1118.1., Clever parrot.]

171   It was the day of the year when the priest gave the sermon on the miracle of the loaves and the fishes. After saying the Mass he began to tell the people of how Christ had performed one of the greatest miracles of all time. He said:

"And Christ, with only five thousand fish and two thousand loaves of bread, was able to feed ten people!"

A man in the church said in a loud voice to the priest:

"That's nothing! I can do that myself!"

The priest, realizing what mistake he had made, said nothing and closed the sermon for the day.

A year later it was the same day on which the miracle of the loaves and the fishes was to be described. The priest said:

"And Christ, with only five fish and two loaves of bread, was able to feed thousands of people!"

"That's nothing," said the man from the year before. "I can do that, too!"

"Really?" asked the priest. "And how do you, an ordinary mortal, propose to perform this miracle?"

"With the loaves and the fishes left over from last year!"

[AT1833**, Other Anecdotes of Sermons: Application of the Sermon; X410., Jokes on parsons.]

The Bible of the Greek Orthodox Church is written in ancient Greek; not all the people understand it today because over time the language has undergone many changes. Old women, particularly those who went to school for only a few years, do not always understand what the priest says. The informant who told me the following joke suggests that sometimes they misunderstand because some words of the ancient language are still used in modern Greek, but with new meanings.

172　One Sunday the priest was reading from the Bible at the Mass, and he said:

"So Christ broke [*éklase*] the bread. . . ."

And one old woman heard the word "broke," but she didn't understand ancient Greek, and so she thought that the priest had said "broke wind."

So she bowed her head and crossed herself three times and said:

"Oh, my golden Christ, even if you *did* do that, they shouldn't have put it in the Bible!"

The next joke deals with the same type of problem as the preceding joke. The *dhimótik* word for "to fuck" is *gamísi*, which is related to more polite words such as *gámos* ("wedding"). Probably in ancient Greek the word had a meaning less vulgar than it has today.

173　One Sunday at church the priest said:

"In the beginning, God created Adam and Eve. . . . And so Adam fucked Eve and then. . . ."

Well, the village policeman was there, and after the service he fined the priest one hundred drachmes for saying "fucked."

The next Sunday the same thing happened. The priest said:

"So Adam fucked Eve. . . ."

And this time the priest was fined two hundred drachmes for using bad language.

So the next Sunday the priest said:

"And so one man fucked Eve and another man paid the bill!"

[X410., Jokes on parsons.]

174　One time, in a village, there was no priest. So the mayor of the village went to a man and told him he would have to be the priest until they could get a real priest.

"But I can't do that! I don't know what to say," protested the man.

"There's no problem," said the mayor. "You will just read the Bible, and, if you make a mistake, we will tell you."

"But how?" said the man. "In front of all the congregation?"

"No, we have a better idea. We'll tie a string around your balls, and, if you make a mistake, we'll pull the string."

So the next Sunday the new "priest" was reading the Bible, and afterwards he had to explain the meaning of some of the passages from the Bible. So he said:

"And so God made the earth with animals, trees, light, and he made the sky with five hundred stars."

Somebody pulled the string.

"With three hundred stars!"

Again the string was pulled, this time harder.

"With one hundred stars!"

Again the string was pulled and even harder.

"With *no* stars! And so God made the sky with no stars, and me with no balls!"

[AT1825, The Peasant As Parson; X434.4.*, The sermon is misinterpreted (Rotunda 1942).]

NUNS

175   During the war [World War II], an English airplane crashed near a nunnery. Everyone was killed but the pilot. So he went to the nunnery and asked for refuge.

Well, the nun who answered the door knew it was forbidden, but she let the young pilot inside (because it was wartime).

The young nun hid the pilot in her room, and so of course he screwed her! Well, she got pregnant.

Well, the Mother Superior came because she had heard that one of the nuns was pregnant. So she held a general inspection of all the nuns, to look at their stomachs. She made them lift their skirts so that she could see their stomachs.

So the young pregnant nun told the pilot that he would have to put a habit on, and to tie a string to his penis and to pull it in back and secure it there so that the Mother Superior wouldn't see the penis when she inspected him. She told him not to worry, the Mother Superior was half-blind and wore thick glasses.

Well, when the Mother Superior told the pilot (she thought that he was a nun since her eyesight was so bad) to raise his skirt, and she looked down, just then the string broke and his penis flew up! When it did that it knocked off her eyeglasses and they landed on his penis!

"Well!" said the Mother Superior. "I've seen a lot in my time, but *never* one wearing glasses!"

[K1836., Disguise of man in woman's dress; K2285., Villain disguised as ascetic or nun; V465.1.2., Incontinent nun.]

The conclusion of the preceding joke is similar to that of joke 331, about another nosy old woman: evidently the very close proximity of the woman's face to the man's genitals causes an erection, which then knocks off the woman's glasses. The over-zealous inspection by the nosy old woman is a caricature of the general inquisitiveness of Greek women (and of many Greek men). I was consistently asked what we in America consider very personal questions (about my religion, my salary, and so on) by total strangers only moments after meeting them. Furthermore, the punch line, "I've seen a lot in my time" (meaning a lot of penises), which occurs also in joke 329, seems to reflect the widespread male attitude in Greece that women are over-sexed and unfaithful. The ancient Greeks also believed that women enjoy sexual intercourse more intensely than do men and that women have a natural inclination toward adultery (Dover 1978:67).

Chapter 6
Transportation Jokes

A number of jokes in Greece involve situations on buses, trains, and airplanes; jokes about automobiles also circulate. Several outstanding characteristics of the various modes of travel in Greece deserve mention here as a basis for appreciating the jokes in this chapter and elsewhere. (Some transportation jokes, particularly those pertaining to a crowded bus, are in chapter one, "Political Jokes"; others are in the scatological joke section of chapter nine, "Light *Sókin* Jokes.")

Public buses in Athens and Piraeus and in other urban areas of Greece have two men on board: the driver and the *ispráktoras*, who collects money and issues a "ticket." (A few "automatic" trolleys that require the passenger to drop the fare into a box at the side of the driver were running in Athens in 1977.) Passengers enter at the rear of the bus, pass the *ispráktoras*, and move forward. Some of the world's most crowded buses are to be found in Athens, but, despite the temptations inherent in the situation, few men take advantage of the crowding to fondle, pinch, or press against women. Buses that travel from town to town are normally not so crowded because the passenger must secure a ticket and reserve a seat in advance of the trip; only on major holidays such as Easter, the First of May, or the Fifteenth of August does one see passengers standing on those buses.

Traveling by bus in rural Greece can be amusing. The *ispráktoras* has many duties in addition to collecting tickets: he ties the extra baggage on top of the bus and removes it at the destination; he opens and closes windows for the passengers.

Usually while performing the latter duty, the poor man gets caught in the middle of very noisy arguments between those passengers who are too hot and those who are too cold. Passengers are frequently entertained with tape-recorded popular Greek music, not only on rural and tour buses, but also in taxis and on ferryboats. The music helps to make the trip more pleasant and to "pass the time."

Another characteristic feature of buses, as well as trucks and even taxis, in Greece is their colorful and varied decoration. A recent article in a Greek magazine devoted to Athens said that this characteristic was being eliminated gradually by the government's takeover of buses that previously had been privately owned.

Many of the decorations are religious objects: ikons of Christ, the Virgin, or the saints, in addition to photographs of famous bishops and archbishops. After the Turkish invasion of Cyprus and the downfall of the Junta in 1974, pictures of Archbishop Makarios were displayed everywhere in Greece, even on buses, for he was the hero of the year. Crosses and other religious objects are used to protect both the driver and the vehicle.

Secular decorations include photographs of pin-up girls and other sexy *gómenes*, and photographs of cats, dogs, and landscapes. Sometimes photographs of ancient Greek art or ancient Greek sites like the Acropolis in Athens or Delphi are displayed. Photographs of the driver's family or loved ones may also be observed. Short fringed curtains, usually scalloped, sometimes hang inside across the top of the windshield, possibly to shield the driver's eyes from the sun; they also provide a "homey" touch. Plastic flowers, little colored lights, and various dangling objects add interest. One of the most remarkable decorative items that I saw, on a bus in Athens, was a plastic model of Laurel and Hardy that lit up every time the bus stopped.

An unusual form of vehicle decoration emerged in late 1976 to become widespread by spring 1977: flat, two-dimensional "hands" made of plastic or heavy paper imprinted with some message such as "Good luck" or "Good trip" that attach to windshields and back windows by means of a suction cup with a spring. As the hands wave from side to side with the motion of the vehicle, they seem to be giving simultaneously the *múntza* curse gesture (see appendix C and the discussion on pages 192–93) and the (American) "hello" gesture. As another use of the *múntza* gesture is to avert the "evil eye," around which concept revolves a complex set of beliefs and practices in Mediterranean and Latin American countries, perhaps the hands on the vehicles enable one to avert the "evil eye." Or perhaps they simply allow an aggressive driver to give with impunity the *múntza* gesture to everyone. (Drivers in Greece, especially in Athens, are indeed aggressive; they blow horns, shout, curse, and insult each other with gestures such as the *múntza* and the "to my balls" gestures (see appendix C and also the discussion on pp. 186–87).

Private automobiles also have decorations. Most popular are the little dolls that attach to the inside rearview mirror and that bounce up and down on a spring. Handmade crocheted pillows lie on the back decks of automobiles. Almost every automobile, to protect it and its passengers, carries religious medallions or ikons, either attached to the dashboard or hung from the rearview mirror.

The first three jokes below involve automobiles, which in Greece usually cost three times as much as equivalent models in America.[1] Greeks pay very high road-use taxes, based on the size and weight of their cars, and high fees for license plates. One is supposed to have had driving lessons before obtaining a driver's license, the cost of the latter also being very high.

176 A Greek was driving a Jaguar on the National Highway toward Athens, and on the way he stopped to help a woman in a stalled Volkswagen.

"My car's out of gas," said the woman.

"Okay, I'll tow you to a gas station," said the man. "But, in case I get carried away and forget that you're behind me and I start speeding, just blow the horn and I'll slow down."

So they took off, and, just as they were approaching a gas station, a Buick blew the horn and went speeding by!

The owner of the Jaguar went crazy and started going very fast to overtake the Buick. So the woman in the Volkswagen started blowing the horn.

Well, a man in the gas station that they passed called his friend in the next gas station down the highway and said:

"You won't believe what I just saw! A Buick going one hundred followed by a Jaguar and then by a Volkswagen trying to pass them both!"

[D1273.1.1., Three as magic number; X583., Jokes about travelers.]

177 One Sunday a man from Athens drove up to the mountains and then left his car and walked in the fresh air. He sat down and dozed off. When he woke up he saw two wolves getting ready to attack him! So he forgot his car and started running down to the highway with the wolves at his heels!

He tried to flag down a car, but it was going too fast and didn't stop. A second speeding car also didn't stop. Finally, a small car was coming, and, as it was going very slow, the man ran and opened the door and jumped in!

When he looked he saw that there was nobody driving the car! It was going all by itself!

He started shaking!

"First the wolves try to eat me, now I've gotten into a car with a ghost driver!"

The car kept going for twenty minutes. Finally, it pulled into a gas station, and the attendant came to put gas into it!

The door by the driver's side opened and a man started to get in.

"If I were you I wouldn't get into this car, it's haunted! It's been driving by itself for twenty minutes!" said the man.

"By itself?" asked the other man. "Don't be ridiculous! I ran out of gas in the mountains and I've been pushing the car for half an hour!"

[X583., Jokes about travelers.]

The preceding joke calls to mind a yearly phenomenon in Greece—reports, usually in the spring, of wolves being sighted, usually by shepherds. When the police question the shepherds in the areas of the sightings, they always say that they didn't see any wolves, that the report must have come from somebody farther up in the mountains. Perhaps the shepherds serve as modern counterparts to the boy who cried wolf.

178 Two friends left a Greek nightclub late at night and very drunk.

They climbed into a Jaguar convertible and took off. About three minutes later, when turning a corner, the car went into a spin and turned
over, and the two men fell out, unharmed.

One friend said to the other:

"It's a good thing that you didn't drive like that all night or we'd be
dead by now!"

The other man said:

"Me? I thought you were driving the car!"

[X583., Jokes about travelers.]

As most of the collected jokes involving buses fall more logically into the categories represented by other chapters, the following single example of a bus joke suffices here.

179 A man on a bus in Athens tapped another man on the shoulder,
and, when the second man turned around, the first man said:

"I'm from Mars!"

So the second man figured that the heat had gotten to the first man,
and so he ignored him.

A while later the first man again tapped the second man on the
shoulder and said:

"I'm from Mars!"

"Oh, go to my balls," said the second man.

"In Mars we don't have balls and penises!" said the first man.

"So how do you fuck then?" asked the second man.

"By tapping people on the shoulder! And now I've fucked you
twice!" said the first man.

[X583., Jokes about travelers.]

The next three jokes involve travel by train. According to a
textbook on modern Greek, the trains in Greece are always late;
indeed, one of the phrases to be learned from the book is *Ta
tréna stin Elláda éhoun pánta kathistérisi*.[2] The alleged tardi-
ness of trains reflects Greek attitudes toward time: events take
place in Greece when the time is "right," rather than "on
time."[3]

180 A man took the train to Thessaloniki from Athens, but he was
only going half of the way, to Lamia.

The man had a sleeper, and so he called a conductor and said:

"Here's a tip. I want you to wake me up when we get to Lamia."

"Yes, sir!" said the conductor.

"But, listen," said the man. "I'm a very heavy sleeper. Don't just call me and leave, because I'll just turn over and go back to sleep. Scream and slap me in the face once or twice! Then for sure I'll wake up!"

"Yes, sir, just as you say," said the conductor.

So the man put his pajamas on and went to sleep. When he woke up he went to shave. He said to a man in the bathroom:

"What time do we arrive in Lamia?"

"Lamia?" asked the man. "Lamia? In ten minutes we'll arrive in Thessaloniki!"

So the man was furious, and he went to find the conductor. But he couldn't find him, he found another one. Well, he started complaining:

"I gave that man a good tip to wake me up in Lamia and here I am arriving in Thessaloniki!"

Two passengers overheard him and one of them said:

"He's right, you know. He paid his money and they didn't wake him!"

The second passenger said:

"But don't you remember all the screaming and shouting we heard in Lamia when they put somebody off the train who didn't want to get off?"

[X583., Jokes about travelers.]

181 Three friends went to the Larissa Train Station in Athens and asked when was the next train to Thessaloniki.

"Nine o'clock sharp," said the stationmaster.

As it was only seven-thirty, the three friends said:

"What can we do to pass the time?"

One saw a *tavérna* across the street.

"Let's go have something to eat in the *tavérna*," he said.

So they went to the *tavérna* and ordered food and wine. Then they had some more wine. Finally, when they saw the time, it was eight-fifty-nine! Well, they ran over to the station, but the train had gone.

"What time is the next train to Thessaloniki?" they asked.

"Eleven o'clock sharp," said the stationmaster.

"Oh, what to do until eleven o'clock?" said one.

"Let's go back to the *tavérna* and continue where we stopped!" said another.

So they went back to the *tavérna* and had lots of *retsína* [resinated wine] and appetizers. And more wine and more food! When they saw the time, it was ten-fifty-five!

"Hurry up," said one, and they all ran over to the station. The train was just pulling out, so they kept on running. Two of the men made it, but the third, who was the heaviest of the three, couldn't make it. So the train pulled away and left! Suddenly the man started laughing hysterically!

Well, the stationmaster saw him and said:

"What? You missed the train and so you're laughing? Are you nuts?"

"I'm laughing," said the man, "because *I* was the one who was supposed to go to Thessaloniki! The other two were just seeing me off!"

[D1273.1.1., Three as magic number; X583., Jokes about travelers.]

182 A man was traveling by train. Next to him, in the aisle, was a suitcase. So the conductor came by and said:

"Please, sir. Put the suitcase inside so nobody will trip and fall."

"Don't bother me about a suitcase!" said the man.

"Please, sir! Be reasonable! Move the suitcase out of the aisle!"

"Leave me alone! Are you going to keep bothering me about a suitcase?"

"Look, sir," said the conductor. "If you don't move that suitcase immediately, I'm going to throw it off the train!"

Still the man ignored the conductor's threats and refused to move the suitcase.

So the conductor picked up the suitcase, opened the window, and threw the suitcase off the train!

"There!" said the conductor. "That will teach you not to leave your suitcase in the aisle!"

"*My* suitcase? Who told you it was *my* suitcase?" asked the man.

[X583., Jokes about travelers.]

Airplane jokes also occur in other chapters because their primary themes fit more logically into other joke categories. The one example of an airplane joke included here pokes fun at the technology of the United States.

183 In America they built the fastest airplane in the world! Well, they got the best of all the test pilots to try it out.

Just after the pilot took off from New York, he said:

"Okay, New York, take-off completed and journey en route."

But he heard a voice saying:

"New York? This is London International!"

"Oh, excuse the mistake, London International! This is test pilot Smith continuing on my journey!"

"London? This is Berlin Airport!" said another voice.

"Oh, Berlin Airport, this is Pilot Smith. Over!"

"Berlin?" answered another voice. "This is Moscow!"

"Hello, Moscow? Oh, my God, is that you?" asked the pilot, beginning to get nervous.

"Yes, my son," said still another voice. "You're in heaven now!"

[X583., Jokes about travelers.]

Chapter 7
Lunatic Jokes

The closest thing that the Greeks have to what we in America call "sick" humor are jokes about "crazy" people and scatalogical jokes (see chapter nine, "Light *Sókin* Jokes"). Interestingly enough, only crazy men are depicted in those jokes; one never hears a joke about a crazy woman. As one informant explained, "In Greece we have other work for women!"

A small island between the shipyards of Perama (part of the port of Piraeus) and the island of Salamis at one time was the site of an extensive colony for the insane. Today the buildings and houses on this island appear deserted, and, according to rumor, Aristotle Onassis once wanted to buy the island on which to build a gambling casino and luxury resort. I never saw any other hospital for the mentally ill in Greece, but many of the jokes I heard refer to one that reputedly is close to Dafni, a few miles west of Athens.[1]

A Greek proverb advises, "From the mouths of children, drunks, and crazy people,/You will always learn the truth." In America we say, "Out of the mouths of babes ..." but that we Americans share the view that the drunk and the crazy have a special veracity is doubtful. In a few of the jokes included here, a crazy person utters a truth, but those jokes do not seem to be trying to demonstrate any philosophical wisdom on the part of a schizophrenic.

The following jokes, which I have labeled "lunatic jokes,"[2] are widespread and very popular in Greece. People of all ages and of both sexes tell them, and seemingly enjoy them. The jokes also frequently appear in Greek humor magazines such as *Trast*.

123

184 A special psychiatrist was sent to the mental hospital in Dafni to examine a patient who was supposedly "cured" and ready to leave the hospital.

The day the doctor arrived had been a holiday, and all the inmates had been having picnics and the like in the gardens of the hospital.

Earlier in the day one of the patients had fallen into the shallow pool, and the supposedly "cured" patient had gone in and saved the man from drowning.

So the psychiatrist was interviewing the "cured" patient:

"I heard that you saved a fellow patient from drowning today," said the doctor.

"Yes, I did!"

"Good! Good! That means you are healthy again. Now, tell me, what did you do next?"

"Then I hung the guy up in a tree so he could dry off!" said the lunatic.

[X540., Jokes on madmen.]

185 There was a crazy man who had to be transferred from one mental hospital to another. So he was sent by plane, in the company of a friend of his.

During the flight the lunatic started playing ball [soccer], and he was really creating a commotion and disturbing all the passengers. So the stewardess went to ask the pilot what to do.

"Is the man traveling alone?" he asked.

"No, he's with a friend."

"Send the friend to talk with me," he said.

When the friend arrived the pilot told him:

"If you get that lunatic to stop playing ball in the plane and disturbing everybody, I'll let you fly the plane for a while."

"Okay," said the friend, and he went back to talk to the lunatic. After ten minutes everything was completely quiet, and the friend returned to the cockpit asking to fly the plane!

"How did you get your friend to behave?" asked the pilot.

"It was easy! I just opened the door and told him to go and play in the garden!"

[X540., Jokes on madmen.]

186 There was a lunatic in the mental hospital in Dafni. After he had been there for one year, the doctor decided that he was well enough to go home. So he called him to his office to tell him that he could go home.

While the patient was in the office, another patient came in with a hammer and a big nail. He was trying to hammer the nail into the wall, but he was hitting the wrong end of the nail, and of course it didn't go into the wall.

So the lunatic that was "cured" said to the other lunatic:

"Hey, you're not doing it right! You've got the wrong wall! It's the opposite wall that you must put the nail into!"

[X540., Jokes on madmen.]

187 A lunatic escaped from Dafni and was walking down the road. Finally, he saw an old house that had some wooden columns in the yard.

So the lunatic went into the yard and started climbing up one of the columns. The man who owned the house saw him and started to go out into the yard, but the lunatic saw him coming and got down and left.

A while later he came back and again started to climb up the column. Again the house owner came outside and the lunatic left!

About an hour later the lunatic came again to the house and again started climbing up the column. This time the owner decided to wait and see what the lunatic was going to do.

When he got to the top, he took a piece of paper out of his pocket, folded it, and then took a thumbtack out of his other pocket and tacked the paper to the top of the column. Then he got down and left.

So the house owner went over to the column, and he climbed up to the top. Then he grabbed the paper and climbed down to read it. He unfolded it and read:

"Attention! Be careful! This is where the column ends!"

[X540., Jokes on madmen.]

188 About ten years ago, when Greece still had a king, the king used to visit hospitals and the like at Christmas.

One Christmas the king visited several hospitals in Athens, and then he went to a psychiatric hospital to visit the patients and to wish them a "Merry Christmas."

As he entered one room, he announced to a patient:

"Hello! I'm your king, and I've come to wish you a Merry Christmas!"

"Better be careful," said the patient. "When I said that *I* was the king, they locked me in this crazy house!"

[X540., Jokes on madmen.]

189   One time, a woman lived next door to a crazy house. She had two small parrots, a red one and a green one. One day the two parrots escaped from their cage and flew into a tree inside the grounds of the hospital.

So one of the doctors told one of the patients to climb up into the tree and catch the two birds that belonged to the nice lady next door.

So the lunatic went up into the tree and caught one of the birds, the red one. Then he came down.

"And the other bird?" asked the doctor. "The green one?"

"It wasn't ripe yet," said the lunatic, "so I left it there."

[X540., Jokes on madmen.]

The next joke is one of my favorites because it is a variant of the classic joke about folklorists and their conventions in America.[3]

190   There was an insane asylum in Greece, and one day all the patients got together in the auditorium by themselves. One of the patients got up on the stage and said:

"Five!"

And all the other patients laughed and laughed and laughed!

Then another patient got up and said:

"Twenty!"

And the patients in the audience laughed like crazy!

Then another patient went to the stage and said:

"Forty-two!"

Well, the patients almost died of hysteria. They laughed for almost a half hour!

One of the doctors was passing by, and he heard the man say "forty-two" and all the laughter. So he went into the auditorium and asked the man who had said "forty-two" to come to his office.

Well, the doctor asked the man:

"Why were all the patients laughing so much? What was so funny?"

"We were telling jokes," said the patient.

"Jokes?" asked the doctor.

"Yes. We know lots and lots of jokes. Since we know so many, and they take so long to tell, we decided to give each joke a number. That way we can just say the number, and everybody remembers the joke, and then we all laugh."

"I want you to teach *me* all of the jokes and the numbers," said the doctor to the patient.

So the doctor learned all the jokes and the numbers!

About a month later he was passing the auditorium, and he saw the patients were again assembled and laughing like before.

So he went inside, and then he went up on the stage and said:

"Twenty-seven!"

But nobody laughed!

So he said:

"Eight!"

But nobody laughed!

Then he said:

"Seventy-five!"

But still nobody laughed!

So he went to the patient who had taught him all the jokes and the numbers and asked him why nobody had laughed.

"Well," explained the patient, "some people know how to tell a joke and other people don't!"

[X540., Jokes on madmen.]

In the following joke three lunatics try to escape by the same means Hermes used when he was one day old and went to steal Apollo's cattle. Undetected, Hermes left by the keyhole and returned to his crib in the same manner.

191 In a mental hospital there were three lunatics locked up in a room together. One of the lunatics said:

"I'll get out of here through the keyhole!"

So he ran across the room and smashed his head into the door and fell down unconscious.

So the second man said:

"Let me try it, I'm stronger!"

So he ran across the room at full speed, and then he also smashed his head against the door and fell down unconscious.

Well, the third man didn't run across the room. Instead he walked over to the door and looked through the keyhole.

"Now I know why they couldn't get out through the keyhole," he said. "Because the key is in the lock on the other side of the door!"

[D1273.1.1., Three as magic number; X540., Jokes on madmen.]

192 One day two lunatics in the hospital at Dafni took the doctor's little Mini-Cooper and put it on top of another small car.

When the doctor saw what they had done, he asked them:

"What did you do that for?"

"We're mating the two little cars so they can make a baby car for us," they said.

"Don't be silly," said the doctor. "Can't you see my car is wearing rubbers?"

[X540., Jokes on madmen.]

193 Once there were two lunatics. One of them put a glass of water on the ground and told his friend that he would climb to the roof of the building and dive into the water.

When the lunatic got to the roof, his friend took away the glass of water.

"Why did you do that?" shouted the lunatic from the roof.

"Because I don't want you to drown!"

[X540., Jokes on madmen.]

194 One time, three lunatics escaped from a hospital and they went to a park. They sat on a park bench, and one of them started gesturing with his two hands; the other held out one hand in front of him; and the third one sat with his arms folded.

So a policeman came by and asked the last man:

"What are those two guys doing?"

"He's fishing, and he's holding the basket for the fish!"

Not realizing that the third man was also crazy, the policeman said:

"Take those two nuts and get out of here!"

"Okay, Captain!" said the third lunatic, and he started moving his arms as if he were rowing a boat!

[D1273.1.1., Three as magic number; X540., Jokes on madmen.]

195 One time, three crazy men decided to escape from the hospital. So they knew of a place in the garden where a tree was growing close to the wall, and they could climb the tree and jump down on the outside.

When they got there, unfortunately, there was a guard sitting under one side of the big tree. So the first man climbed up, and, when the guard heard the leaves rustling, he said:

"What's that?"

And the crazy man went, "Meow, meow!" So the guard thought it was a cat!

Then the second crazy man climbed up into the tree to escape. When the guard heard the leaves rustling again, he asked:

"What's that?"

"Meow, meow, meow!" went the second crazy man.

So he escaped, too!

When the third man got up into the tree and the leaves began to rustle and the guard asked, "What's that?" —

"I'm a cat, too!" said the lunatic.

[AT1363*, The Second Cat; D1273.1.1., Three as magic number; X540., Jokes on madmen.]

196 One time, a psychiatrist saw a friend of his in the mental hospital.

"George, what are you in here for?" he asked the man.

"I'm in here because I prefer black shoes to red shoes," said the man.

"Well, I prefer black shoes to red shoes, too!" said the doctor. "That's no reason to put you in here."

"Really?" asked the lunatic. "How do you prefer them, boiled or fried?"

[X540., Jokes on madmen.]

In ancient Greece the fig was the symbol of the testicle and the gift of Dionysus.[4] The old association survives in the next joke.

197 One time, two lunatics escaped from the mental hospital and ran into the woods. They saw a fig tree, so they climbed up into the tree and were hanging from the branches.

Finally, one of them let go of the branch and fell down!

"What happened?" asked the other lunatic.

"I came!" said the first.

[X540., Jokes on madmen.]

198 Two lunatics were walking down the street, and they saw a pile of shit in the middle of the road.

"What's that?" asked one. So he stuck his finger in the shit and tasted it and said:

"Oh, it's chocolate cake!"

"Let me see," said the other. So he put his finger in the shit and licked his finger and said:

"No, it's *baklavás* [a Greek pastry]!"

"No, it's chocolate cake," insisted the first.

"No, it's *baklavás!*" said the second.

So they started to fight. Well, a policeman heard all the racket and came over and pulled them apart.

"What's going on here?" he demanded.

"I say that's chocolate cake and he says it's *baklavás*," said one of the lunatics, pointing to the pile of shit.

"That's shit!" said the policeman.

"Oh, then it's a good thing you came along and told us," said one of the lunatics. "We almost stepped in it!"

[Legman II:942; AT1832B, What Kind of Dung? J1772.9., Excrements eaten by mistake; X540., Jokes on madmen.]

Chapter 8
Very *Sókin* Jokes

By far the largest number of jokes that I collected fall into what Greeks call the *sókin* category. The Greek word *sókin* has been borrowed from the English word "shocking." In the last twenty years, *sókin* has been used instead of Greek words (*eskrá, vrómica, akatálila*) to describe what we in America call "dirty" jokes. If a joke deals with or describes sexual acts, or uses very vulgar language, it is considered *sókin*. *Sókin* jokes may be either very *sókin* or a little *sókin*.

Whereas some of the jokes in other chapters may be considered *sókin*, their primary associations are with other humorous elements; the jokes in this chapter deal with sex *per se*. Although sex is the main theme of all the jokes in this chapter, the material is very diverse, and, as indicated by the subheadings throughout the chapter, I have grouped jokes by subthemes. *Sókin* jokes seem to cover the full range of possible sexual behavior between human beings (with the exception of lesbianism).[1] Jokes about sexual acts with animals add another dimension, but, although I understand that such jokes were very popular in Greece about twenty years ago, I heard very few.

If Greeks seem preoccupied with sex, it may be pointed out that all successful animal species that procreate by sexual reproduction are "preoccupied" with sex. Human societies are no different; those that did not emphasize sexual reproduction became "extinct." However, the occurrence of dirty jokes in the folklore of all nations is perhaps a recent development in world events, a result of the sexual revolution that originated in the West and that by 1979 had a worldwide impact. Dirty jokes now

seem to leap cultural and linguistic boundaries with the speed
of light. Although anthropologists have described some aborigi-
nal peoples as "puritanical" and lacking "obscene" folklore at
the time of their contact with Europeans, the geographic isolation that is necessary to sustain cultural isolation no longer
exists.

Obviously, however, not everybody in every group engages
in telling or listening to dirty jokes. Some individuals, because
of their own values and inhibitions, find such material dis-
tasteful. Moreover, the element of context is very important in
regard to telling dirty jokes. For example, in America dirty jokes
are not supposed to be told in mixed company; that is, men are
supposed to exchange dirty jokes with other men, women with
other women, and children with other children. Those are the
"ideal" rules; actual joke-telling practice may be very different.
In Greece the following places and social situations appear to
be proper contexts for telling *sókin* jokes:

(1) The coffeehouse, usually an all-male domain, is the principal place where men exchange news, rumors, and gossip, discuss sports and politics, and tell and listen to *sókin* jokes.

(2) The *paréa*, or informal friendship group, is another principal context in which *sókin* jokes are exchanged. The members
of a *paréa*, a mixed company in many cases, may get together for
outings that usually involve food, drink, and perhaps dancing.
In Greece young, unmarried people seldom, if ever, "date" in
the American sense. They go out with a *paréa* of other single
people for an evening of fun. During the evening, usually after
a few glasses of wine, the conversation may turn to jokes, and
sókin examples are normally included. In the case of married
couples who go out with the *paréa* (which may, of course, also
include some single people), *sókin* jokes are normally told by
the husbands, again usually after a few drinks have been consumed. (Greeks often say that the wine does the talking.)

It was my observation that women only occasionally partici-
pate in the telling of *sókin* jokes in the presence of a mixed
paréa, and that those who do are either very well educated and
"liberated" or married, or both. Uneducated, single women
normally would be afraid to ruin their reputations by telling

such jokes, since unmarried Greek women are expected to remain virginal and should never demonstrate any knowledge of sexual matters in public. To do so would lead them to be considered "bad" girls, and such a reputation would make it very difficult for them to be married.

(3) Women, who meet for coffee, sewing, or the like in each other's homes, usually in the afternoons, may exchange *sókin* jokes. In many cases the women have initially heard *sókin* jokes from men—from their husbands if they are married or from their brothers, fathers, and other male relatives if they are single. Often they do not hear the jokes directly, but rather overhear them from another part of the house.[2] Contrary to the belief among men in Greece that women tell dirtier jokes than men do, I found that they usually tell the same jokes as men do. Women, however, primarily tell *sókin* jokes only in the presence of other women.

(4) Children are often separated by sex a great deal of the time during their education and probably exchange *sókin* jokes mostly with children of the same sex. However, the opportunities for material to pass from one group to the other through brothers and sisters are ample. Greek boys that I interviewed (from nine to twelve years old) seemed quite spontaneous in their telling of *sókin* (usually light) jokes for adults in mixed company. Little girls that I interviewed for jokes never told *sókin* jokes although they may well have known some. That Greeks share many adult activities, even the telling of *sókin* jokes, with children is remarkable, but doing so may be in the main a rural, or peasant, practice. The teenagers that I interviewed in the classroom told light *sókin* jokes, with boys and girls seeming to be equal participants. (The principal of the night school where I taught had forbidden me to allow them to tell *sókin* jokes in class.)

Greek attitudes toward sex and the sexes are clearly illustrated in the collected material. Some of the attitudes reflect a traditional society's views that are rooted in the past and sustained mainly in the rural areas of Greece. The traditional view of dirty jokes is that they are created and exchanged principally by men and that they tend to ridicule women (see Legman

1968). The traditional view is a male chauvinistic one, and it is not entirely supported by the material that I collected, much of which ridicules men.

Still another aspect of the *sókin* jokes is their use. Among youths, telling *sókin* jokes is a means of flirting. The boys who tell the jokes carefully observe the girls' reactions, to see whether they laugh or not, whether they blush or not, and so on. Boys presumably typecast the girls on the basis of their reactions as "good" or "bad" girls. For some individuals, telling *sókin* jokes seems to function as a means of expressing normally repressed drives. The verbalization of sexual acts seems, for some, to offer a type of sexual satisfaction, especially if one of the listeners is a member of the opposite sex. The many restrictions on sexual behavior in traditional Greek society (still found in many parts of Greece today) must create a great deal of sexual anxiety in the population, and *sókin* jokes, which are extremely popular and widespread among the population, give some relief from sexual tension and anxiety.

The sexual revolution has only begun to reach Greece, usually in the form of tourists, magazines, movies, and traveling Greeks (sailors and others who seek employment outside Greece) who return to Greece with stories of how it is elsewhere. A great deal of sexual repression and frustration remains in most of the towns and villages of Greece. Indeed, throughout Greece the double standard and traditional attitudes toward women prevail.

The average Greek man marries a girl who is anywhere from two to twenty years younger than he. She must be sexually pure, whereas he is expected to be experienced, and he sees her, in sexual terms, as the mother of his children and as a personification of the Virgin. He normally does not experiment with her sexually, but seeks fulfillment of his sexual fantasies (if he has any and is so inclined) outside the marriage.

Greek men often expressed their views to me that Greek wives are characteristically unfaithful.[3] If they are (and I doubt that the percentage of unfaithful women is any higher in Greece than it is in the United States or in France, for example), it may be that the Greek woman, too, seeks romance and the fulfillment of her own sexual needs outside the marriage. A Greek wife dare not reveal her sexual needs to her husband for fear of his divorcing her as an "anomalous" or "impure" woman.

As most Greeks accept the biblical story of Adam and Eve as literal truth, they believe that women are both conniving and inferior to men.[4] Also a common belief is that women are by their very nature evil, whereas men are by nature good. Women are seen as seductresses, as oversexed temptresses, who, therefore, must be protected (by seclusion in the home and by chaperoning) from acting out their inclinations. In other words, women must be protected from themselves and are, for that reason, expected to remain in the home except during morning and mid-afternoon hours, when they have legitimate tasks to perform elsewhere. While women are at home, they are expected to keep busy with domestic chores, including sewing, embroidering, crocheting, or weaving even in their free time. They should not admit men to their homes during the day. Traveling about at all hours, unchaperoned, as foreign women do, is still not considered appropriate behavior for a decent Greek woman or girl, particularly in the villages or in rural areas.

The most commonly used epithets heard in Greece are *poutána* ("whore," or "prostitute"); *keratás* ("cuckold"), from *kéras* ("horn"); *malákas* (a man who constantly masturbates, or who does not give proper protection to his women or who is inefficient or foolish); *poústis* (a male homosexual of the passive type). Women, since they are blamed for being the instigators of all sexual affairs, usually have only themselves to blame if they lose their virginity and are considered *poutánes* by others. Men are, to a degree, responsible for protecting the honor of their women, but "protection" usually involves their keeping the women at home or arranging for the marriage of any unmarried women in their domain as quickly as possible.

Women cannot be disgraced by the sexual conduct of male relatives. Men, on the other hand, can be disgraced by women's behavior. An unmarried girl can disgrace the *timí*, or honor, of the entire family by losing her virginity, becoming pregnant, or carrying on a long-term love affair. Among the Sarakatsani

(Greek-speaking transhumant shepherds of northern Greece) such a girl should, ideally, be killed by either her father or her brother in order to restore the *timí* of the family. If these male kinsmen did not have the courage to kill the girl, or if they were convinced by the girl that she was raped rather than having acted voluntarily, then the dishonored girl might escape death as punishment (see Campbell 1974:187).[5]

The greatest threat to the Greek male is the possibility of being cuckolded. Unable to keep their wives in pumpkin shells, as Peter the Pumpkin Eater did, many Greek men suffer some anxiety about their wives' activities when the husbands are away from the house, especially in cities such as Athens. Gossip, one traditional means of social control in Greece, is much less efficient in large urban areas; once people leave their neighborhoods, they can act as they please with little fear that their behavior will be observed by neighbors, relatives, or friends and will be reported to their families. I was led to believe that private detectives who spy on married women find easy employment in the Athens-Piraeus area.

Homosexuality is found in Greece, but it does not appear to be an exceptionally pronounced phenomenon if one is objective in one's observations. Traditional relationships among Greek men often have been misunderstood probably since classical times.[6] What is difficult, if not impossible, for most foreigners (especially Americans) to understand is that two Greek men can embrace each other, kiss each other, dance with each other, and engage in other affectionate behavior toward each other in public without either being a homosexual. Because of the traditional separation of the sexes and the seclusion of the women inside the house (practiced since classical times and still practiced in much of Greece today), boys and men associate principally with each other; "best friend" relationships develop very early and may be very long lasting. Greek boys and men traditionally go out in all-male *paréas*. It is widely believed among Greeks that, if a male is sodomized, he will automatically become a homosexual because he will find sodomy with other males more satisfying than heterosexual sex. That particular folk belief probably functions to keep sexual experimentation in the all-male friendship groups at a minimum.

It is my theory that most Greek men find the buttocks the most sexually attractive part of the body. The heavy emphasis placed on the derriere in visual advertising in Greece tends to support my theory.[7] For the Greek male, anal intercourse involves probably the most sexually attractive part of the body (the buttocks), and it possibly is more stimulating and satisfying. Obviously it can also be performed with both sexes. Hollander wrote in *The Happy Hooker* (1972) that her Greek clients were excellent lovers, but unanimously wanted anal intercourse in addition to "regular" sex. Sodomy is an age-old solution to sexual frustration when "normal" heterosexual sex is unavailable (as in prisons, during long sea voyages, or when all the women are secluded, chaperoned, and so on). Anal intercourse with women is also a solution to sexual frustration when "normal" heterosexual sex is impractical because of fear of pregnancy or during menstruation. Anal intercourse is a means of satisfying sexual urges with a woman while leaving her virginity intact, an important factor in the Mediterranean region, where the emphasis on virginity at marriage is widespread. It is also a fairly effective means of birth control. The strong taboos placed on menstruating women in Greece (DuBoulay 1974:102) and in the entire Mediterranean region suggest that anal sex would be the logical solution to sexual urges during menstruation (see also joke 211, below).

A large proportion of the jokes in this collection deals with anal intercourse, or sodomy, and Legman (1975) suggests an explanation for the prevalence of such jokes. He equates the cult of machismo with the fear of pederastic rape, and believes that both are derived from intensely patriarchal cultures such as those in the Mediterranean region. Those aspects have been further intensified in Greece and in Spain during the Moslem occupations of those areas, and Legman suggests (1975:160) that the fear of pederastic rape is the heritage of those areas once occupied by Moslems, whom he asserts still castrate or sodomize their captives in war. If it is true that many generations of Greek men were subject to castration and pederastic rape by their Turkish captors, then the historical memory of that experience might be the reason for the apparent Greek preoccupation with sodomy (especially as a means of revenge by the cuckold in the many jokes that I collected). Although most of Greece has been independent of Turkey since 1833, other regions such as Crete achieved liberation only as late as 1898, and the memory of such practices must be strong, particularly in Crete. Moreover, the constant Turkish threat to Greece, exhibited only recently in the 1974 Turkish invasion of Cyprus, could serve to keep alive the fear of pederastic rape.

Also, according to Legman, the typical view of Greeks in American humor is that they are still given to homosexuality (presumably from the Golden Age) and anal intercourse, and this predilection is "proved" in the American mind by the Evzone soldiers' tradition of wearing skirts and petticoats. Legman also points out (1975:78) that during the late Renaissance the British and the French believed the Italians to be inclined toward homosexuality. Why the Greeks replaced the Italians in these European and American folk stereotypes is unclear, but I believe that the explanation that the apparent Greek preoccupation with sodomy (especially as a means of revenge) is a result of the Turkish occupation is more convincing than the assumption that it derives from the Golden Age.

JOKES ABOUT HETEROSEXUAL RELATIONS

Jokes about Women

The Innocent Girl Who Becomes Oversexed After First Time
199 A young girl who was a virgin went to the seamstress to try on a dress that she was having made. The seamstress accidentally stuck her with a pin, and the girl screamed in pain.

"My, my," said the seamstress, "if you scream like that from just a pin prick, what will you do on your wedding night, when your husband will stick his big sword inside you and break you open?"

Well, the girl was really worried about that. So she thought:

"I'll find a man to marry who has a small penis!"

So during the summer, when she went swimming, she looked at all the boys on the beach in their bathing suits to try to find one with a small penis.

She saw a boy who wore a loose-fitting, trunk-type bathing suit, and she couldn't even see the outline of a penis!

"That's the boy I want," she thought.

So she told her father, and he arranged the engagement and the wedding.

Well, on the wedding night, when the husband got undressed, the girl saw that despite his appearance in his bathing suit, he was normal in size or even a little more!

The girl begged him not to make love to her because she was afraid of the pain because his penis was so big.

"Don't worry," said the husband. "Tomorrow I'll go to a hardware store and buy a carpenter's plane, and I'll shave it down to the size that you want!"

So the next night they got ready for bed. So the husband showed her the plane. Then he turned off the lights and went over to the wooden wardrobe and started shaving wood off of it! After about ten minutes he told her that it was ready.

So he got in bed and started making love to her. And she really liked it very much! After they finished the girl reached down and touched his balls.

"What's that?" she asked.

"Oh, just some shavings that didn't come off."

"Oh, maybe you can glue them back on the staff and put them inside me, too?"

[Legman I:463; K2052.2., Girl who is frightened of love becomes insatiable; X735.1.4., After first penetration, wife wants husband to put his testicles in as well.]

200 A long time ago, when there were Turks living in Greece, a Turkish man wanted to marry a Greek girl.

So he went to a matchmaker and asked him to find him a girl who was afraid of sex.

"Why?" asked the matchmaker.

"Because I have a problem. I used to have a big penis, but when I was a boy, one night when I was asleep, the cat thought it was a mouse and ate a big piece of it! So now it's rather small. But don't tell the girl anything."

So the matchmaker found a girl who was afraid to lose her virginity. He told her that he had a marriage prospect for her, but she said she was afraid of sex because she had heard that it was more pain than pleasure.

"Don't worry!" said the matchmaker. "This man has a small penis because the cat ate it up when he was a boy!"

So they got married, and on the wedding night the girl found out that she liked having sex very much!

"Ah!" she sighed. "If only we had that extra piece that the cat ate, it would be even better!"

[K2052.2., Girl who is frightened of love becomes insatiable.]

201 Sometime, a boy and a girl were in love, and they wanted to have sex together. But the girl was afraid of losing her virginity, so she didn't let the boy make love to her.

One night the boy said:

"I have a plan so we can make love and you'll still be a virgin."

"How?" asked the girl.

"We'll put a bunch of grape leaves inside you, and they'll be like insulation. That way we won't break it!"

So they put about twenty leaves inside the girl's pussy, and they started to fuck.

After a while the girl said:

"Let's take out a few leaves, it'll feel better."

So the boy took out five leaves. And after a while the girl said:

"Let's take out some more leaves, it'll feel better."

So he took out about ten leaves. And later she said:

"Take out a few more!"

So he took all of them out, but he didn't tell her.

After a while she said:

"Why don't you take out a few more leaves so it'll feel better?"

So the boy said:

"I've already taken out all of the leaves! What do you think my penis is? A grape vine?"

[Legman I:463; K2052.2., Girl who is frightened of love becomes insatiable; X735.9.3.3., "Do you think my balls are the regimental pot?" Asked by soldier who seeks to seduce woman and then finds her insatiable.]

202 There was an innocent young virgin who was soon to be married. So her mother decided it was time to give her instructions for her wedding night.

So the mother made the girl get undressed and lie on the bed. Then she put the smallest Greek coin, the *fránco*, under one armpit. Then she put the next coin, worth two drachmes [the *dífranco*], under the other armpit. Then she put the coin worth five drachmes [the *táliro*] into the girl's pussy.

"When your husband starts to make love to you, you must learn to move correctly," said the girl's mother. "First you must move one shoulder, where the *fránco* is. Then you must move the other shoulder, where the *dífranco* is. Then you must raise up the part down there where the *táliro* is."

So, they had a practice session, and the mother told her:

"*Fránco, dífranco, táliro! Fránco, dífranco, táliro!*"*

And so the girl practiced over and over how to move correctly on her wedding night to please her husband.

On the wedding night she remembered her mother's instructions. So, when her husband started to fuck her, she thought:

"*Fránco, dífranco, táliro,*" over and over, and she moved her body the way her mother had told her. But after a while she really got excited, and so she said:

"Forget the small change, mother! *Táliro, táliro, táliro!*"

[Legman I:463; Legman II:263; D1273.1.1., Three as magic number; K2052.2., Girl who is frightened of love becomes insatiable.]

Tourists and Other Horny Women

203 (In the mountains of Crete, there are many villages that are separated into two halves, with the one half being high on the mountain, and the other half being on the lower part of the mountain. High in these "upper" villages, the people gather a wild plant that is called *éronta* in parts of Crete and that is used to brew an herbal tea.)

Well, one summer a tourist woman visited one of the *lower* mountain villages, and she met a shepherd who was very handsome. Although he couldn't speak English, he invited her to his house, where he lived alone, and offered her hospitality.

Well, the tourist wanted to have sex with the shepherd, but she didn't speak Greek at all. So she looked at him lovingly and said:

"I love you!"†

Realizing that the girl wanted *something*, but not understanding *at all*, the shepherd thought to himself:

"What does she want? Maybe some *mizíthra* cheese?"

When the shepherd offered the girl the cheese, she said:

"No, no! I *love* you!"

---

*Body movements often accompany this joke: the right shoulder and hip are thrust to the right, the left shoulder and hip are thrust to the left, followed by a pelvic thrust at the word *táliro*.

†This joke was told in Greek, but "I love you" was said in English throughout.

Thinking that maybe the girl was thirsty, he offered her a glass of water.

"No, no! I LOVE you!"

Finally, she remembered that she had a small dictionary in her purse, and after a quick search was able to find the word for love: *érota*. So she showed it to the shepherd, who mistook it for the word *éronta*, for the mountain tea.

"Oh, such bad luck!" he said. "You can *only* find what you want in the *upper* mountain village; down here we don't have any at all!"

[D1273.1.1., Three as magic number.]

204 A woman tourist went up to the mountains in Greece. She saw a handsome shepherd, and she asked him:

"How long has it been since you had a woman?"

"Oh, a long, long time," said the shepherd.

"What a pity!" she said. "Well, I feel sorry for you, so I'll let you fuck me. But first let me put this prophylactic on you so we won't make a baby."

So they had a good time, and the tourist woman left.

Further down the mountain she saw another handsome young shepherd playing the panpipe.

"How long has it been since you had a woman?" she asked him.

"Over a year," said the boy.

So she felt sorry for him and said:

"I'll fuck you, but first let me put this prophylactic on you so we won't make a baby."

Later in the day the two shepherds met on a mountain path.

"Guess what?" said one. "A tourist woman put a rubber on me and fucked me!"

"The same thing happened to me," said the other, "and I haven't had a piss all day!"

"Me too," said the first.

"Well," said the second, "baby or no baby, I'm taking the damn thing off!"

[Legman I:120; Legman II:307; J2321., Man made to believe that he is pregnant.]

205 There was a woman from Sweden who got her vacation earlier than her husband. So she went by herself to Hydra to wait for him.

She rented a cheap room in a small hotel, the kind that has thin walls, and doors that don't close well, and beds with rusty springs.

Well, after she was there for two or three days, she found a Greek boyfriend and took him to her room every night, and they made love.

Well, after ten days she told the boyfriend that her husband was coming the next day so she couldn't see him anymore.

Well, the first night that her husband came, he took his wife to bed early because he hadn't had sex for so long.

Well, they were making love and the rusty springs were really making a racket! Finally, a woman in the next room pounded on the wall and said:

"For the last two weeks we can't get any sleep with the bed squeaking so much! When is the honeymoon going to end?"

206 Two women who were good friends were having coffee together, and the one who was married to a sailor said to the other:

"I can't stand it anymore without sex! My husband's been gone for ten months, and I don't know what to do!"

"Haven't you heard the news?" asked the other woman. "There are plastic penises now for sale, and they have batteries inside them, and they screw like the real thing! The French make them thick and short, and the British make them long and thin, and you can buy them at the drugstore!"

So later that day the woman went to a drugstore and asked the clerk for a plastic penis.

"Do you want a British one or a French one?" he asked.

The woman thought and thought. Finally, she said:

"I'll take an Anglo-French one!"

[Legman I:327.]

207 A girl was walking along a road in the country, and she had to go to the toilet. So she went in the bushes and made pee-pee.

Well, she didn't have any paper, so she wiped herself with some leaves. But the leaves had some sticky substance on them, and this irritated her. Her pussy really burned!

"Now, now," she said to her pussy, "don't complain! After *all* the meat you've eaten, a little greens won't hurt you!"

Women Who Cuckold Their Husbands

208 A young girl from a well-to-do family loved a poor boy and wanted to marry him. But her mother wanted her to marry a rich man. Finally, the old woman consented, and the girl married her sweetheart.

Well, the poor boy was an orphan, and he didn't have work. So their life was very hard together without any money.

So the girl's mother found a rich man who wanted to sleep with the girl and who would give her money.

So the girl said okay, and her mother brought the man to her daughter's house one day when the young husband was gone. Well, just when they were in bed together, the husband came home! So the rich old man hid under the bed, and the mother-in-law went to talk to the husband.

"Oh, your poor wife, she's so upset!" said the old woman.

"Why?" asked the husband.

"Well, I made her a new blanket for the bed, but she says that it's too short."

So the husband went into the bedroom and found his wife in bed crying.

"Why don't you get into the bed with her, and we'll see if the blanket is big enough," said the mother-in-law.

So the husband got into bed with his wife, and the mother-in-law pulled the blanket over his head. At the same time the rich man got out from under the bed and quickly left the house.

"Well, do you like the blanket?" asked the mother-in-law.

"Yes, it's very nice," said the husband.

"I thought you would like it," said the mother-in-law. "I've been fixing blankets like that for years now for *my* husband, and he always liked them!"

[Legman II:951; AT1355, The Man Hidden under the Bed; inversion of AT1418*, The Father Overhears; AT1419, The Returning Husband Hoodwinked; K1521.5.1., Lover escapes behind the sheet which wife holds up to show husband; L113.1.0.1., Heroine endures hardships with menial husband; L161.1., Marriage of poor boy to rich girl.]

209 One time there was an Englishman who went to a small village in Greece. It was in the old days, before so many tourists came and before so many hotels were built. Well, in those days it was the custom for the mayor of the village to give a foreigner hospitality.

So the mayor of the village invited the man to his house, and they ate and drank well. When it was time for bed, the mayor told his wife to fix the bed. Then they put the Englishman on one side of the bed, and the husband and wife got in the same bed! But the wife was in the middle. During the night, when the husband was asleep, well, the Englishman fucked the wife!

The next day the mayor asked his wife if anything had happened during the night.

"Well, the Englishman took advantage of the situation and he fucked me!" she said.

"What? You let him do that and you didn't say anything?"

"How could I?" asked the wife. "I can't speak English!"

[Legman I:260; J2496.2., Misunderstandings because of ignorance of different language; K1544., Husband unwittingly instrumental in wife's adultery.]

210 There was a Greek sailor who was about to leave for a year on board a ship.

Before he left he told his wife:

"Well, I'll be gone for a year, and you know that I can't do without sex for a whole year, so naturally I'll go with other women."

So the wife said:

"Well, if you go with other women, then I'll go with other men during the year because I can't wait a year without sex either!"

So they agreed to keep track of how many times they had been with another by putting a grain of rice in an envelope each time they had sex with somebody else.

The sailor left and was gone for a year as he had said. When he returned to Greece, he went to his house and greeted his wife:

"Here's my envelope with the grains of rice, so you can count them."

So she counted the grains, and there were thirty.

"Let me see your bag with the rice grains," said the husband.

So the wife gave him the small sack, and he counted. There were only twenty-five grains of rice.

"Only twenty-five!" he said. "What will we do now to make it even?"

"Oh, don't bother," said the wife. "While you were gone, I cooked *dolmádes* five times!" [An average pot of *dolmádes*, vine leaves stuffed with rice, uses a cup of rice.]

[T230., Faithlessness in marriage.]

The following joke is reminiscent of a saying attributed to soldiers: "In war, any trench is good."

211 Once there was a seaman who had been away from home for over two years. So he was really horny for his wife when he got home! So the first thing he did was to grab her and throw her on the bed!

But the wife had been screwing all the neighbors while he was away, so she tried to put him off:

"Oh, no, not now! I'm having my period!"

"Never mind, then, just lean over," said the husband.

"No, no! I've got hemorrhoids really bad!" she said.

"Okay then, but if you tell me your tonsils hurt, I'm going to kill you!"

[Legman I:279; D1273.1.1., Three as magic number; T288., Wife refuses to sleep with husband.]

The next joke has many versions, most of which begin differently, but have the same ending. Most of them tell of the separation of a couple for some extended period of time and of the couple's attempts to be faithful.

212 One time, there was a couple who was really poor. So finally the husband took a job on a ship that paid well so that they could have some money.

When he told his wife that he would be gone for a year, she was very sad. They both promised to remain faithful to each other during that time and bid a sad farewell to their married life together for a year.

When the husband returned after a year, he told his wife:

"I was faithful to you all year, really! A few times I almost went with another woman, but at the last minute I remembered our promise, so I got up and got dressed and left!"

"I tried to do the same thing when I changed my mind," said the wife, "but, since I was on the bottom, it was impossible!"

[T61.2.1., Parting lovers swear faithfulness; T218., The faithful husband.]

Women Tricksters: The Widow

An old man in Crete once told me, "I never met a bad widow!" The implication was that widows are easy to take to bed. Greek widows have the most difficult lot of all Greek women: they are not expected to remarry, to wear jewelry, to sing, or to dance; they are expected to wear black for the rest of their lives; they are the objects of gossip and scandal, especially if they take part in any festivities or talk with men (see DuBoulay 1974:122). The widow is no longer a full member of her family or origin, and the connection to her family of marriage (her husband) has been severed. A Greek widow is without the essential factor that she needs to validate her life (a man) since her husband is dead and her father is no longer responsible for her. She is potentially dangerous because she has "too much freedom" for a woman. Thus the Greek widow, like the Greek priest, represents an anomaly. Greek culture, by prescribing black clothing for both priests and widows, provides an easy means of recognizing these anomalous and potentially dangerous individuals so that the proper magical precautions to avert harm to the innocent may be taken.

I heard only two jokes about widows, and in each the widow is a trickster. In the second joke, however, the trick is uncovered.

213   One day a fisherman went fishing and he caught about five kilos of fish. On the way back home, he passed the house of a young and beautiful widow.

"Hey, fisherman!" she called. "Come here!"

So he went to her house.

"Um, you have a lot of nice fish! Let's make a bet, and if you win you can fuck me. But if I win I get your fish."

"Okay," said the fisherman, "what's the deal?"

"Can you tell me where my pussy is? Is it in the front or in the back?"

"Oh, that's easy," said the fisherman. "It's in the front."

"Wrong!" said the widow as she turned around, pulled up her skirt, spread her legs (she wasn't wearing any underwear), leaned over, and showed him her pussy from behind!

So she took his fish, and he went home with nothing!

The next day he caught about ten kilos of fish, and on his way home the widow called him to come over again.

"Want to make the same bet again?" she asked.

"Sure," said the fisherman, thinking this time he'd easily get to fuck the widow since he knew her pussy was in the back. "It's in the back," he said.

"Wrong again!" she said as she raised her skirts, and, since she wasn't wearing any underwear, showed him that her pussy was in the front.

So again he lost the bet, and she took all his fish!

When he got home his wife said:

"What? Two days with no fish?"

"Look," said the husband, "if that pussy doesn't stay in the same place, we'll never eat fish again!"*

[A1313.3., Misplaced genitals; F547.5., Extraordinary vagina; X253., Jokes on fishermen.]

214   There was a young widow who wanted to get married again. She found a young man to marry, but since he wanted only to marry a virgin, she didn't tell him that she was a widow.

About a week before the wedding, she went to a doctor and told him her problem.

"Get up on the table so I can have a look," he said.

So she got onto the table and spread her legs.

"Oh, I'll need to do a lot of work!" he said. "Go to the butcher's and get a piece of lambskin about eight inches long."

So she came back with the piece of lambskin, and the doctor sewed it in her, closing her up like a virgin!

On her wedding night everything seemed to be just fine. As her husband started to fuck her, she screamed in pretended pain as the lambskin broke. Afterwards there was some blood on the sheet (she was having her period), so the husband was pleased and convinced that he had married a virgin.

They went to sleep, but later he woke up and wanted a cigarette. So he turned on the light to get a cigarette, and when he did he looked at his wife's pussy. What did he see? He saw a meat stamp that said, GOVERNMENT INSPECTED, FIRST-CLASS LAMB FROM HOLLAND!†

[Legman I:498; K1912., The false virgin; K2052.2.4., The hypocritical widow.)

---

*The Greek folk illness known as the "Wandering Navel," in which the navel is said to move about, indicates that, in the Greek folk mind, the ability of body parts to move their location is not peculiar. An apt title for this joke would be "The Wandering Pussy."

†In the last few years, Greece found it necessary to import lamb from other European countries. Greek lamb does not bear government-inspection stamps; only the imported meat does. Hymen-restoration operations are a common form of "cosmetic" surgery in the entire Mediterranean region since most men insist on marrying virgins.

Old Women

215   One day somebody asked an old lady:

"Grandmother, which would you rather have? Some *loukoúmia* [a soft, jelly-like candy called "Turkish Delight"] or a man?"

She replied:

"My child, you know I don't have any teeth to eat *loukoúmia!*"

[J1391.6., Lame excuse: one cannot drink because of no teeth.]

216   There was a shepherd who had been way, way up in the mountains for over a year. So he was really crazy to have sex with a woman. He was so horny that he made a vow that he would fuck the first person that he saw on his way to his village, once for every tooth that the person would have.

Well, after five days he passed a house, and he saw an old widow woman in front of the house.

He went over to her and saw that she was about ninety years old.

"Excuse me, old lady, but I've been a year in the mountains, and I'm very horny, and I must fuck you because I made a vow that I'd fuck the first person that I met on my way to the village, once for every tooth the person has."

"But I'm so old," said the woman, "and I have only one tooth," she said as she opened her mouth to show him.

"Never mind," said the shepherd, "I'll fuck you anyway."

So he fucked her once and went to his village. He stayed there about three days and then he returned to the mountains and his flock.

On his way he passed the widow's house again.

"Hey, shepherd, come here!" yelled the old woman.

When he got to her house, she said:

"Look! On the other side of my mouth I have another tooth!" And she opened her mouth wide to show him the tooth.

[F513.1., Person unusual as to his teeth; K2312., Oath literally obeyed; M130., Vows concerning sex.]

217   During the last war [World War II], an old woman went from her small village to Athens. When she was crossing Omonia Square, she passed the clinic where the Germans had stationed physicians to give weekly examinations of the local prostitutes. So there was a long line of women and girls waiting to go inside the building.

The old lady asked one of the girls waiting in line:

"What are you doing here?"

"We're waiting for free chocolates," said the girl.

"So! I'll wait in line, too!" said the old woman.

After a long wait she finally got to the physician's office. There was a clerk taking names, and when he saw her he said:

"What are you doing here, grandmother?* You mean that you eat [slang for "fuck"] too?"

"No, no, my son," said the old woman [thinking the doctor referred to chocolates]. "I don't have any teeth, so I only lick them!"

[Legman II:279.]

Princesses and Other Unattainable Women

The Grimm Brothers collected fairy tales and folktales of Europe for the purpose of studying linguistic change in and relationships among the languages spoken in Europe at the beginning of the nineteenth century. As far as I know, their printed collections contain no obscene examples and thus probably reflect the standards and customs of the day. In Greece I collected many stories that are reminiscent of the old European fairy tales with the unattainable princess and the suitor task as themes. But, unlike the Grimm fairy tales, all the tales I collected describe sexual behavior as well. The first example below also contains a trickster figure, who is anonymous in the versions of the tale that I heard.

218   A clever village boy told his friend one day:

"I'm going to Athens and fuck the king's daughter!"

"Are you crazy?" asked his friend. "They'll catch you and kill you!"

"No, because I have a special plan how to do it and get away!"

So he went to the palace, and he asked to see the king. When he finally saw the king, he asked for work in the royal gardens.

"Okay," said the king, "we can always use another gardener. But tell me, what's your name?"

"Oh, please, sir, don't ask," said the boy. "I have a very strange name."

"Never mind, never mind! We *must* know your name!"

"Well, it's Penis!" said the boy.

"Okay, Penis, go to work in the garden," said the king.

---

*Kinship terms such as grandmother, grandfather, aunt, and uncle are often used in Greece as polite forms of address for nonrelatives and strangers.

The next day the princess was walking in the garden, and she saw the new boy and said to him:

"You're new here. I've never seen you before. Who are you?"

"I just started working here yesterday, and my name is very strange and it embarrasses me to tell you."

"Never mind," she said, "what is it?"

"Big Meatball!" he said.

"Well, it's nice to meet you, Big Meatball," she said as she walked away.

The next day the queen saw the boy and said:

"Who are you? I've never seen you before."

"I just started working here two days ago, and my name is very peculiar and I'd prefer not to tell you."

"But I must know your name!" said the queen.

"Okay, then, it's Pussy!" said the boy.

"Very well, Pussy," said the queen. "I hope that you'll enjoy working here."

Well, the next night the boy waited until everybody was sleeping; then he went up the trellis and climbed into the princess's bedroom. She was sleeping, and so he started to fuck her!

Suddenly, she woke up and started screaming:

"Mother, Mother! Come quickly! The Big Meatball is bothering me!"

The queen, who was very tired and didn't understand what was really going on, said:

"I told you not to eat so much at dinner! Drink some water and you'll feel better."

"No, you don't understand! Come here quickly!" screamed the princess.

So the queen went into the princess's bedroom, and, when she saw what was happening, she screamed to the king:

"King, come here! The Pussy is on top of our daughter's legs!"

The king answered her:

"So where do you want it to be, on top of her head?"

"No, no! You don't understand! Come here quickly!"

So the king went to his daughter's room, and, when he saw what was happening, he shouted to the guards:

"Guards! Drop your weapons and grab [your] Penis!"

So the guards all started playing with themselves, and the boy, who had finished his "work" by then, grabbed his clothes and escaped!

[AT1545, The Boy with Many Names; D1273.1.1., Three as magic number; T475.2.1., Intercourse with sleeping girl.]

The clever use of an unusual name to achieve seduction is also the theme of the next joke.

219 One time, a priest was looking for a young man to be a servant in his house. But he was afraid because he had a pretty young daughter.

So he decided he would find a young man who didn't know about sex.

So he went up to a boy and asked him:

"*Kséreis apó gamíssi* [Do you know what fucking is]?"

Well, that boy knew, and so did the next ten boys that he asked. Finally, he met a boy who mistook the *kséreis apó gamíssi* for *kséreis tó ipokámiso* and thought the priest was asking him if he knew his shirt. So he said yes and pointed to his shirt.

"Ah!" thought the priest. "I've found the right boy to be our servant." "Would you like to work for me?" he asked.

The boy agreed.

When he started working for the priest, the boy told the priest's pretty young daughter that his name was Trahana.

One night, after the family had finished a heavy meal that included *trahanás* [a pasty soup or porridge made from coarse flour and sour milk], they all went to bed and fell into a heavy sleep.

So the young man decided it was the right moment, and he crept into the daughter's bed and started fucking her!

Finally, the girl awakened, and she screamed:

"Mama! Come help me! The Trahana is bothering me!"

"Go and drink some water, child," said the mother. "I told you not to eat so much soup at dinner!"

[AT1545B, The Boy Who Knew Nothing of Women; K1399.2., The unusual names; T475.2.1., Intercourse with sleeping girl.]

220 One time, a young man wanted to marry a girl named Kiki. So he went to her father and asked for her hand. The man said he would have to think about it. So he went to his daughter and asked her if she wanted to marry the boy.

"Not that stupid guy," she said.

"How will I get rid of him, then?" asked her father.

"Tell him I'll marry him only if he can do something impossible to do. That way we can get rid of him."

So when the boy came back to the house, the girl's father told him:

"My daughter says she'll marry you only if you can pick up an automobile with your hands."

"Oh, that's easy," said the boy. So they went outside where there was a midget car parked, and the boy lifted it off the ground with two hands.

So the girl's father said:

"My daughter will marry you only if you can beat up the five brothers who live next door!"

"That's easy," said the boy. So he went to the next house and started a fight, and one by one he beat up all the five brothers!

Finally, the girl's father said:

"Kiki will marry you only if you have a penis that is fifteen inches long!"

Now the father was certain that he had found the impossible request to get rid of the boy!

Well, the boy scratched his head and thought a bit. Finally, he said:

"Okay, I guess it's worth it to marry your daughter to have five inches cut off of my penis!"

[Legman II:466; D1273.1.1., Three as magic number; H301., Excessive demands to prevent marriage; H310., Suitor tests; H335., Tasks assigned suitors.]

The preceding joke depicts the traditional situation found in many fairy tales: the hero must perform three impossible tasks if he is to marry the princess. The following joke describes the same situation, but the ending is also that of joke 152, which involves the "priestwife."

221 One time, there was a princess who announced that she would marry the man who brought her the fruit that most pleased her. But, for those who brought her fruit that she didn't like, there would be a punishment.

Well, the first man who came to see her brought her an eggplant.*

"Ugh! I hate eggplant!" said the princess. "Take him away and punish him."

So the guards took the man into the next room, pulled down his pants, and shoved the eggplant up his ass! And his screams could be heard for miles!

Well, the next man who came brought her a cucumber.

"Oh, I detest cucumbers," said the princess. "Take him away and punish him!"

*"Eggplant" and "cucumber" are slang terms in Greek for the male sexual organ.

So the guards took the man into the next room and pulled down his pants and shoved the cucumber up his ass! Well, the man was really screaming in pain, but, suddenly, as he was looking out of the window, he started laughing hysterically!

"What's so funny?" asked the guards.

"Look out the window and you'll see," said the man.

So they looked, and they saw a man coming to the palace carrying a huge watermelon!

[Legman II:157; AT1689, "Thank God They Weren't Peaches!"; D1273.1.1., Three as magic number; H310., Suitor tests; H313.1., Princess shall marry whoever gives her all she wishes; H335., Tasks assigned suitors; H1333., Quest for extraordinary plants; T75.0.1., Suitors ill-treated.]

Jokes about Men

Shepherds, Vláhi, and Other Sexually Stupid Men

According to Campbell (1974:1–2), the word "Vlachs" was already in use during the Byzantine period as a general occupational reference for Greek-speaking transhumant pastoralists. In its original sense, however, it was used to describe the Koutsovláchs, an ethnic minority in northern Greece that speaks a Romance language akin to Romanian. Today, however, "Vlachs" has so many different connotations that a general confusion exists in regard to the term's specific meaning. In the jokes included in this section, the term that I transliterate as *Vláhos* (*Vláhi* in the plural) was used by informants to indicate a very dumb shepherd, much as we use "hillbilly" or "hick" to indicate an ignorant rural person.

222 A shepherd got married, but he didn't know how to make love, so on the wedding night nothing happened.

The next day the wife went to his mother and complained.

The mother called the village doctor and he came. They told him their problem.

So the doctor called the shepherd and said:

"Your wife is very sick, and if you don't help her, she'll die!"

"What can I do?" asked the shepherd.

"Put your penis inside her hole and move it around and that'll be the medicine to make her get better!"

So the shepherd went to his wife, who was in bed pretending to be sick, and he fucked her once, twice, and three times! By that time she was really feeling good.

"Ah!" said the shepherd. "Such good medicine! Too bad I didn't know about it when my father was dying! I could have saved his life!"

[AT1685, The Foolish Bridegroom; D1273.1.1., Three as magic number; F950.4., Sexual intercourse as illness cure; J1744.1., Ignorance of bridegroom on wedding night; K1326., Seduction by feigned illness; P412., Shepherd.]

223 Once a shepherd had a terrible pain in his leg, and he could hardly walk. So he went to see a doctor. Well, the doctor was very busy. After giving him a brief examination, he told the shepherd to wait in one of the reception rooms. Well, there was a woman in the room who was waiting to see the doctor, too.

Well, after a while the woman invited the shepherd to fuck her. He didn't really know how to do it, but she showed him how. As soon as they finished, his leg stopped hurting him.

When the doctor came back, the shepherd told him:

"You're not the doctor, she is! She fixed my leg so that it stopped hurting!"

[J1745., Ignorance of sex; K1363., Seduction through ignorance of sex; P412., Shepherd; T25., Miraculous healing from a passionate love.]

224 A shepherd got married, but he didn't know how to make love, so nothing happened on his wedding night.

The next day he went to visit his uncle.

"How was it last night, my boy?" said the uncle.

"We slept," said the shepherd.

"Why?" asked the uncle.

"Because I don't know how to screw women," said the boy.

"Well, just watch what I do, and you'll learn," said the uncle.

So they went into the kitchen, and the uncle's wife was leaning over making bread, kneading the dough. So the uncle went behind her and raised her skirts and started fucking her!

So the shepherd went home, and that night he told his wife:

"Make some bread. I'm hungry!"

"Now, at this hour?" asked the wife.

"Yes, now," said the shepherd.

So while she was leaning over, kneading the bread, he went behind her and raised her skirts and started fucking her!

A month later the shepherd saw his uncle.

"How's the sex life going?" asked the old man.

"Just fine," said the shepherd, "but we have more bread than we know what to do with!"

[AT1685, The Foolish Bridegroom; J50., Knowledge acquired from observation; J1744.1., Ignorance of bridegroom on wedding night; J2450., Literal fool; P412., Shepherd; T166.2., Bridegroom must be taught sexual intercourse.]

225 A shepherd got engaged through a matchmaker to a school-teacher, and they got married. On their wedding night nothing happened because the shepherd didn't know how to screw.

So the teacher complained to her mother and her mother-in-law. Well, the shepherd went off with his sheep into the mountains, and when he came back he went to his mother's house first.

"Why didn't you screw your wife on your wedding night?"

"What's that? I don't understand," he said.

So then he went to his mother-in-law's house, and she said to him:

"Why don't you sleep with your wife?"

"We slept together," he said.

"But no sex," she said.

"What's that?" he asked.

So the mother-in-law took the shepherd to her bed, and she taught him to screw!

"That's what you must do to your wife," she said.

So after that the shepherd and his wife passed their life together well!

[AT1685, The Foolish Bridegroom; J1744.1., Ignorance of bridegroom on wedding night; K1363., Seduction through ignorance of sex; P412., Shepherd; T166.2., Bridegroom must be taught sexual intercourse; T417.1., Mother-in-law seduces son-in-law.]

The preceding joke brings to mind a problem that can result from Greek marriage customs. Since men traditionally marry women much younger than they, the man's mother-in-law, in many instances, is only a few years his senior. Such a situation can lead to unusual stress in the relationship when the father-in-law is much older and sexually inactive. As far as I am aware, however, mother-in-law avoidance, a custom practiced by some New World Indians, was never practiced by the Greeks.

226 Sometime, a couple married. Well, on the wedding night, the bride's mother peeped through the keyhole to see what the newlyweds were doing.

Well, what did she see? Her daughter, dressed in her new negligee, was lying on the bed, and the groom was sitting in a chair reading a book!

So the next day the woman told her daughter to strip down to her bra and panties to get her husband excited so he would make love to her.

Well, that night she again peeped through the keyhole, and she saw her daughter on the bed wearing only her bra and panties, and the groom was sitting in the chair reading his book!

So the next day the woman told her daughter to get completely naked and to lie on the bed with her legs open. Then the groom would get excited and make love to her.

So that night she again peeped through the keyhole to see what was going on. And she saw her daughter, naked on the bed with her legs spread open, and the groom, still in the chair reading the book! But every few minutes he would stick his finger in his wife's pussy to moisten it to turn the page of the book!

[Legman I:668; AT1685, The Foolish Bridegroom; D1273.1.1., Three as magic number; J1744.1., Ignorance of bridegroom on wedding night; J1745., Ignorance of sex; X735.2.2., Bridegroom reads magazines. . . .]

The last joke in this group about sexually stupid men concerns the supposedly supermacho Greeks, the *mánges.* They typically button only the last two buttons of their shirts to display very hairy chests, usually with a heavy gold chain bearing a golden cross nestled in the hair. They affect very deep, strong voices and use a lot of slang and braggadocio. They try to be what Greeks call "heavy." They often hang around the plazas and the *piátsas,* the areas where taxi stands are situated, in Athens and Piraeus. They are the tough, lower-class, uneducated Greek men who frequent the bordellos and the *bouzoúkia,* the nightclubs that play popular Greek music. The joke below is about a typical *mángas* who is called Vangos. He indeed may become the "hero" of a new joke cycle.

227 Vangos married a high-class woman. So, after the wedding night had passed, his friends asked him how he spent his wedding night.

"Well, I took her to a really fine fourth-class hotel."

"And then what did you do?" they asked.

"Well, I started kissing her and stroking her, to get her warmed up."

"Then what did you do?"

"Then I farted, to create the right atmosphere," said Vangos.

"Then what did you do?" they asked.

"Then I kissed her some more, to get her excited."

"Then what happened?"

"Then I slapped her in the face a few times, so she'd know what a heavy guy I am," said Vangos.

"Then what did you do?" they asked.

"Then I kissed her a little more and a little more and rubbed her a lot to get her *really* excited."

"Then what did you do, Vangos?"

"When she was very, very horny and excited, I went over in the corner and masturbated to show her that I *really* don't need women!"

The Big Penis: Fantasy Jokes

Sexual stereotyping of other ethnic groups vis-à-vis penis size was reflected in some of the jokes that I heard in Greece. Blacks are believed to have very big penises, and Orientals, especially the Chinese, are believed to have very small penises. However, the Greeks usually find big penises the most interesting to joke about.[8]

228 This couple got married, and the wife told her husband that, if he saw anything unusual or strange during the day, to bring it back home for her to see because she liked strange things.

So one day, on his way home for lunch, the husband saw a man wearing a suit, but he looked very strange. His shoulders were very narrow, and his legs were very thin, but he had a big bulge around his middle.

"That's a strange looking man," thought the husband. So he went over to the man and asked him why he had the bulge in his middle.

"Well, you see, I have a very big penis, and so I have to wrap it around my waist so it won't drag on the ground!"

"Oh, that's really strange," said the husband. "Would you please come over to my house to meet my wife? She likes to see strange things."

So the two men went to the couple's house, and when they arrived the husband said to the man:

"You wait here and I'll go upstairs first. But give me the end of your penis, and I'll take it upstairs with me to surprise my wife."

The man agreed, so the husband took the man's penis (like a fire hose) and walked up two flights of stairs to his apartment! He rang the bell, and his wife came to the door.

"My Virgin! What's that in your hand?" asked the wife.

"It's the biggest penis in the world! I brought it to show you because you like strange things."

"Well, bring the man who belongs to this penis upstairs so that I can meet him," said the wife.

So the husband went down one flight of stairs and called down to the man:

"Come on up, my wife wants to meet you!"

"Sorry," said the man. "I can't come up just now. My penis is doing its work upstairs *somewhere,* and you'll just have to wait until it finishes!"

[F547.3., Extraordinary penis; F547.3.1., Long penis; X749.4.1., Man with huge member.]

229 There were three men who made a bet about who had the biggest penis.

So they went to a bordello, and a prostitute fucked the first man, an Englishman, and she measured him: he had a twenty-five-centimeter penis.

Then the German went to the woman, and she measured him and found that he was twenty-seven centimeters long.

Then the Greek went into her room, and the other two men heard the woman screaming, "Help! Help!" And then she ran out!

So the Greek came out, and the other men said:

"What? Is your penis more than twenty-seven centimeters?"

"Yes, in diameter it's twenty-nine centimeters," said the Greek. "In length it's much longer!"

[D1273.1.1., Three as magic number; F547.3., Extraordinary penis; F547.3.1., Long penis; X749.4.1., Man with huge member.]

230 There was a man with a huge penis, fifty centimeters long, who called himself "The World's Biggest Penis." Well, one day somebody told him there was a man in Greece with a bigger penis, so he went to Greece to see if it was true.

When he arrived at the man's house, a woman answered the door.

"Hello! I'm The World's Biggest Penis, and I heard that your chief has a penis bigger than mine. So I want to meet him to see if it is true."

"You'll have to talk to the lieutenant first before you can see the

chief," said the woman. So she took him to the room where the lieutenant was.

"I'm The World's Biggest Penis," announced the man, "and I heard
your chief has a penis bigger than mine, but I don't believe it and I
want to see if it is true."

"Well, let me see your penis," said the lieutenant.

So The World's Biggest Penis took out his penis and they measured
it. It was fifty centimeters long!

"Oh, that's nothing," said the lieutenant.

"Well, let me see yours," said The World's Biggest Penis.

So the lieutenant dropped his pants, and he had his penis tied up in
a bow! (It was much longer than fifty centimeters!)

"Oh, my God!" said The World's Biggest Penis. "And where is the
chief so I can see him?"

"He's down at the harbor fishing with his penis!"

[Legman I:296; F547.3., Extraordinary penis; F547.3.1., Long penis;
F547.3.7., Man ties penis in knot; X749.4.1., Man with huge member.]

231 One time, a donkey went into a bar to have a drink. Well, he
seemed very depressed, so the bartender said to one of his regular
customers:

"Tell him something to cheer him up!"

So the man whispered something in the donkey's ear, and suddenly
the donkey started laughing like crazy! Well, he kept on and on until
he was really annoying all the customers.

So the bartender said to the man:

"Tell him something to calm him down!"

So the man whispered something in the donkey's ear, and then the
two of them went outside the bar for a few minutes. When they returned the donkey sat down at the bar and was very depressed again.

After the donkey left the bartender asked the man:

"What did you say to the donkey to first make him laugh like crazy,
then later to depress him again?"

"First, I told him that I had a bigger penis than he did."

"And then?" asked the bartender.

"Then we went outside, and I proved it to him!"

[F547.3., Extraordinary penis; F547.3.1., Long peinis; X749.4.1., Man
with huge member.]

In another version (231a) of the joke above, a Chinese man
tells the donkey that his penis is bigger, and then when the

donkey sees the Chinese man's little penis, he feels so sorry for
him that he cries.

232 One Sunday a man took his son to the zoo. The little boy asked
many questions about all the animals.

When they were watching the elephant, the little boy said:

"What's that thing hanging down?"

"That's the elephant's nose; it's called a trunk," said the boy's father.

"No, no! I mean at the other end," said the boy.

"That's the elephant's tail."

"No, no! I mean the thing in between," said the boy.

"That's the elephant's penis," said the father.

"But when I asked Mommy, she said it was nothing."

"Never mind," said the father. "It's because she's used to something
else!"

[Legman I:56; F547.3., Extraordinary penis; X749.4.1., Man with
huge member.]

233 A man went to a whorehouse. Well, he was going upstairs with a
woman, and they passed a room where there was a naked woman sitting on top of a naked Black man in a chair, but they weren't moving
around at all.

So the man went with the prostitute, and he paid her. Then he went
downstairs again, and, as he passed the room, he saw the woman was
still sitting on top of the Black man. And they had been like that for a
long time!

So he asked the woman who ran the bordello, what was going on in
that room?

"Oh, that's a new girl who had a small pussy. So we're using the
Black man like a shoe last (*kalapódi*) to stretch her pussy out!"

[F547.3., Extraordinary penis; X749.4.1., Man with huge member.]

234 Once there was a man with a very big penis. Well, he had it
tatooed with stripes of different colors, like a rainbow. And he was in
big demand by all of the women of the neighborhood! He made his
living by fucking women for money!

So he went to one house, and the maid said:

"Oh, give me ten drachmes' worth."

So he put his penis into her up to the first stripe of color, and he
screwed her like that.

Then at the next house, the maid wanted thirty drachmes' worth. So
he put his penis into her up to the third stripe and fucked her like that.

At the next house the maid had just gotten paid, so she wanted fifty drachmes' worth. So he put his penis into her up to the fifth stripe. Well, she got really warmed up!

"Give me thirty drachmes more!" she said.

So he put it into her up to the eighth stripe!

"Give me thirty drachmes more!" she said.

So he put it in up to the eleventh stripe.

"Give me ten more!" she said.

Well, the man got really hot, and he put his penis all the way inside and started to put his balls inside her, too!

"Stop! Stop! Stop!" said the woman. "I'm up to here!" [pointing to the throat].

[F547.3., Extraordinary penis; F547.3.1., Long penis; F547.3.4., Tattoo on penis; K1398., Trickster with painted member; X749.4.1., Man with a huge member.]

The preceding joke was told once in a *paréa* of mixed company when one of the women in the group refused more food, saying, "I can't eat more. I'm up to here!" and pointed to her throat. "To eat," as explained before, is also slang for "to fuck."

Male Sexual Tricksters

Several jokes already included in other chapters, especially some of the Bobos jokes, could be placed here. The following are other examples of jokes about tricksters who use their cleverness for sexual purposes.

235 Two men who had been best friends for years made a bet one night. They bet that the first to deny the other something that he wanted would lose five hundred drachmes.

One night they went to one of the friends' house for dinner. After dinner the friend who was the guest said:

"Give me your wife!"

Since the host didn't want to refuse his friend something and thus lose the bet, he asked:

"What do you want my wife for?"

Of course, if the guest said that he wanted to fuck his friend's wife, the host would then have to say no. So instead the guest said:

"I want to make her into an automobile!"

"Okay," said the man, and he called his wife to come.

Very Sókin Jokes

"Tell your wife to take off her clothes and sit on t
So the woman took off her clothes and sat on the
"But an automobile has four wheels," protested t'
So the guest took four plates and put them aroun
"Those are the four wheels," said the guest.
"But an automobile has an engine that works," s
"Wait until I put the crank in the automobile," said tne cuc.
"Then you'll see how the engine works!"

[An automobile-age version of AT1315.3.2., Seduction Attempted on Promise of Magic Transformation of Woman to Mare.]

236 Once there was a young boy about eighteen working in a furniture-making shop. Well, the owner of the store had a pretty young daughter, and so the boy wanted to fuck her, but he couldn't figure how to do it. "How? How to do it?" he thought.

Well, one day he asked his boss if he could leave for half an hour to get something to eat since he hadn't eaten any breakfast. (The boss was very strict and never gave the men any time off.) So the boss said:

"You don't have to go for half an hour. Just go upstairs and tell my daughter to fix you some eggs and to make it fast! We have a lot of work today."

So the boy went upstairs and told the girl:

"Your father said that I could fuck you!"

"That's impossible!"

"Just ask him!" said the boy.

Well, there was a hole in the floor that opened into the ceiling of the workshop so that the family could talk back and forth.

"Papa—yes?" asked the girl.

"Yes, and make it quick!" said the father.

So the boy put her down on the floor, on top of the hole, and fucked her! After they finished some of the semen fell out and fell through the hole in the floor. It fell and hit the father on the head. Well, the man wiped his head and looked at his fingers.

"Stupid girl," he said, licking his fingers. "Wasting the best part of the egg!"

[Legman II:378; K1354., Seduction by bearing false order from father or husband; 1563B., Give Him "That."]

The Cuckold

237 Sometime, there was a married man who only went to his house for dinner. All the day he worked; then he went to the coffeehouse.

Later he went home for dinner; then he went out again with his [male] friends every evening and only returned home late at night.

Well, for years, every night his wife had meat for dinner. So one night when the man got home for dinner, his wife served him beans.

"What's that! Beans? Why isn't there any meat?" demanded the man.

"Because you didn't bring me any meat, so we only have beans," said the wife.

Well, the man thought about that. Since he *never* went shopping and never brought meat to his wife, he understood, and said (pointing to his plate of beans):

"Take it away! It's not proper food for a cuckold!"

[K1501., Cuckold.]

238 One time, there were two enemies. One of them sent the other one a box that contained a pair of horns (implying that he was a cuckold).

So the man realized who had sent the horns. So he filled the horns with rose petals and returned the box with a card that read:

"We each sent the other that which he had. You had the horns, I had the roses!"

[H425.2., Horns grow on cuckold; J156.3., Present returned to giver; K1501., Cuckold.]

239 One day, while the husband was away from home, the *kumbáros* came over to visit. Well, after a while he and the wife were in bed together having a good time!

Just then the husband came home and walked in on them!

"Eh, *kumbáre*, what are you doing here?" asked the husband.

"It started raining, so I stopped working. Then I thought I'd come over here and do your work for you!"

[K1501., Cuckold.]

Old Men

240 An old man, eighty-five, married a thirty-year-old woman.

Well, before the wedding he went to see his doctor and said:

"Doctor, you're my friend. So you must help me. Next week I'm marrying a young woman, and I can get an erection only once a month! What can I do?"

"Don't worry," said the doctor. "Come back in three days, and I'll have something for you."

So in three days the man returned to the doctor.

"Look, I've built an artificial penis. You can strap it on before you want to fuck your wife. And in this little hole, you can pour milk in before you make love. Then, when you want to pretend you've had an ejaculation, just push this button and the milk will squirt out!"

So the man was very happy, and on his wedding night his wife was happy too! She didn't suspect anything.

Well, the wife got pregnant, and when it was time for the baby to be born, the doctor told her she would have to have a cesarean operation because the baby was so big.

When they cut her open to deliver the baby, what did they find? A twenty pound cheese!

[Legman I:315; J445.2., Foolish marriage of old man to young girl.]

241 Sometime, there was an old couple that had been married many years. They rented two rooms of their house to a newly married couple to make a little money.

One afternoon, when the old man was in the coffeehouse, the old woman heard loud noises in the rented rooms. She peeked through the keyhole to see what the trouble was, and she saw the man fucking the woman on the top of the table!

When the old man came home, she said to him:

"Get ready! We're going to do something new!"

So the old woman got undressed and got on the table. The old man stood up next to the table and started to screw her.

Suddenly the old man started screaming!

"What's the matter?" asked the old woman.

"With all the pushing, pushing, pushing, my balls got caught in the drawer under the table!"

[Legman II:455.]

242 There were two men who were best friends for fifty years. One was sixty, the other was sixty-five.

One day they saw each other on the street:

"Where have you been for six months?" asked the older man.

"I found a nudist colony, and I go there all the time to see naked girls, fifteen years old," said the other man.

"Let's go together so I can see naked girls," said the older.

So they went, and they saw two beautiful young girls. So they went with these girls and they fucked them!

The next day there were more naked girls. So the two men took two more girls upstairs to fuck them.

But the old man, the sixty-five-year-old one, couldn't get a hard-on!

All he could do was fart when he tried to get an erection!

So he went downstairs, and later his friend who was sixty came down.

"What's wrong?" asked the friend.

"Let's go," said the older man. "Once a month I can screw. The other twenty-nine days, all I can do is fart!"

[Legman I:627.]

Jokes about Bordellos and Prostitutes

243 A Greek went to France on a business trip. So when he was in his hotel, he sent for a prostitute.

So she came to the room, and they started screwing.

"A little more to the left," said the Greek.

So the woman moved to the left.

"A little more to the right," said the man.

So the woman moved to the right.

"Oh, go up a little higher," said the Greek.

So the woman moved up a little bit.

"Oh, oh, move down just a little bit," said the man.

Finally, in exasperation, the woman said:

"Look! Make up your mind! What do you want to do: park or fuck?"

[X520., Jokes concerning prostitutes.]

244 A Greek ship went to Japan, and immediately about ten prostitutes came on board.

The captain had a beautiful prostitute in his cabin. So he showed her to the bed, and then he started fucking her.

Every time that he fucked her, she would say, *"Táka máka!"* But he didn't understand Japanese.

After he left Japan, during the voyage he kept thinking about *táka máka* and what it meant. So when he got back to Greece, he went by the Japanese Embassy and asked somebody to translate for him.

"What does *táka máka* mean?" he asked.

"It means 'wrong hole'!" the translator told him.

[Legman II:165; X520., Jokes concerning prostitutes; X733.1.1., Man mounts Indian squaw who continually shouts "Wahoo" as he has her. Later he is told that "Wahoo" means wrong hole.]

245 One time, a man owned a whorehouse, and he had one hundred women. So he decided to make a bet with his clients. The clients who could fuck all one hundred women could fuck the man's wife and daughter *and* get a huge dowry! But if the client failed the owner would cut off his head!

So a *mángas* type came and took the bet. Well, he fucked fifty women, and an employee ran to the owner and said:

"Boss! The *mángas* has fucked fifty!"

"Never mind," said the boss. "His penis will drop soon!"

So the *mángas* fucked ten more women, and then his penis dropped! So the *mángas* was beheaded.

Well, other men came to take the bet. One fucked seventy, another seventy-five, another did eighty. But none of them could fuck all one hundred women!

So one day a sailor who had been at sea for five years and who was really horny heard about the bet, so he went to the whorehouse and started fucking.

After a while the employee ran to the boss:

"Boss, he's fucked eighty-three!"

"Never mind, it will fall down soon," said the boss.

A while later the employee returned:

"Boss, he's fucked ninety-five!"

"Don't worry, he'll pass out soon," said the boss.

Later the servant returned:

"Boss, he did it! He fucked all one hundred!"

"And where is he now?" asked the boss.

"Sitting on the balcony masturbating!" said the employee.

[X520., Jokes concerning prostitutes; X735.8.1.1., Man fucks whores to death, then chases heifers in field; X749.4.3.1., Man wagers he can mount one hundred women in succession.]

246 One time, a *Vláhos* went to Athens, and he decided to go to a bordello. After he picked out a woman, he told her:

"I want something extra. I want the *tsimboúki* [literally, a long-stemmed pipe; in slang, oral sex, fellatio, or 'a blow job']."

So they got into bed, and he told her:

"Suck! Suck!"

So she started to suck him.

"Suck! Suck!" he continued.

So she sucked even harder.

"Blow! Blow!" suddenly shouted the *Vláhos*.

"Make up your mind!" yelled the woman. "First you say 'suck', then you say 'blow'!"

"Blow fast!" yelled the *Vláhos*. "The sheet is going up my asshole!"

[X520., Jokes concerning prostitutes.]

247 One time, two prostitutes had a fight about what kind of penis was the best: a short, thick one or a long, thin one. So they took their arguments to court and asked a judge to decide.

After hearing their arguments the judge told them that he would consider the case overnight and give them his decision the next day.

That evening he told his wife about the case.

"But the size has nothing to do with it!" protested his wife. "It's the hardness that matters," she said.

The next day the judge told the two women that their arguments were irrelevant because size was unimportant and that the hardness was the main factor.

"And which old whore told you that?" they asked.

[J1170., Clever or wise judgment; X520., Jokes concerning prostitutes.]

248 A soldier and a prostitute were making love. Well, the man lost his ring; it fell inside the woman's pussy. So he put his finger inside, but he couldn't find it.

Then he put his hand inside her, but he still couldn't find his ring.

So he put his head inside the woman's pussy, and what did he see? An army captain! The captain said:

"What are you doing in here?"

"I'm looking for my ring; I lost it in here," said the soldier.

"Don't feel bad!" said the captain. "I lost my whole platoon in here!"

[Legman II:453; F547.5., Extraordinary vagina; X520., Jokes concerning prostitutes.]

249 A *Vláhos* went to Athens for the first time. Well, he wanted a woman, so he decided to go to a bordello. He asked somebody where he could find a bordello, and they told him to look for a narrow street and a dark house with only a small light on and with lots of people waiting in the hall.

So the *Vláhos* walked around the district close to the main train station in Athens because he heard that's where a lot of bordellos were. But by mistake he went into a house where there was a wake in progress, because the house was dark, with only one small lamp burning, and there were lots of people waiting in the hallway, seated.

So he went inside and took a seat. Someone came up to him and asked him if he wanted some coffee.

"No," said the *Vláhos*, "I just came to stick my cock in a little bit!"

250 A Greek went to America, and he went to a bordello. He asked how much the charge was, and they told him they would pay him three hundred dollars!

"So it's true what they say about America!" he thought.

The next time that he went there, he was paid four hundred dollars! He was really happy that he had come to America!

Well, the next time that he went, they told him it would cost thirty dollars!

"Thirty dollars! But the last two times you paid me to screw!"

"Yes, but today we're not shooting porno movies like the other times!"

[Legman II:244.]

251 A man went to a bordello and went with a whore to her room.

"Do you have a rubber?" she asked.

"Er, no," said the man.

"No rubber, no fucking!" said the woman.

"But, er, couldn't we, er—just—er—" he said.

"No! But I've got an idea. Do you have a five-hundred-drachme bill?"

"Yes."

"Then fold it up like a cone, and put it inside me, and it'll act like a rubber. Then we can fuck!"

So the man folded up the money and put it inside the whore and fucked her and left.

A while later the woman had another customer.

"Do you have a rubber?" she asked him.

"No," said the man.

"Well, do you have a five-hundred-drachme bill?"

"No, the smallest bill I have is one thousand drachmes."

"Never mind. Just fold it up like a cone, and put it inside me, and then we can fuck," said the woman.

So the man put the money "cone" inside the whore, and he fucked her! When he finished, the five-hundred-drachme bill that the first man had put inside came out!

"My Virgin!" he said. "I've seen a lot of pussies in my time, but never one that makes change!"

[F547.5., Extraordinary vagina; X520., Jokes concerning prostitutes.]

JOKES INVOLVING SEXUAL ACTS BETWEEN MEN

Jokes about Homosexuals

The first joke in this section is probably the classic joke in Greece about homosexuals. In addition to being very widely known, it also exists in many different versions. Principally, however, the homosexual is an Englishman. In many of these jokes, only the male taking the passive role is considered homosexual.

252 There was an Englishman, a queer, who came to Greece for his vacation because he had heard that Greece was the homeland of homosexuality.

Well, on his first night he met a *paréa* of young Greek men in a *tavérna* in Plaka [Athens' old quarter], and, seeing that the Englishman was alone, they invited him to join their *paréa*.

After several bottles of *oúzo* [Greek aperitif tasting like licorice] and appetizers, the group left the *tavérna*. Since the Englishman was obviously a queer, and very drunk, they went to one of the narrow, dark alleys in Plaka, and all the Greeks (about ten of them) took turns screwing the Englishman!

Well, the next day, when the Englishman woke up, he said to his traveling companion:

"Oh! What a hangover I've got! But things are really different here! In England, when I drink Scotch my head aches. But, in Greece, when I drink *oúzo* my ass aches!"

[Legman II:756; T463., Sodomy.]

253 A man driving a truck passed a nun on the road. So he stopped to give her a ride.

As she was young and pretty, he was constantly changing gears so he could touch her leg. So he got excited, and she seemed to be getting excited, too.

"Let's stop for a while and enjoy ourselves," said the driver.

So they stopped by some woods and went into the woods.

"But wait a minute," said the nun. "I'm a virgin, so I don't know—I wouldn't want to go back to the convent if I wasn't a virgin any more."

"Never mind," said the driver, "we'll do it from behind, and that way you'll stay a virgin."

So he fucked her from behind, and they enjoyed themselves.

After they continued their journey, the driver said:

"I have a confession to make. I'm really a medical student, not a truck driver. That's why I didn't take your virginity by force!"

"And I have a confession to make," said the nun. "I'm really a homosexual, and not a nun, but I wear the habit to fool people like you!"

[K2285., Villain disguised as ascetic or nun; T463., Sodomy; X724.1.8.1., Man disguises himself as girl to effect seduction; X749.12.1.1., Man makes advances to another man who is disguised as woman.]

On the sixth of January, the Epiphany, the Greek Orthodox Church celebrates the baptism of Christ by a custom in which the seas are also blessed. On this day, called popularly "The Day of the Cross," the town priest tosses a silver or gold cross into the harbor (if available), and the boys of the town dive to compete in retrieving the cross. The lad who succeeds at the task earns much honor and prestige. The following joke relates to the custom.

254 In Heraklion one time, when the bishop threw the small cross into the harbor, as is the custom, the six or seven boys who were dressed in swimsuits and who were supposed to dive into the sea to compete to retrieve the cross were shivering from the cold and had no enthusiasm for their task. So they just kept standing and shivering on the pier.

The people in the crowd urged the boys to be strong, to go on in, et cetera. Finally, one of the boys dived into the water, found the cross, and brought it to the bishop.

"*Brávo!*" said the bishop to the boy. But he noticed that the boy was looking around in the crowd.

"What's the matter?" asked the bishop.

"I'm looking for the queer who goosed me [*mou ésprokse ápo píso:* literally 'pushed me from behind'] so that I would jump into the sea!"

[K16., Diving match won by deception.]

255 A queer went to a grocery store and asked for a kilo of salami. When the grocer started to slice it up, the queer said:

"What do you think, you dummy? That I put it up my ass piece by piece?"

256 Sometime, a man went to a nudist beach. Well, as he was walking around, he saw a big sign that read:

BEWARE! ACTIVE HOMOSEXUALS IN THE VICINITY!

As he continued his walk, he saw a second sign that also warned of the homosexuals. A bit farther down one of the paths, there was still another sign on a tree to beware of the active homosexuals.

Finally, as he rounded a curve in the path, he saw a small sign on the grass. He went over to read the sign, and as he leaned over, somebody fucked him in the ass!

The sign had said:

DON'T COMPLAIN! YOU WERE WARNED!

[T463., Sodomy.]

The *Vláhos* in the following joke is not considered a homosexual because he assumes the active male role in the sexual encounter with another man. The joke also illustrates the traditional Greek leniency toward bisexual males who always take the active, aggressive role in sex. Indeed, Greeks have regarded male homosexual desire as "natural" for the active partner, but "unnatural" for the passive male who chooses a "prostitute's role" (Dover 1978: 67–68). Whereas in the classical period Greeks were lenient to both partners in male homosexual encounters, by 346 B.C. sentiment had changed. Men who submitted to anal penetration by other males were considered degenerate; by law they were barred from addressing the assembly and denied other civic rights. The law did not penalize the active male in the homosexual encounters (Dover 1978: 14, 19), however.

257 One time, a *Vláhos* from the mountains of northern Greece came to Athens for the first time. He was a tall and handsome young man wearing the typical skirt of the Vláchs and shoes with pompoms, and sporting a big moustache.

The *Vláhos* went to a coffeehouse in Omonia Square in Athens and ordered a coffee.

A dissolute old gentleman eyed the *Vláhos* appreciatively and ordered an *oúzo* to be sent to the young man.

"What's that?" asked the *Vláhos* as the waiter brought him the drink.

"That gentleman over there has sent it to you," said the waiter, pointing to the old man.

Well, at first the *Vláhos* worried about accepting the *oúzo* because he remembered stories his grandfather had told him about the evils and vices of Athens. So he twisted his moustache again and again pensively and finally asked himself, "What can I lose?" And he drank the *oúzo*.

The old gentleman sent another, then another, then another. Finally, he came over to the table where the young man was sitting and asked permission to sit down.

"Is this your first time in Athens?" asked the old man.

"Yes," admitted the *Vláhos*.

"Do you have a place to stay?"

"Not yet."

"Then let me invite you to my house. It's not far from here."

Again the *Vláhos* twisted and pulled his moustache, thinking what to do. Finally, he thought, "What can I lose?" He accepted. So they went to the old man's apartment.

"Make yourself at home," he told his guest.

As there was only one double bed, the *Vláhos* settled in the bed, stretching out. The old man came and got into the bed with him.

"Since you're here," said the old man, "er, could we do it?"

Again the *Vláhos* pulled his moustache, thinking what to do. But what could he lose?

So he screwed the old man!

This was repeated several times through the night, as the old man asked the *Vláhos* to do it again and again.

In the morning, when the *Vláhos* was getting dressed to leave, the old man asked if they could do it again.

"What can I lose?" said the *Vláhos*.

After they finished the old man begged the *Vláhos* not to leave, to stay with him so they could do it again.

The *Vláhos* turned to the old man and scrutinized him from head to toe.

"What are you? A queer?"

[T463., Sodomy.]

258 Sometime, one of Socrates' students, Alkibiades, cut the tip of his finger. Well, the finger was bleeding a lot and it wouldn't stop. So the student told Socrates of his problem, and the teacher said (dropping his pants and pointing to his rear end):

"Put your finger in there and that will stop the bleeding!"

So the boy put his finger into Socrates' ass, and it stopped bleeding.

"Oh! Very good!" said the student.

One day, however, the sneaky Socrates purposely cut his own finger when Alkibiades was nearby, and his finger was really bleeding.

"Oh, never mind, teacher," said the boy. "Put your finger in here" (lifting his skirts and showing his rear).

But Socrates took advantage of the offer and put his penis inside, and not his finger!

[T463., Sodomy.]

259 A village man was in Athens, and he saw a sign that read:
BECOME A MAGICIAN FOR ONLY TEN DRACHMES.

So the villager went down the stairs into the basement where the magician lived, and he saw a Black man with a turban on his head.

"I want to become a magician," said the villager.

"First, give me the ten drachmes," said the Black man.

So the villager paid him.

"Okay now, take off your coat," said the Black man. And the villager took off his coat.

"Now take off your shirt," said the Black man. And the villager took off his shirt.

"Now, take off your pants," said the Black man. So the villager took off his pants.

"Now get onto that bed," said the Black man.

"Are you going to fuck me?" asked the villager.

"Oh, so, you're a magician!"* said the Black man.

[D1711., Magician; D1711.0.3., Means of becoming magician; K1315.3., Seduction by posing as a magician.]

260 A missionary went to an island, and when he got there he discovered there were no women on the entire island!

So when he met the mayor, he asked him:

"Since there are no women here, what do you do for sex?"

"We have a barrel with a hole in it, and every Sunday we go to the village square and have sex with the barrel!"

Well, on Sunday, after the missionary had given his sermon, he saw all the men getting in line in the village square. And then the village mayor came over to him and said:

"Aren't you going to get in line and fuck the barrel, too?"

---

*The expression *"Mágos eísai"* (literally "You are a magician?") is said to someone who remarks on something that is obvious. This joke plays on this expression.

"Me? With a barrel? Never!" said the missionary.

"Really, it's very good," insisted the mayor.

Well, after much coaxing the missionary decided he'd try it. After he finished he said to the mayor:

"You were right; it was really good. Better than a woman! Terrific! I liked it!"

Then he heard a voice from inside the barrel saying:

"You like it now, but just wait until it's your turn inside the barrel! *Then* how will you like it?"

[Legman I:659; T463., Sodomy.]

261 Three soldiers were given an overnight leave. The next day, when they returned to the base, the sergeant looked at the first one and said:

"You look all worn out! What did you do all night?"

"I was fucking Kaiti," said the first soldier.

Then the sergeant looked at the second soldier and said:

"And you look really exhausted! What were you doing all night?"

"I was fucking Kaiti," said the second.

So the sergeant turned to the third soldier and said:

"You look great! You must have taken care of yourself last night."

"Yes," said the third soldier. "I was Kaiti last night!"

[Legman II:172; D1273.1.1., Three as magic number; T463., Sodomy.]

262 A man from a mountain village went on a trip to sell his oil in a large town nearby. On his donkey he had two goatskins full of oil. On the road, before he reached the town, he met a stranger.

"Eh, *kumbáre*, what are you doing here?"

"I'm going to the town to sell my oil."

"Oh? Well, let me sample the oil, and if I like it I'll buy it from you and save you the trip."

"But the goatskin is sealed," said the farmer.

"Never mind. Just cut the skin with your knife and let a few drops out."

So the farmer cut the skin and let a few drops of oil out. Then he held the skin closed with his fingers.

"Oh, that's bitter oil! How about the other skin?"

So the stranger cut the other skin open to taste the oil, and the farmer had to hold it closed with his other hand so that the oil wouldn't pour out.

"Ugh! That's even worse oil!" said the stranger.

Seeing that the farmer had his two hands occupied holding the goatskins closed to keep the oil from spilling, the stranger took advantage of the farmer. He pulled down the farmer's pants and fucked him! The poor farmer couldn't do anything to stop him, or he would lose all of his valuable oil!

So the stranger left, and a while later a man from the farmer's village came by and helped the farmer to sew up the goatskins.

Well, the farmer went to the town and sold his oil. When he returned to his village, he saw his cousin, Maria, who was pregnant.

"Eh, Maria, do you have pain in your stomach from the baby?"

"Of course, what do you think?" she said. "The baby is always kicking me, and it hurts a lot!"

(Since the farmer was a bit ignorant, he thought he could get pregnant, too!)

"Oh, curse that stupid cuckold on the road! Now what will I do?"

[Legman I:601; J2321., Man made to believe that he is pregnant; T463., Sodomy.]

263 One time, there was an English governor of a colony in Africa. One day he asked his aide to find him a woman.

"Okay, my lord," said the aide, "but I'm afraid it will have to be a Black woman!"

"Never mind, then," said the bigoted English governor.

"But," said the aide, "there is one very handsome young Chinese boy that I probably could get for you!"

"Well, okay then," said the governor, "but be sure to be very discreet!"

"Certainly, my lord," said the aide. "Only five will know about it!"

"Five?" asked the governor. "Why five?"

"Well, the Chinese boy and the four men to hold him down!"

[Legman II:158; T463., Sodomy.]

Sodomy for Revenge

264 A long time ago we used to have Turks here. So we had a school for the children to learn Greek, but the Turkish kids went to the school, too.

There was a young Turkish boy named Ismayo, who had a very pretty mother.

So the teacher in the Greek school saw her, and then one day he told Ismayo:

"I send many greetings to your mother."

This continued for many days, and then the teacher told Ismayo:

"Greetings to your mother, and tell her that I love her!"

So Ismayo conveyed this message to his parents, and they devised a plan for the schoolteacher. The next day, when the boy went to school, he said to the teacher:

"My mother sends you her greetings and says for you to come to our house tonight."

So that night, when the teacher went to Ismayo's house, he brought a big turkey to offer to the woman. When he arrived he asked where Ismayo's father was.

"Oh, he's off in the woods chopping firewood," was the reply.

So he offered the turkey, and he sat and talked with Ismayo's mother, making plans all the time to get her into bed. Suddenly, there was a knock on the door.

"Quick, hide, it's Ismayo's father," said the woman.

"Where to hide?" asked the teacher.

"In the back room where we keep the calves,"* said the woman.

So the teacher hid, and the husband asked what was for dinner.

"A rock fell on a turkey's head and killed it, so we have turkey for dinner," said the wife.

So they ate and drank, and then the husband told his wife to get undressed so that he could fuck her.

"No, no," said the woman. "I don't feel like it!"

"Take off your clothes, I said!" shouted the husband.

"No, no, I don't want to!" screamed the wife.

"Okay, then, I'll go fuck the calves!"

So he went and fucked the teacher! The teacher didn't say anything; he pretended to be a calf! When the family was asleep, he left the house.

The next day at school, Ismayo said to the teacher:

"You have many greetings from my father!"

"To the whores with your mother, to the cuckolds with your father, and tell him not to fuck the calves again!"

[AT1730, The Entrapped Suitors; T463., Sodomy.]

*It is common in rural areas of Greece for domestic animals to be housed in the family home (see DuBoulay: 1974).

265 A condemned man was on the way to his execution. On the way he passed a skull that had the words *mí hirótera** written on it.

"That's stupid!" thought the condemned man. "Nothing is worse than death!"

Well, before the man faced the firing squad, all the soldiers took turns fucking him! And he said:

"Now I understand what the words on the skull meant!"

[T463., Sodomy.]

266 One time, there was a championship soccer game in Germany between a German team and a Greek team.

A Greek went to a hotel there for a room, but was told that the hotel was full, but that, if he wanted to share a room with a German, he could.

So he said okay.

"But the German is a sleepwalker."

"Never mind!"

So the Greek went to bed and went to sleep. During the night the German came over to his bed and fucked the Greek and shouted: "GOAL!"

Later, when the German was sleeping, the Greek went over and started fucking him. While he was doing that, he was making hissing noises.

"What are you doing?" asked the German.

"I'm filling up my balls for the soccer game tomorrow!" said the Greek, and he kept on fucking the German all night!

[T463., Sodomy.]

267 Sometime, on a train, there were two men sitting face to face. One was an Englishman; the other was Greek.

Just after the train left the station, the Englishman pulled a gun out of his pocket and ordered the Greek to masturbate! So the Greek masturbated. After the poor man had masturbated ten times, he said:

"Please, my back is killing me from all this! Why are you doing this to me?"

"Because the last time I traveled by train, there was another Greek, and my ass is still hurting from that trip! So keep on masturbating!"

[T463., Sodomy.]

*Mí hirótera is an expression advising somebody who's already had some misfortune to be careful not to have even worse trouble.

AMBISEXUAL JOKES

Joke about a Bisexual Man

268 A [bisexual] Greek captain was arriving in port in Japan. Before he went out he took a bath to be ready for the evening.

As he was bathing he started lathering his penis, and he said to his penis:

"Oh, you little devil! All the hundreds of beautiful women all over the world that you've fucked!"

Just then he dropped the soap, and, as he leaned over to pick it up, he farted loudly.

"Shut up, you queer!" said the captain talking to his rectum. "We weren't talking to you!"

[Legman II:875–76; H451., Talking private parts betray unchastity.]

Jokes That Begin with Heterosexual Sex and End with Sodomy

269 Sometime, there was a clever young man who married a girl from a nearby village. Well, the girl was very pretty, but she had no brains at all.

About a month after they were married, the husband complained to the wife:

"You're no good in bed at all! You don't know what to do, and you don't even try to please me!"

So the next day the poor wife went to see a doctor.

"What's the problem, my child?" asked the doctor.

"My husband says that I'm no good in bed, so there must be something wrong with me. Maybe you know what I can do?"

"Don't worry about a thing," said the clever doctor. "Let's go to my other office, at my house, and I'll take care of the problem for you!"

So they went to the doctor's house, and he told her:

"First, you have to learn to move your hips!" So he explained that she had to move her hips first to the right, then to the left, then she had to thrust her pelvis out in front. But the poor woman was too stupid to understand! So he gave her some rhyming words to chant while she moved to help her remember the motions:

"Wool [*mallí*], move to the right; flax [*stoupí*], move to the left; cotton [*babáki*], make a pelvic thrust."

So for about thirty minutes they practiced moving:

"Wool, flax, cotton! Wool, flax, cotton! Wool, flax, cotton!"

After they had practiced the doctor told the woman:

"That's fine! Now I'll give you an examination to see if you have learned to do it right!"

So the doctor fucked her!

So that night, when the woman was making love to her husband, she started saying, "Wool, flax, cotton!" And right away her husband knew she had been doing something with another man.

"Who taught you about the 'wool, flax, cotton'?"

"The doctor," said the dumb wife.

"Good. Tell him that you want one more lesson tomorrow at three o'clock at your house."

So the next day the doctor and the wife were continuing their "practice" in bed at her house, and the doctor was saying:

"Wool, flax, cotton! Wool, flax, cotton!"

Suddenly, the husband jumped out of the closet, where he had been hiding, jumped on top of the doctor, and screwed him in the ass! As he did that, he said:

"Here's the *spindle* to spin the wool, the flax, and the cotton into thread!"

[AT1359, The Husband Outwits Adulteress and Paramour; D1273. 1.1., Three as magic number; K1315.7.1., Seduction by instruction in marital duties; T463., Sodomy.]

270   There was a Greek apprentice seaman who was always asking the captain for money when they got into port so he could go with a woman. And so the captain always gave him money.

One time, the ship was in the port where the captain's family lived. So the seaman asked for some money to go ashore, and the captain gave him some money.

Well, when the seaman was walking through the town, he heard a "psst, psst" from a balcony. He looked up and saw a woman beckoning him into her house. (Well, it was the captain's wife, but the sailor didn't know.) So he went into her house and he fucked her! Then she gave him some money and told him he must leave because her husband was coming home. But she told him to return the next evening at six-thirty.

So the next day, when the captain saw the seaman, he said:

"I suppose you're going to ask me for some money?"

"No, I've got plenty!" said the seaman. "Last night when I was walking in the town, a woman took me into her house and fucked me and gave *me* money!"

"Incredible!" said the captain. "Where did she live?"

So the seaman told him, and the captain realized that it was his own house. But he didn't say anything.

"When are you going back?" asked the captain.

"Tonight at six-thirty," said the seaman.

So at six-thirty the seaman went to the captain's house, and, just as he was fucking the captain's wife, the bell rang.

"Quick! Hide under the bed; it's my husband," she said.

So the captain came in, but he didn't find the seaman! So he stayed awhile, then he went back to the ship.

[The episode is repeated several times.]

After the captain left, the woman told him:

"I want you to do me a favor. Take this money (about twenty dollars), and tomorrow go and buy some flowers and take them to my daughters, who live in the boarding school!"

So the next day the seaman took the money and bought flowers and went to the boarding school where the girls were kept to protect their virginity. Well, he pretended to be their cousin, so he got into their room. And he fucked both of the girls!

When he got back to the ship, he went to see the captain to ask him for some money. So the captain asked him how things were going.

"Great!" he said. "I'm still fucking the old lady, and today I fucked her two daughters as well!"

Hearing this, the captain pulled down his pants, turned around, leaned over, and pointed to his ass:

"In that case, fuck me too and make it the entire family!"

[Legman I:405; Legman II:98–99; AT1364:II, The Hidden Lover; T463., Sodomy.]

271 A shepherd got married, but he didn't know how to make love. On the day after his wedding night, the couple went to the bride's house. The girl's father asked them how they spent the night.

"We slept," said the daughter, "because he doesn't know how to make love."

So the girl's father said:

"We'll fix that! I'll show him! At dinner tonight we'll eat without our clothes!"

So at dinner, when they were eating, the father-in-law said to the shepherd:

"See that hole?" (pointing to the mother-in-law's pussy).

"Yes," said the shepherd.

So the father-in-law started screwing the mother-in-law!

Well, the shepherd's penis got hard while he was watching them. Finally, the shepherd asked his wife:

"See that hole?" (pointing to his father-in-law's ass).

And so he went over and fucked his father-in-law in the ass!

[AT1685, The Foolish Bridegroom; T463., Sodomy.]

The adulterous wife who betrays her husband with a low-status Black servant or slave, a common theme in Arab folklore (Slater 1968:247), is also the basis of the following joke.

272 One time, a married couple had a Black male servant. Well, every time that the husband went out, the Black man went and fucked the wife! Well, the Black man really pleased the wife because he had a big penis, but the woman's husband had a very small penis.

Well, the husband got back from London, and he said to his wife that he had some business in America, and he wanted her to go along on the trip.

"What will I do? What will I do?" thought the wife because she didn't want to do without all the good sex from the servant.

That night she told the servant:

"Dimitri, what will I do? My husband will take me with him to America on a trip, and you know he doesn't satisfy me because his penis is so small. What will I do without you?"

"Don't worry at all!" he said. "At night, when you get into bed to go to sleep, you will say, 'Abdulláh! Abdulláh!' and I'll come and fuck you!"

"Really?" said the woman.

"Yes, I promise," said the servant.

Well, the couple went to America, and the first night the woman was very horny. So when she got into bed, she said:

"Abdulláh! Abdulláh!"

And the servant came during her sleep, and he pleased her.

And the next night she did the same, and the servant came and pleased her.

The next night the husband heard her, so the following day he asked:

"Wife, did you have bad dreams last night? I heard you talking in your sleep! You were saying 'Abdulláh! Abdulláh!' What is the meaning of that?"

"Oh, that's nothing," said the wife. "Say it yourself and you will see."

So that night, before the wife said anything, the husband said:

"Abdulláh! Abdullá—ah, ah, ah!" (The Black man came and fucked him! That's why he said "ah, ah, ah!")

[D1420.4., Helper summoned by calling name; T463., Sodomy; T481.4., Wife seduces husband's servant.]

273   One time, there were two friends. One of them decided to go to America to visit some friends he had there. So he took an airplane, but, as it was flying over Africa, the plane had engine trouble, and so the man had to parachute out of the plane! Well, he went down, and he landed in a Mau Mau village.

So all the Africans were looking him up and down because they had never seen a white man like him before. So they bathed him and gave him clothes and fed him. Then they asked him:

"What torture do you want? The five or the ten? Now that we've been good to you, you must have some punishment."

So the Greek, thinking they would kill him, said:

"Better give me the ten so I can die faster!"

So they put him into a room and said:

"Are you sure that you want the ten torture?"

"Yes," said the Greek.

So they put ten Black women into the room with him, and he fucked all of them!

Later they gave him money, and so he returned to Greece and told his friend what had happened to him.

"*Po, po, po* [a Greek exclamatory, similar to 'Wow']! I'll go there too, then!"

So he took a plane, and, as it was flying over Africa, he parachuted down. Well, the Blacks looked him up and down. Then they gave him food, a bath, and clothing.

"What torture do you want? The fifteen or the thirty?"

"What will I do with the fifteen? Give me the thirty!"

So they put him into a room with thirty African men with huge penises, and they all fucked him!

Afterward, they sent him to Greece, and he saw his friend who had gone first to Africa.

"What happened?" asked the friend. "What torture did they give you?"

"The thirty," said the man. "Thirty Black *men!*"

"*Po, po, po!*" said the friend, looking at the other's backside in sympathy.

The man, turning to look at his own ass, said:
"Why? Does it show?"
[T463., Sodomy.]

BESTIALITY JOKES

274 One time, a village priest called all the men of the village to the church to have a talk with them. He began:

"It has come to my attention that many of you are ignoring your wives and having sex with animals instead! I want to know how widespread this problem is because I need to give you counseling. Therefore, all the men who have had sex with goats will please go out the right door, and all of the men who have been having sex with sheep will please go out of the left door."

In a few minutes all the church was empty except for one man standing in the middle.

"*Brávo!*" said the priest. "At least one man in our village doesn't have sex with sheep or goats!"

"No, you don't understand," said the man. "I go with *both* sheep and goats, so I didn't know what to do."

[T465., Bestiality; X734.3., Intercourse between male and animal.]

The following is an example of a "catch" joke. This particular joke is normally told in a group, and its object is to catch one of the unsuspecting listeners in an embarrassing position.

275 One time, there was a *Vláhos* who was engaged to a beautiful girl. So he promised himself that he would be faithful to his fiancée.

Well, after he was up in the mountains for four or five months tending his flock, he got so horny that he couldn't stand it any more.

So he picked the prettiest ewe, and he started to screw her. Well, the ewe started moving her head up and down [teller moves head up and down in a funny way], er, well, the way they do, you know?

[Someone in the group will usually say, "Yes," to indicate he or she knows the way sheep move their heads. So the teller says:]

So! How many sheep have you screwed?

[T465., Bestiality.]

The next joke involves another category of humor, the lie, as well as bestiality.

276   One time, a group of friends who were hunting enthusiasts were spending an evening together telling hunting stories. Well, most of the stories were just lies, incredible lies.

So one man said:

"Last week I went hunting in the woods, and I had my rifle loaded in my hands. Well, I pushed through some bushes, and I stumbled upon a huge she-bear! As soon as I saw her, I raised up my rifle, and the bear raised up on her hind legs to attack me—"

Just at that moment the telephone rang, and so the man telling the story excused himself to answer the phone.

When he returned after a few moments, he said:

"Where were we when I left? Oh, yes, the bear raised up on her hind legs!"

"So what did you do then?" asked one in the group.

"I fucked her, of course!" said the liar.

[T465., Bestiality; X584., Jokes about hunters; X1130., Lie: hunter's unusual experience; X734.3., Intercourse between male and animal.]

The last joke in this section may not be the usual type of bestiality joke, but it seems to fit in with the material of this section as well as with any other. I first heard it from a ten-year-old boy in Crete. Later in Athens I heard different versions from adults, but it seems the type of joke that children normally tell.

277   Once there were two fleas hiding in the navel of a lady's stomach. One said to the other:

"Let's separate and go in opposite directions to see what's out there, and then we'll meet here again after an hour."

So an hour later they returned to the navel.

"*Po, po, po!*" said the first flea. "I crossed a big plain; then I saw two huge mountains on the other side!"

"That's nothing," said the second flea. "I crossed a forest, then I saw a cave, so I went inside. Just then a man with two suitcases came inside and got me all wet!"

[Legman I:585; Legman II:320.]

JOKES INVOLVING OBSCENE GESTURES

It has often been remarked that one can watch a Greek conversation, but not hear it, and still understand it. Greeks, as

others in the Mediterranean region, communicate extensively
with their hands, arms, eyes, facial expressions, head movements, and the like. There is even a book (Papas 1972), written
in four languages and available to tourists in Greece, that
teaches, by illustration, most of the Greek system of body language, or kinesics. However, the book does not contain any of
the obscene or insult gestures (with the exception of the
múntza), which are very important to learn if one is spending
any time in the country.

The most widely used obscene gesture, which is also highly
insulting, is the "To my balls!" gesture. Normally performed by
men only, it may be directed to either men or women. Usually
at the same time, the insulted party is told, "Write your name on
my balls!" or "Go to my balls!" The gesture exists in two standard versions: in the first, the two hands are raised to the level
of the shoulders, right hand by right shoulder and left hand by
left shoulder, and then the two hands are rather rapidly jerked
down to the region of the genitals, where the two hands are
brought together; in the second, one hand alone is raised, usually the right one, to the level of the right shoulder, then
brought down suddenly to the region of the groin. If a respect-
able lady is present and if the man is polite, he may tell the
other man to "Write your name on my old shoes." Sometimes
the gesture alone is used since everybody knows the meaning.

A variation of "Write your name on my balls!" is "I've written
your name on my balls!" By the latter expression the teller indicates his low opinion of the other person. Also, it is a way of
saying that the other person has been tricked. In America an
equivalent gesture—although it bears only slight resemblance
to the Greek "To my balls!"—may be one I have overheard
American soldiers use, saying at the same time, "I've got your
idea right here!" (as one grabs or clutches his groin). The American gesture is not as widely used or understood in the United
States, however, as the "To my balls!" gesture is in Greece.

Finally, the "To my balls!" gesture may be used by men to
imply copulation. One Greek may be overheard bragging
to another, "I really fucked a hot piece of ass!" or "I gave it to
her!" as he uses the "To my balls!" gesture.

Many, many *sókin* jokes told in Greece use gestures as the punch line. If one is unfamiliar with the gestures, one cannot understand the jokes. Jokes with accompanying gestures translate only with some difficulty into foreign languages, but I include them here to give a more complete understanding of Greek humor. (See appendix C for illustrations of the gestures.)

"To My Balls!" Jokes

278 (Have you heard of Dr. Barnard, the famous surgeon who does all the transplants?)

Well, one time, Dr. Barnard was going on a trip. Well, on the way to the airport, his car was intercepted by an ambulance that was carrying a very badly injured man inside. The man's wife begged the doctor to operate since it was the only hope to save her husband's life. But since the doctor was in such a hurry to catch his flight, he performed the operation in a big rush so that he could still make his flight.

Well, when he came back from his trip, he went to see the patient in the hospital where he was convalescing.

"How are you doing, my boy?" asked Dr. Barnard.

"I'm okay, I guess," said the young man, "but that night you were in such a hurry that you made three mistakes!"

"Three! Oh, my God! What were they?"

"Well, first you put my left leg where my right leg should be, and my right leg where my left leg should be. But that's okay, it doesn't bother me very much now."

"And the second mistake?"

"Well, you cut off a piece of my penis by accident!"

"Oh, my God! What else?"

"Well, you put my testicles where my ears should be! But it's okay; now I can tell people to 'Write their name on my balls' [raises hands to ears and brushes ears with fingertips several times] much easier!"

[Legman II:639; D1273.1.1., Three as magic number; X372.4., Foolish doctor performs useless operation.]

279 A man went into a coffeehouse in Athens. When the waiter came he said:

"Bring me a piece of cake. But not too sweet and not too bitter. Just in between."

So the waiter brought him the cake. A while later the same customer called the waiter again:

"Bring me a cup of coffee, but not too hot and not too cold, but just in the middle."

So the waiter brought him the coffee. Later the customer called the waiter again and said:

"Bring me an orangeade, but not too sweet and not too sour, but just in the middle."

So the waiter brought him the orangeade. When the customer was ready to leave, the waiter said:

"I'm going to fix your bill now. It won't be too high, and it won't be too low, it'll be just in the middle [gives 'To my balls!' gesture]!"

[D1273.1.1., Three as magic number.]

280 One time, a man went rabbit hunting with his hunting dog. But the dog wasn't too bright and would often chase other animals (goats, sheep) as well as rabbits.

Well, the dog took off after what appeared to be a rabbit. And he chased and ran and chased the animal.

Finally, the rabbit was exhausted, so he decided to try to trick the dog. At the edge of the village, the rabbit stopped still in the middle of the road and dropped his ears so that he would resemble another hunting dog.

Well, the hunter's dog came running up and saw the rabbit, but, thinking that it was a dog, asked:

"Which way did the rabbit go?"

So the rabbit lifted one of its ears and pointed in the opposite direction, and the dog went charging off!

Then the man came up and, seeing the rabbit, exclaimed:

"What are *you* doing here? My hunting dog just passed by and is looking for you! He should have torn you to pieces!"

"Don't tell me about your dog," said the rabbit. "I just wrote his name here [gives 'To my balls!' gesture]!"

[B211.2.6., Speaking hare.]

The following joke is a picture riddle that involves a drawing. It also is another type of catch joke, as the listener is the unwitting victim of the "To my balls!" gesture.

281 Question: Can you draw the number seven [European style, drawn with two strokes as 7] without lifting the pen from the paper?

Answer: Draw the number four without lifting the pen and then give the "To my balls!" gesture and say:

"Four plus three is seven!"

The next joke must be acted out to "catch" the listener.

282 Stand on the right leg with the foot of the left leg touching the right knee. In this position the legs resemble the number four. The person then asks another which number he represents. The other will immediately recognize the number four. Then the teller gives the "To my balls!" gesture and says, "Plus three is seven!"

283 One time, two homosexuals bought a new car. So on Sunday they went for a drive. Since they were very nervous, they drove very slowly, causing the drivers in back of them to get very nervous. Finally, Gregoris, who was driving, stopped the car very suddenly, and the car in back of them struck their new car!

Everybody got out of the two automobiles to assess the damages. There was a small dent in the back of the queer's new car.

"Don't call the police; I'll give you five hundred drachmes!" said the driver of the other car.

"Stamatis, call one hundred [the telephone number of the police in Athens]!"

"I'll give you one thousand drachmes," said the other driver.

"Stamatis, call one hundred!"

"Okay, I'll give you five thousand drachmes!"

"Stamatis, call one hundred!"

"Oh, write your names on my balls!" [gives gesture].

"Stop, Stamatis!" said Gregoris. "We've made a deal!"

[Legman II:91.]

Jokes with Gestures Indicating Sexual Intercourse

Greeks use at least three different gestures to mean sexual intercourse. These gestures do not indicate the insulting retort "Fuck you!" as "giving the finger," or "shooting the bird," does in America; they simply imply copulation and thus are not insult gestures. In the first gesture, the two index fingers are rubbed together, back and forth. This gesture can mean simply "together," but it is often used in reference to two people who are "going together" and having sex together. The following is an example of a joke that uses this gesture.

284 One time, a young man saw a sexy young girl on the street of Athens wearing a miniskirt. So he started following her:

"Psst, psst, hey, beautiful, let's get together," said the boy.

But the girl ignored him and kept walking.

"Psst, psst, hey, gorgeous, tell me something! Tell me pussy!"

"Don't you have any shame?" asked the girl, and she kept on walking.

"Psst, psst, hey, sexy, tell me something! Tell me cock!"

"If I wouldn't say pussy, what makes you think I'd say cock?" asked the stupid girl.

"Ah, that's even better," said the boy, rubbing his two index fingers together back and forth, implying copulation. "You said both of the words at the same time!"

The second gesture that means copulation is what I call the "sidewinder" gesture. The hand, usually the right hand, is halfway closed. One of the middle fingers, either the third or the fourth finger, is held down, almost touching the palm of the hand. Then the entire hand is moved rapidly sideways, from left to right, several times. It is a much more subtle gesture than the American "finger," or "bird," gesture and sometimes cannot be seen except by those who are intended to see it. A joke that involves this gesture follows.

285 One time, there was a bachelor who had a very scrofulous parrot. Everytime a woman would come into the bachelor's apartment, the parrot would shriek:

"Fuck her! Fuck her!"

Well, one day a special girlfriend was coming to dinner, and so the man took the parrot and wrapped tape around its beak so it couldn't say those bad things!

Well, the man and his girlfriend were sitting on the sofa, and the parrot slowly crept over, little by little, and climbed up onto the coffee table in front of the couple. Then, he started doing this [gives sidewinder gesture]!

The third gesture that means copulation is widely known and used in Latin American and Mediterranean countries; I call it the "jump." However, I don't believe it is understood or used in America. The two hands are clenched into fists (palms up), and the arms are first held away from the trunk of the body. The two arms are then brought straight toward the trunk of the body until the fists reach the abdomen. Sometimes a pelvic thrust accompanies the arm motion. It is often a very subtle gesture in Greece, whereas in Mexico it usually is performed in a violent jerking motion. My favorite joke that involves this gesture is one that also plays on a common Greek theme. To appreciate the joke, which follows, it is helpful to know that Greeks are extremely fun-loving people and spend hours eating and drinking instead of the shorter period of time normally spent at the table in America. When, finally, the meal is finished, Greeks will often say, "We ate, we drank, now if we only had a good woman!"

286 Two Greeks are overheard at a table in a *tavérna* in Plaka:
"We ate, we drank, now if only we had a good *newspaper* [gestures to indicate opening a newspaper] to *read* [gives the jump gesture of copulation]!"

The following is another joke that uses the jump gesture of copulation. As understanding it greatly depends on seeing the accompanying gestures, it may lose much in the transcription.

287 One time, there was a couple. Well, the husband had a job in a factory, and one day his boss told him that they didn't need him any more, that he was fired. So he went home and told his wife that he had lost his job.
"Well," said the wife, "if you don't find another job, I'm leaving you!"
So the man went to another factory, a mill where cloth was made, and said to the foreman:
"Please, I don't have work. Can you give me a job?"
"Sorry," said the man, "we don't have any work now."
"Please, please," said the man, "if I don't get a job, my wife will leave me!"
"Okay," said the foreman, "if you let me fuck your wife every day, then I'll give you a job. Otherwise, nothing!"
"But that's not right," protested the man.
"If you want to work, then bring me your wife tomorrow morning. If not, then forget it!"
So the man went to his wife, and she agreed to the plan. So the next

day they went to the factory together, and the foreman took the wife, and the husband got the job.

So the husband was working on a weaving machine. And as he pushed the spindle to the left, he said to himself, "You wanted it!" And as he pushed the spindle to the right, he said, "You did it!" And as he pulled the comb down on the cloth, he said, "Now pull out your hair!" [The three comments are made with three gestures: first, the hand is brought to the left; then the other hand is brought to the right; then the two hands are brought toward the trunk of the body in the gesture implying copulation. This part of the joke is repeated several times.]

One day the wife of the foreman saw the man working at the loom and heard what he was saying.

"Come here, my boy," said the woman.

"Yes, madam, what do you want?" asked the man.

"What are you doing with the 'you wanted it, you did it, now pull your hair out'?"

"Well, I needed a job, and the only way the foreman would give me one was if I let him fuck my wife every day!"

"Well," said the woman, "I'm the foreman's wife and so I'll let you fuck *me* every day!"

So later that day, when the man was fucking the foreman's wife, he started saying:

"*My* wife [right hand pushing to the left]!"

"*Your* wife [left hand pushing to the right]!"

"And *that's* how it is [two fists brought toward trunk of the body]!"

[The punchline is performed three times.]

[D1273.1.1., Three as magic number; F856.1., Loom made of woman's breasts with vagina as shuttle; X251., Jokes on weavers.]

Jokes with the Múntza Gesture

One of the most interesting of all Greek gestures is the *múntza*: the open palm, with a various number of fingers, faces the person to be insulted. In its mildest form it is similar to the "victory" sign of World War II or to the "peace" sign of more recent times. Usually, in the case of the *múntza*, however, two fingers are thrust violently toward the person to be insulted. In a yet more aggressive form, the gesturer strikes the top of one hand with the other hand, then violently thrusts the two hands, with all ten fingers outstretched, to the insulted party. For even greater, more dramatic insults, one can add the feet, one at a time, or both together if one is seated, to the thrusting motion. Greeks speak of two (as first described), five (the open hand with five fingers), ten (the two hands), fifteen (two hands and one foot), or twenty (two hands and two feet) as a measure of the intensity of the insult that, using the *múntza*, they direct toward others.

The origin of the *múntza* gesture is obscure. The word itself has been borrowed from Romany, the language of the Gypsies who live in Greece; it means "pussy," or "cunt." One popular explanation of the origin of the *múntza* that I collected is the following:

> In the olden times, when someone was thrown out of a village, all of the villagers would rub charcoal and other black filth on their hands and wait in line. The person who was being ejected would have to pass through this line of hostile villagers, who would thrust their hands, dirty with filth of various types, into the face of the damned. This is the origin of the *múntza* curse.

There seems to be no equivalent English expression to substitute for either the *múntza* gesture or its implied insult. Books that I am familiar with translate the *múntza* curse as "Go to Hell!" But translated as such, the curse is not nearly strong enough to produce the extreme reaction of most Greeks on the receiving end of the insult. For instance, one Cretan woman I know told me how she cured her small daughter from making the evocative gesture. After the child first gave her mother the *múntza*, the woman slapped the girl (probably about four years old). The child, in stubbornness, repeated the gesture. The woman spanked her. The arrogant child defiantly gave the *múntza* again. The woman picked up a rock and beat the girl's hand until it was bloody so that she would learn never to insult her mother like that.

The following joke illustrates and utilizes the *múntza*.

288 One time, a man got really angry with the owner of the village coffeehouse. Well, one day when he was drunk, he went into the coffeehouse and said to somebody sitting there:

"Want to bet me that I'll break all the windows in the place?"

"Sit down, sit down!" the man told him.

So he said to somebody else in the place:

"Want to bet me that I'll break all the tables and chairs in here?"

Well, the owner heard what the drunk man was saying. So the owner came over and told him:

"You look tired! Sit down and let me fix you a coffee, and then have a brandy, and you'll feel better."

"Take that!" said the drunk, giving the man the five-finger *múntza* curse.

Then the drunk asked another man in the place:

"Do you mind if I say something to your donkey that is outside?" (The donkey was standing in front of the coffeehouse.) "I know how to talk to donkeys!"

So the drunk went outside and went over to the donkey and said something into the donkey's ear. (The drunk had a lit cigarette in his mouth, so he really just burned the donkey in the ear!)

Well, the poor donkey went crazy and went running inside the coffeehouse and broke all the tables, chairs, cups, glasses, and even the windows! The place was smashed to bits!

So the owner of the coffeehouse took the drunk man to court for making the donkey break everything in his coffeehouse.

Well, the judge said that they couldn't fine the drunk man since it was the donkey who broke everything in the shop.

"But," said the judge to the offender, "since you cursed the owner of the coffeehouse with the *múntza*, I'm going to fine you half a *líre!*"

Well, the man reached into his pocket and took out a one-*líre* gold coin and gave it to the judge.

So the judge asked the clerk of court to get change for the *líre*, but he couldn't find any change.

So the man told the judge:

"Here, take this [gives the five-finger *múntza*] and keep the whole *líre* instead!"

[J1193.2.1., The court keeps the change; X16.1.*, Mule goes on a rampage and causes melee (Rotunda 1942).]

Other obscene gestures are in use in Greece today (the "finger," or "bird," is understood and used on occasion, for example), but none of them are pertinent to any of the jokes that I collected. One of those gestures, however, was used in joke

48, and a description of it seems in order here: the right hand is held with fingers up and in imitation of the shape of the fig; the hand is lowered about two inches as weighing something. In ancient Greece, as mentioned above in connection with joke 197, the fig was the symbol of the male genitals, particularly the testicles. Today, in popular Greek slang, to call a man a "fig" is to call him a homosexual, a "queer"; the implication is that he is "nothing but balls."[9]

ANIMAL JOKES

Animals, particularly talking animals, appear in the folklore of all peoples of the world. Talking animals are also very important figures in the world's mythology. Some good examples of animal jokes that are not *sókin* must circulate in Greece, but I heard few; indeed, most animal jokes told in Greece are very *sókin*. (Exceptions are "elephant jokes," which constituted a joke fad in America a few years ago and which are also told in Greece.) Moreover, Greek jokes that involve animals place heavy emphasis on the parrot as a trickster figure.

Parrots, and birds in general, probably symbolize the penis, if a Freudian interpretation is taken. For example, in the "bird" gesture—which means "Fuck you!"—the middle, or third, finger is thrust upward as the other fingers are bent down. The raised finger, the "bird," is a symbol of the penis. Another indication that the bird is a male symbol is that in many languages "bird" is often used as a euphemism for "penis." In Greek the word for "little bird" (*pouláki*) can have many meanings, including "penis."

The parrot is a very male symbol, traditionally associated with bad language, with sailors, and, for some reason, with shaving. Two widely known parrot jokes in Greece involve shaving. In America the parrot was the mascot for a well-known company that manufactures razors and blades and that used to sponsor boxing matches on television. The rooster is another supermale symbol. I heard one rooster joke in Greece, but I remember also hearing it years ago in America.

Other animals appearing in Greek humor are elephants and fleas, also found in jokes heard in America. Of the jokes I heard in Greece, the owl appears in only one, the first joke below.

289 One time, a couple was making love in the woods. A wise old owl was watching them. After they finished the woman (naked) sat on a pine needle and screamed in pain!

"People are so strange!" said the wise owl. "First he puts a big stick in her, and nothing! Then she sits on a little stick, and she screams!"

[B122.0.3., Wise owl; B210., Talking animals.]

290 A man from a village went to Athens. As he was passing a store in the big open-air market, he saw a man selling a rooster.

"How much is that rooster?" asked the villager.

"Ten thousand drachmes," said the man.

"Are you crazy? Ten thousand drachmes for a rooster?"

"Yes, but this rooster is really something! He never stops screwing! He screws all the chickens night and day!"

So the villager bought the rooster and took him home.

Well, the next morning when the man woke up, he saw that all his hens were dead! They had been screwed to death! And there on the ground was the rooster, and he was dead, too!

There were buzzards circling overhead, and when the man started to shoo them away, the rooster opened one eye and said:

"Wait, stay back! Let them come down a bit closer so I can screw them, too!"

[B211.3.2., Speaking cock.]

291 Sometime, Tarzan was the *kumbáros* [wedding sponsor] for Cheeta, the chimpanzee, and a lady giraffe.

About a month later Cheeta came over to visit Tarzan, and he couldn't walk straight!

"What's the matter?" asked Tarzan. "Don't you like married life?"

"Oh, yes, yes! But, you see, I have to climb up to kiss her, then climb down to fuck her, and all the running up and down is killing me!"

[Legman I:196; B210., Talking animals; B280., Animal weddings.]

The next joke could fit easily into the section on scatalogical humor in chapter nine, "Light *Sókin* Jokes."

292 Tarzan was leaving the jungle for a month to go to the city. Before he left he built a big latrine and ordered all the animals to shit in the latrine and not to mess up the jungle!

Well, when he returned he saw Mr. Hare shitting under a bush!

"Hey! What are you doing? Don't you remember what I said about using the latrine?"

"Yes, I remember," said the rabbit. "But you don't know what happened to me! The first time I went to shit in the latrine, there was an elephant in there doing his work. And he asked me if I was losing my hair! Well, when I told him no, he picked me up with his trunk and used me to wipe his ass. That's why I'm not in the latrine anymore!"

[B210., Talking animals; J1882., Foolish attempt to educate animals.]

293 One time, a bird went to fuck an elephant. Well, just as he was getting ready, the elephant farted, and all the bird's feathers were blown away!

"Ha, ha, ha!" said the elephant.

"What so funny?" asked the bird. "Doesn't the husband take off his clothes before he fucks his wife?"

[B210., Talking animals; 244A**, Sparrow's Courtship of the Mare.]

294 One time, in the jungle, an ant said to an elephant:

"I'm going to fuck you!"

"Ha, ha," said the elephant. "You're so small, it's impossible!"

So the ant climbed up the elephant's leg, and, just when he went inside the elephant's asshole, a coconut fell and hit the elephant on the head. So the elephant yelled in pain!

"Ah, ha! It really hurts, eh?" said the ant.

[Legman I:196; B210., Talking animals; X734.5.3., Sparrow has intercourse with elephant; wonders if he is hurting her.]

295 An elephant and a flea were best friends. One day the flea complained to the elephant:

"I'm really jealous of you! You have such a big penis, and mine is so small that none of the women want me!"

So the elephant said:

"That's no problem any more. Down in Cape Town Dr. Barnard can fix you with a big penis if you want!"

"But I don't have any money," said the flea.

"Never mind, I'll pay the bills," said the elephant.

So they went to Cape Town and to Dr. Barnard's office.

"Can you graft him a big penis?" asked the elephant.

"Of course I can," said the doctor.

So after the operation the flea was sleeping, and he dreamed that he was having sex. Well, he had an orgasm, and he drowned in his own sperm!

[B210., Talking animals; X372.4., Foolish doctor performs useless operation.]

The remaining animal jokes deal with the star of this section, the parrot. In Greece the teller typically tries to imitate a parrot's voice when he or she tells the jokes. Pertinent also in the first joke to follow is that in Greek folklore, as in the folklore of other Mediterranean countries where Christians live, the Holy Ghost is often depicted as a bird, a dove or a pigeon. According to my informants, God sent with a dove the message to Mary that she was to be the Mother of God. Crude jokes often depict the Holy Ghost as a pigeon.

296 A parrot died and went to heaven. A week after he was there, he saw Saint Peter.

"How do you like it in heaven?" asked St. Peter.

"Terrible," replied the parrot. "There's no good sex up here at all!"

Two weeks passed, and again Saint Peter saw the parrot.

"How's everything going?" he asked.

"Just great!" he replied. "I've met this super pigeon, and we're really having a good time [gives the sidewinder gesture of copulation]!"

"Oh, my God!" said Saint Peter. "You're fucking the Holy Ghost!"

[B211.3.4., Speaking parrot; J1118.1., Clever parrot.]

297 A man had a parrot. Well, across the street, on the opposite balcony, lived a female parrot.

So the parrot went across the street and asked the owner of the female parrot:

"Can I fuck your parrot?"

"Yes," replied the man, "but you'll have to pay one hundred drachmes!"

So the parrot got the money from his owner, and he fucked the female parrot.

Well, the owner of the female parrot kept raising the price, from one hundred to two, then three, then five. So after that the owner of the parrot didn't want to pay and told the parrot that he couldn't go with the parrot across the street any more.

A month later the parrot again wanted to fuck the female parrot. But this time her owner wanted one thousand drachmes!

"No, that's too much," said the parrot's owner.

"Please, just this last time," pleaded the parrot.

So the owner agreed, but he insisted that it was absolutely the last time!

So the two parrots were together in the room for one, then two, then three hours! Finally, the two owners opened the door to see what was going on.

Well, the male parrot had plucked all the feathers out of the female!

"What did you do that for?" asked the owner of the female.

"What do you think," asked the parrot, "we'd pay one thousand drachmes to fuck her with her clothes on?"

[B211.3.4., Speaking parrot; J1118.1., Clever parrot; K2382.1., Bird plucks out another bird's feathers.]

Perhaps the oversexed parrot has replaced the rooster in the animal jokes, for, as in the following, he is often depicted as screwing chickens.

298 One time, a truck driver was on his way to Athens from Thessaloniki with a load of live chickens. In the cab of his truck was his parrot, a scrofulous bird that always said obscenities. He kept the parrot to amuse himself and help pass the time.

Well, he saw a girl hitchhiking, so he stopped the truck, put the parrot in back with the chickens (so as not to embarrass the girl), and let the girl into the cab.

"How far are you going?" she asked.

"To Athens," he said.

"Great, me too!" said the girl.

A few minutes later the truck driver said:

"You're really a pretty girl, and I like you a lot!"

"Thank you," said the girl.

"After a while can I kiss you?"

"No! Of course not!" said the girl.

"Can I caress you then?"

"No! What do you think?"

"Then can I fuck you?"

"Of course not!"

"No? Then get out of the truck," said the man, stopping and opening the door for the girl to get out.

But after a minute he thought, "Maybe I was being too hasty. Maybe she'll change her mind later." So he opened the door again and motioned for her to get back into the truck.

[The teller repeats the episode about four times.]

Finally, they arrived in Athens, and the truck driver still hadn't gotten even a little kiss! He let the girl out of the truck and drove to the market.

When he opened the door of the truck to take out the chickens, what did he see? Nothing! All the chickens were gone, except for one or two. And the parrot was saying:

"Can I kiss you? Can I fuck you? No? Then get out of the truck!"

[Legman I:202; B211.3.4., Speaking parrot; J1118.1., Clever parrot.]

299 Sometime, there was a man who had a parrot. Well, the parrot was always saying bad words. So the man put the parrot out with the chickens one day when his wife had some ladies over for coffee so that the women wouldn't be embarrassed.

Well, when he went to get the parrot, he saw that the parrot had fucked all of the chickens! So the man got angry and plucked all of the parrot's feathers out!

"There, you bald fucker!" he told the bird.

Well, one night some friends came over to the man's house for an unexpected visit. There was one man who was bald. So the parrot started shrieking:

"Ladies to the left, gentlemen to the right, and bald fuckers to the back!"

[Legman I:201; B211.3.4., Speaking parrot; D1273.1.1., Three as magic number; J1118.1., Clever parrot.]

In another version (299a) of the preceding joke, a priest has the bad parrot who fucks the chickens and then gets the feathers plucked out of his head. Then the next Sunday the priest takes the parrot to church (men and women usually stand on opposite sides of the church in Orthodox services in rural Greece), where he begins directing the people: "Ladies to the left, men to the right, bald-headed fuckers up here with me!" (Legman I:201; D1273.1.1., Three as magic number.)

The Greek word *pinélo* is used for a painter's (artist's) brush and for a man's shaving brush. The slang expression "doing the *pinélo*" means performing sexual acts involving the tongue or the penis when either is used to stroke the partner's body in sexual foreplay. The following joke involves an understanding of this popular expression.

300 A lady had a parrot, and one day when she got home she saw him swallowing her husband's shaving brush!

Naturally, the poor bird's belly was about to pop open, so right away she took the parrot to the nearest clinic.

Well, it was a maternity clinic, and, as they were waiting their turn to see the doctor, a lady about to deliver her baby came in and sat in the waiting room.

"I know what you've been doing!" shrieked the parrot. "The shaving brush, the shaving brush [*To pinélo, to pinélo*]!"

[B211.3.4., Speaking parrot; J1118.1., Clever parrot.]

The following is another version of the preceding joke.

300a One time, a barber had a parrot. Well, one day, the barber got carried away while lathering one of his customers; his hand was flinging the shaving brush back and forth like crazy! Well, the brush slipped out of his hand, went flying across the room, and at that moment the parrot was shrieking and the brush flew into the parrot's mouth and he swallowed it! Well, naturally, the parrot's stomach was bulging!

Just then, a pregnant woman passed the barber shop. And the parrot yelled:

"She ate the *pinélo*, she ate the *pinélo*!"

[B211.3.4., Speaking parrot; J1118.1., Clever parrot.]

301 Sometime, a married couple had a parrot. Well, one day when the husband went to the bathroom to shave, the parrot followed him and started to shriek:

"You're going to cut yourself! You're going to cut yourself!"

"Shut up," said the man. "You're making me nervous!"

But the parrot went right on:

"You're going to cut yourself! You're going to cut yourself!"

So the man got angry and grabbed the parrot and put him inside the toilet and closed the lid on top of him! That way he couldn't hear the bird.

When he finished shaving he forgot to remove the parrot from the toilet!

A while later his wife went to the bathroom and went to use the toilet. She opened the lid and sat down, not realizing that the parrot was inside! She was having her period, too! So the parrot looked up at her pussy and said:

"I told you that you'd cut yourself, and you didn't get all the hair off, either!"

[Legman I:204; B211.3.4., Speaking parrot; J1118.1., Clever parrot.]

302   Once there was a magician on a cruise ship. Every night he had a show, and he would produce unusual items from his pockets. He also had a parrot, and the parrot was part of the act. Sometimes the magician would also make things disappear into his pockets!

Well, one day the ship sank! The magician managed to rescue himself and his parrot on a piece of floating wood.

Well, the parrot was perched on his shoulder, and it said to him:

"Okay, wise guy! Take the ship out of your pocket or I'll bite your ear off!"

[Legman II:981; B211.3.4., Speaking parrot; J1118.1., Clever parrot.]

303   One time, a Greek ship sank, and in one lifeboat was the captain, the chief engineer, and a sailor with a parrot.

Well, after a week the food ran out. There was just some rice left.

"What will we eat now?" asked the captain.

"Let's kill the parrot and fix *piláfi* [similar to chicken and rice]," said the chief engineer.

The sailor, who didn't want to lose his parrot, said:

"I have a better idea! Let's all masturbate, and then we can fix *rizógala* [rice with milk, similar to rice pudding]!"

[D1273.1.1., Three as magic number.]

Chapter 9
Light *Sókin* Jokes

The jokes in this chapter are only "a little" *sókin*, or, rather than being explicit, they leave the vulgar conclusion to the imagination of the listener. Most of them do not have any offensive words in the texts, and they frequently recount family situations. Many of them depict relatives within the nuclear or the extended family. Other jokes, such as those at the end of the chapter, deal with villagers and village life, which are described in slightly *sókin* terms.

The jokes collected here were told in mixed groups when the tellers didn't want to offend someone, usually a lady, who was present. I collected many of the jokes from teenagers in a night-school class that I taught for two months. Others I heard from children. The primary theme of the jokes is still sex, but it is veiled, rather than explicit, sex. The first several jokes to follow involve family situations. The first seven depict parents and children.

304 One time, in a village, a mother told her little eight-year-old son to take the she-goat out to the enclosure where the billy goat was and to wait and then later to bring the she-goat back to the house. She thought that her son was too young to understand that she wanted to mate the two animals.

When the little boy returned after an hour, his mother asked him what had happened.

"The billy goat spoke to her and spoke to her, but she didn't understand what he said! So the billy goat took out a red pencil and wrote it down on her back side so she could understand!"

[Legman I:52.]

305 One day Helenitsa went to play jump rope with her brother and his friend Johnny.

"Now don't jump too high," said her mother, "or the boys will see your under pants!"

When she came back her mother asked:

"Helenitsa, did you remember not to jump too high as I told you?"

"No," said the girl. "But I took off my panties so the boys wouldn't see them!"

[Legman I:226.]

Greek girls are traditionally trained to have "shame" (*tropí*) concerning their bodies. The implication of the preceding joke is that, not only does the girl behave immodestly, but she also at a very early age fits the stereotypical image of the oversexed female.

306 Sometime, there was a poor couple who didn't have enough money to buy beds for their two sons. So the parents slept in the same bed with the two boys!

Well, when the boys were five and six, one night the younger boy was awakened and said to his brother:

"Hey! Stop rocking me!"

"I'm not doing it!" said the older brother. "Father is rocking Mother, so we are rocking us!"

307 One day a little boy asked his father:

"Daddy, can I have permission to marry Grandmother?"

"Are you crazy?" asked the father. "How can you marry my mother?"

"In that case," said the boy, "how did you marry *my* mother?"

308 There was a married couple who had a very small house, so their children slept in the same room with them. Well, the children started getting older and started asking questions.

One morning the oldest son asked:

"Daddy, what were you and Mama doing last night that made so much noise?"

"Johnny," said the father, "Mama and I were writing a letter on the typewriter."

Since the boy was young, that answer satisfied him.

A few days later the parents had an argument, and so they stopped talking to each other.

One afternoon, when Johnny came home from school, his father said to him:

"Johnny, go tell Mother to come here so we can write a letter on the typewriter."

So the boy left, and when he returned he said:

"Mama says she's busy and for you to write the letter by hand!"

309   One time, a small boy saw his mother naked in the bathroom.

"What's that?" he asked, pointing to her.

"That's my garage," said the mother.

"What's that?" he asked, pointing to himself.

"That's your little car," said the mother.

"Can I put my little car inside your garage?" asked the boy.

"No, no, because tonight your daddy is going to put his big truck inside."

So that night the boy went sneaking into his parents' bedroom, and he saw them in bed together.

"Daddy," he said, "you forgot to put the two back wheels of your truck inside Mama's garage!"

[Legman I:52.]

The next joke involves the universal problem of the nosy younger sibling, but, as Greek boys are responsible for the chaperoning of their sisters, in this joke the boy is merely fulfilling his duty to his family.

310   A boy was sent to the store to buy a jar of mustard. On the way home he saw his sister sneaking out of the house. So he decided to follow her so later he could tattletale to his father.

Well, the girl went to a park and sat down on a bench. So the brother climbed up into a tree behind her and watched.

After a while the girl's boyfriend came and sat next to her. They were holding hands and kissing.

"Ah, my love," said the girl, "my pussy is like bread!"

"Oh, my little doll," said the boyfriend, "my pee-pee is like a salami!"

So the little brother said:

"Would you like some mustard, maybe, so you can make a sandwich?"

[T35., Lovers' rendezvous.]

311 A village girl went to town. It was very windy, and the wind kept blowing her skirt up.

As she passed a shop whose owner was from her village, she went inside.

"Oh, my Virgin!" she exclaimed. "It's so windy that my skirt keeps blowing up and embarrassing me. I don't know what to do!"

"Listen, my child," said the shopowner, "go to the hardware store and buy two weights and sew them inside the hem of your skirt. They will keep it down."

So the girl left the store to go and get the weights.

After a few hours she passed by the store again.

"Is everything okay now?" asked the man who owned the store.

"Yes, but I'm really perplexed," said the girl.

"Why?"

"Because you men have two weights (implying balls), and they don't keep it from flying up!"

The next joke refers to a universal custom in Greece: children are named after their grandparents. Usually, the oldest son is named after the paternal grandfather, and the eldest daughter after the paternal grandmother; subsequent children are often named after the maternal grandparents. The custom of naming children after one of the parents, not uncommon in America, is almost nonexistent in Greece.

312 George was named after his grandfather. After the grandfather died his grandmother took special interest in the boy. He became her "pet."

When George finished high school, he decided to study in a university in Italy. He would be gone for four years. So his grandmother promised to send him money, but he had to promise to write to her and send her some photos of himself from time to time.

After George had been gone for two years, he met some tourists one time on the beach, and they all went swimming in the nude. Later they took some photos in the nude on the beach, and they gave George one of the photos of himself.

A few months later Geroge needed some money, so he decided to write to his grandmother. Then he remembered that she wanted him to send her a photo, but he only had the one in which he was nude. So he cut the nude photo in half, to send her the upper half of the picture.

Well, by mistake he enclosed the bottom half of the picture with his letter!

When his grandmother received the letter, she took out the photo and stared at it. But her eyesight was very bad, and she wasn't wearing her glasses.

"Just look at that!" she said. "He's the image of his grandfather, except that his tie is crooked!"

[N825.3.3., Help from grandmother.]

313 One time, a foolish man went to visit his married sister. He hadn't been to see her for a long time. So his sister gave him a big welcome and said:

"Sit down here in the living room. Would you like some coffee?"

The brother accepted. Well, the woman had a small son about eighteen months old, so she left the baby with her brother in the living room and went to the kitchen to fix the coffee.

Well, the baby got restless and wouldn't sit still. Then the baby started to cry and scream.

So the man was holding the baby, and he didn't know what to do, so in exasperation he opened his fly and pulled out his penis! And the baby started playing with his penis and stopped crying!

When the sister came into the living room and saw the baby playing with her brother's penis, she screamed and dropped the coffee on the floor!

"You crazy jackass! Aren't you ashamed of yourself, letting the baby play with your penis?"

"What else should I have done?" asked the man. "Was it better to give him a spoon to gouge his eyes out with?"

[Legman I:603; Variant of AT1408, Man Who Does His Wife's Work, Does Everything Wrong; Variant of AT1681B, Fool As Custodian of Home and Animals.]

The next joke illustrates the customs of the arranged marriage and the dowry still practiced in some parts of Greece.

314 One day two friends were talking in the coffeehouse.

"I've got a big dilemma," said one of the men. "The matchmaker has found me two girls to marry. One is a telephone operator; the other is a schoolteacher."

"Two girls! That's great! Which will you marry?"

"I can't decide. They're both pretty, but the telephone operator is prettier. And they both have nice dowries, but the telephone operator's dowry is worth more money. But I can't decide what to do!"

So the other friend said:

"Well, take the telephone operator if she's prettier and has a bigger dowry."

"I don't know. I've got to think it over."

Well, two weeks later the two friends saw each other.

"I finally made up my mind," said the first.

"Oh? You'll marry the telephone operator?"

"No, the schoolteacher."

"The schoolteacher? But why?"

"Well, I thought it over, and I realized something. After three minutes the telephone operator always tells you you're finished. But the schoolteacher always makes you do your work over and over again!"

[T52.4., Dowry given at marriage of daughter; T53.0.1., Matchmakers arrange weddings.]

The next two jokes involve the honeymoon situation. Greeks usually marry on a Sunday evening and may spend the first night in a hotel, but rarely more than the one night. Very few couples in Greece take what we call a "honeymoon trip," for most of them move directly into their new home to begin married life there. Increasing numbers of young people today move into an apartment that they have furnished prior to the wedding instead of into a new house.

315 Three couples got married on the same Sunday and went to the same hotel for their wedding nights.

The next day the three husbands were talking about how they passed the night:

"My wife kept blowing the horn all night, so I'm really tired today," said the first.

"That's nothing," said the second. "My wife kept changing gears all night, and I'm really tired today!"

The third man said:

"I'm the tiredest of all of you, because my wife kept putting in more gasoline and going again!"

[Legman I:239; D1273.1.1., Three as magic number.]

316   Three couples got married on the same day, and, after the honeymoon was over, the three husbands got together to talk.

"We really had a great time! We went sightseeing, walking, dancing, and the like. It was great!"

The second man said:

"We had a better time because we didn't leave the room!"

"How did you enjoy yourself?" they asked the third man.

"Thursday morning—" he began.

They interrupted him:

"Never mind Thursday morning, what did you do on Sunday night?"

"Thursday morning," continued the man, "my wife asked me to stop so she could go to the toilet!"

[Legman I:239; D1273.1.1., Three as magic number.]

In the following jokes the honeymoon is over.

317   Once a man and his wife had a fight. So she got really angry and cut off his pee-pee and threw it out the window!

Well, a little boy passed by and saw it and picked it up and took it home. When his mother saw it, she screamed, and she threw it out the window!

Then a priest saw it and picked it up and put it into his pocket.

Later, in church, when the priest was giving his sermon, he reached into his pocket to take out his cross, but by mistake he pulled out the pee-pee instead and said:

"And this, my children, is what Christians believe in!"

318   Sometime, there was an old-fashioned couple who had seven children. So the wife went to the doctor and asked him what to do so she wouldn't get pregnant again.

Well, in those days there was no birth control.

So the doctor told her:

"When you see your husband looking at you, and his eyes are burning with desire, get away from him fast!"

"But, doctor," protested the wife, "at that moment, I don't see *anything!*"

[Legman II:233; D1273.1.1., Three as magic number.]

319   A man in a village had nine children. The last child was baptized by a doctor. So one day the father went to the doctor and said:

"Eh, *kumbáre*, can you do me a favor?"

"Of course, what do you want?"

"Can you give me some medicine to take so that my wife won't get pregnant again?"

So the doctor gave the man a box of prophylactics and said:

"Before you go with your wife, put one of these on."

Well, the man had never seen rubbers before, so he didn't understand. So, before he had sex with his wife the next time, he swallowed one of the rubbers with a glass of water.

Well, the wife got pregnant again. And one day the man saw the doctor on the street.

"Hey, *kumbáre*, how's everything?" asked the doctor.

"Terrible!" said the man. "Not only is my wife pregnant again, but I keep pissing balloons all the time!"

[Legman I:430–31; AT1349N*, Leaches Eaten by Patient; X727.3., Contraceptives mistaken for something else.]

320   There was a pregnant woman on the train. In the same compart-ment was a man who started smoking a cigar.

"Please, sir," she said, "will you stop smoking that cigar? It's not for me that I ask, but for my—" (points to her stomach).

Later, when the man opened the window in the compartment, the woman asked him to close the window.

"It's not for me that I ask, it's for my—" (points to her stomach again).

After a while, to relax a bit, the woman put her legs up on the opposite seat. Her skirt got pulled up, and the man was looking at her legs and up her skirt and got excited.

"Please, madam," he said, "put your legs down. It's not for me that I ask, it's for my—" (points to his penis)!

321   One time, a woman was pregnant, and she had twins inside her. Well, the twins would play together, and sometimes they would fight.

One day one of the twins said to the other:

"I'm going outside; I'm tired of being in here all the time!"

So the other twin said:

"You can't go out now; it's raining! Didn't you see the other guy who came in just now wearing a raincoat?"

[Legman I:584; A511.1.2.1., Twins quarrel before birth; T575.1., Child speaks in mother's womb.]

322 A grandmother was keeping her little grandson. And she was having trouble getting him to eat his dinner.

"Eat your spinach," said the grandmother. "It will make your hair curly."

"No!" said the boy.

"Eat the spinach. It will make you grow tall!"

"No, I don't want it!"

"Eat your spinach, and it will make your little penis get bigger."

"No," said the boy.

Well, the grandfather heard what she said, and he came into the kitchen and said:

"Give *me* some spinach to eat in that case!"

323 One time, there were two women: an old woman and her daughter. Well, they went for a walk down to the harbor.

"Oh, look at that beautiful ship!" said the daughter.

"Where? I don't see it," said the woman. "But look at that sailor pissing over there!"

"Oh, yes, I see him. He's on the deck of the ship that you didn't see!"

324 A salesman knocked at the door of a house. An attractive woman answered the door:

"Yes, what do you want?"

"Excuse me, but is your husband home?"

"No, he went out of town on business."

"When will he return?"

"Oh, in two or three days," said the woman.

"Well, do you mind if I come inside and wait for him?"

325 A woman went shopping one day to buy underwear. She went into one store and saw that the undershirts were thirty drachmes and the underpants were fifty drachmes.

So she went to another store, and the undershirts were forty-five drachmes, and the underpants were forty drachmes.

"What's going on?" she said out loud. "The undershirts are going up and the underpants are going down!"

Professional fortune telling is a popular and thriving business in Greece. One of the most widely practiced nonprofessional ways of telling the future is by having someone, usually a woman, read the patterns of sediment left in a coffeecup after the liquid has been consumed. The following joke plays on that popular form of divination.

326   Once a man had hemorrhoids, and he tried several folk remedies. He used butter, he sat in cold water, and the like. One day he tried applying some coffee sediment left from his afternoon coffee. Well, the coffee sediment burned really badly, so he ran to his doctor for help.

"Let me look," said the doctor. "Oh, I see the Big Door; you're going to take a trip! And I see that you're going to win the lottery! Et cetera, et cetera!"

[X461., Jokes on fortune tellers.]

327   There was this couple who had a lot of money, but they were "new rich" because the husband had made the money himself.

Well, they sent their daughter to an expensive boarding school so that she could meet other rich people of the "aristocratic" class.

During the spring the daughter was invited to lots of parties. And the parents were also invited.

At one party there was a buffet meal, and when the family went to sit down, the wife sat down very slowly and in obvious pain.

"What's wrong?" asked one curious woman.

"Oh, it's nothing," said the husband. "My wife's got a pimple on her ass!"

Later on the daughter told her father:

"Don't call Mother's ass like that! Use the word 'popó' with these high-class people."

Well, later in the evening again the wife went to sit down, and again some curious woman asked what was the matter. This time the daughter was not standing close by, and the father couldn't remember the word his daughter had told him to say. So he shouted to her across the room:

"Loula! What's the name of your mother's ass?"

328   A vegetable man was selling fresh cucumbers. A woman came up and asked:

"How much are the cucumbers?"

"Five drachmes a kilo, madam."

Another woman came to ask how much the cucumbers were. The vendor told her:

"Five drachmes a kilo, miss."

A man who was standing by and overheard this asked the vendor:

"How can you tell if the woman is single or married?"

"Easy. If they grab hold of the cucumber, they're married. If they pick it up with two fingers, they're single!"

The following several jokes deal with villagers or with aspects of traditional village life, still preserved in some areas of Greece. In some of the jokes, the villagers are portrayed as dumb; in others, as clever. All of these jokes are slightly *sókin*.

329 A farmer from a small village in Crete went to Heraklion to sell some turkeys. Well, he sold all but one of them.

As he had four hours to wait for a bus back to his village, he decided to go to a movie to pass the time.

So he went to the theatre and asked for a ticket. Well, the cashier saw the turkey and said:

"Sorry, but you can't come in here with a turkey."

So the old man left, and he couldn't figure what to do to pass the time. Well, he was wearing *vrákes*, the strange baggy trousers worn occasionally in Crete today. Well, he had an idea! He shoved the turkey inside his trousers and went back to the theatre! The cashier didn't notice a thing, and the old man went inside and sat down.

A little while later the turkey managed to find an opening in the trousers, and he put his head out.

After a while two women schoolteachers came and sat down next to the farmer. They started eating dried pumpkin seeds [*passatémpo*].

Well, the turkey saw the seeds in the woman's hand, and he started pecking them out of her hand!

"Look at that!" said one woman to the other. "Have you *ever*?"

"No! I've seen a lot [of penises] in my day, but never one that eats pumpkin seeds!"

[Legman I:213–14; Inversion of J1771.3., Object thought to be turkey.]

The next joke is widespread and very popular in Greece. As first given below the joke is set in Crete.

330 There was a young shepherd who lived up in the mountains in Crete and only came down twice or three times a year to his village.

Well, his family decided it was time for him to get married, so they arranged an engagement for him.

The night that he was supposed to go to his fiancée's house to celebrate their engagement, he got all dressed up. He put on new *vrákes*, the typical Cretan pants of the past, and inside them he put a lot of material to make the *vrákes* stand out more. (He was trying to impress his fiancée's family, because the more material used in the *vrákes*, the more expensive they are.)

So he went to her house and sat at the table next to his fiancée, and they drank and ate, and ate and drank, and drank and ate!

With so much eating and drinking, the young man had to loosen his sash several times, and, finally, his *vrákes* became unfastened in front (without his knowing it)! His fiancée was staring at the opening because his penis was showing!

"Oh," she said, "it's really a big one!"

The shepherd, thinking that she was looking at his *vrákes*, said:

"Oh, that's nothing! I have two or three bigger ones at home!"

[Legman I:225.]

Northern Greece, homeland of the Koutsovlachs, is the setting of another version of the preceding joke.

330a One time, a *Vláhos* who was engaged to be married went to Athens to buy bride gifts. He was overwhelmed with the city, and it took him ages to muster up the courage to go inside a big department store near Omonia Square.

He decided to buy some cloth of the type that the women of his village could not weave. Then he spotted a bolt of silk, and it was the first time he had ever seen that fabric. He was captivated by the luxurious texture, but he told the saleswoman that it was probably impractical for clothing.

She explained that it was used for undergarments, and the *Vláhos* decided to buy the whole bolt! Part of it he would use for a *sóvrako* (the sash worn under the skirts used by the *Vláhi*; it is wound around the waist and under the groin to form underpants) for himself. The rest would go to his bride.

So he returned to his village and got all dressed up to go and visit his fiancée. In his excitement about the silk, he forgot to put on his *sóvrako* of the new cloth!

So he went to his fiancée's house for a visit. While he was drinking coffee, he put one leg up on a stool, and, since he was naked under his skirt, his fiancée was staring at him!

Thinking that she was looking at the new silk *sóvrako* that he *thought* he was wearing, he said:

"You like it, eh? Don't worry, I have ten meters more of it at home for you!"

[Legman I:225.]

331 Sometime, long ago, there was a wedding in a village. In those days they made a big celebration, with music, lots of food and drink, dancing, and the like.

Somebody who liked to play jokes went to the bride's house before the wedding and said to the bride's mother:

"Too bad for your daughter!"

"What do you mean?" asked the woman.

"The groom-to-be, he doesn't have a tool!"

When she heard that the old woman went outside where the musicians were playing and told them:

"Stop the music! I have to check something!"

So she called for the groom to come to her, and she took him into one of the empty rooms in her house and told him to take down his pants!

Well, the groom was shocked, but he complied.

Well, she put her head down to inspect him carefully, and as she did his penis jumped up and knocked off her spectacles! And they landed on the top of his penis!

So she went outside again and said:

"Start the music again; everything is okay! I saw something and it was wearing glasses!"

[Legman I:447; T132., Preparation for wedding; T136.3., Amusements at wedding; T150., Happenings at wedding.]

332 One time, a Gypsy went to a village in Crete and asked for hospitality. So, of course, the mayor of the village took him home and offered him dinner, and wine, then a bed for the night.

"Well, okay," said the Gypsy. "But I have a problem. My head smells like cheese, and so I'm afraid that during the night the rats will come and eat me. So I'll stay only if you put a maid to watch over me during the night!"

"Of course, we'll have the maid guard you through the night," said the mayor.

So the Gypsy went to bed and the maid put a chair by the bed. She put her hand on his head to guard it.

Well, somehow during the night the Gypsy turned around in the bed, and so after a while the maid was holding his penis and not his head!

Well, in the morning, when the maid woke up and saw what was in her hand, she screamed:

"Mistress! Come quickly! The rats have eaten all of the Gypsy's head and there's only his neck left!"

[A1662., Peculiar smell of body.]

333   One time, a villager went to Athens for the first time. Well, he went to Omonia Square, underground, where all those vending machines are.

So he saw a machine that had a sign that said:

REPLACES THE WOMAN!

So he watched the machine. And one man went over to the machine, unbuttoned his pants, leaned against the machine, put a coin into the machine, and the machine went "Whrrr, whrrr, whrrr!" Then the man buttoned his pants up and left.

After a few minutes another man went over to the machine and did the same thing.

"So!" thought the villager. "It does the work of a woman! Ha! Well, I'll try it, too!"

So he went over to the machine, unbuttoned his pants, took out his penis and put it inside the little window of the machine, and put a *táliro* [five-drachme coin] into the machine.

Again the machine went "Whrrr, whrrr, whrrr!" and sewed a button on the tip of his penis!

[D1273.1.1., Three as magic number.]

334   One time, a *Vláhos* went to Athens for the first time. Well, he took a trolley to the center of town. After a while he noticed that a man got onto the trolley and showed the ticket taker a piece of paper and then he didn't pay the fare. (The man was an off-duty policeman out of uniform.)

So the man turned to the man sitting next to him and said:

"Why didn't that man have to pay?"

Deciding to play a joke on the *Vláhos*, the Athenian said:

"Didn't you know? There is a new law that married men don't have to pay to ride the trolley!"

After a few days the *Vláhos* went back to his village and got married. The next time that he went to Athens, when he boarded the trolley, he showed the ticket taker his marriage certificate.

"What's that?" asked the ticket taker.

"I'm married, so I don't have to pay," said the *Vláhos*.

"Look, that paper may give you the right to ride your wife for free, but it's no good for riding a trolley for free!"

Basic to the remaining jokes in this chapter are scatalogical themes. The word *scatalogical*, as do many other words in English, comes from the Greek: *skatá* ("feces," or "shit"). The jokes in this section deal with all types of body filth, including menstrual blood. An American classicist and archeologist who has resided and taught in Greece for many years told me that erotic and scatalogical themes predominate in Greek humor. They certainly did in classic Greek humor, as in the plays of Aristophanes; however, by 1977, the fascination with feces seemed to have dwindled. I collected only about twenty-five different scatalogical jokes, whereas I heard hundreds of erotic jokes and jokes dealing with deception. Perhaps the fact that I am a woman had something to do with the kind of jokes inform-ants elected to tell me; or perhaps I didn't meet the right inform-ants. But the small percentage of scatalogical jokes in this col-lection indicates that Greeks are not preoccupied with *skatá*.

American humor does not seem to indicate a preoccupation with scatology (see Legman 1968, 1975), but certain American behavior does. Americans spend millions of dollars every year on bathroom deodorants and cleansers of all types; liquid, spray, solid, and in every conceivable fragrance.[1] Greeks, on the other hand, take a more straightforward attitude; for instance, they treat public toilets, "shit houses," as something contempt-ible and disgusting, as indeed they are. Dirty and smelly, they are littered with toilet paper that is not supposed to be flushed down the toilets since the plumbing usually can not handle it.

The first joke below is what I believe to be the most popular scatalogical joke that I heard in Greece. Following it is a variant version that also seems to be very popular.

335 There was a contest in Patras, Greece, to see who could fart the strongest. And there were three entries: a Frenchman, an Italian, and a Greek.

Before the contest, the Frenchman drank a gallon of milk. The Italian ate a kilo of spaghetti, and the Greek ate a kilo of beans. When the men finished eating, each one put a cork in his ass.

After half an hour the Frenchman said, "I'm ready!" So he pulled down his pants and farted, and the cork flew out. The referees counted the distance: it was fifty meters!

Then the Italian said, "*Avánti* [I'm ready]!" And he farted, and the cork went flying. The referees measured the distance: it was fifty-eight meters!

Finally, after an hour, the Greek said, "Okay, I'm ready!" So he pulled down his pants and really farted loudly! The referees went to measure the distance, but they couldn't find the cork! So the contest was in a stalemate.

The next day the town crier passed the stadium where the men were still waiting and announced:

"News from Athens: Shit, rain, and high winds!"

So they knew the Greek had won!

[D1273.1.1., Three as magic number; H1568., Champion test.]

335a A Greek went to America to seek his fortune. Well, he went to California, and he saw that there was a contest, and if he won he could win one million dollars!

It was a contest to see who could shit the most pounds of shit, and the entry fee was twenty-five dollars. Well, the Greek scraped up the last of his money and entered the contest. To prepare himself he ate beans for ten days straight and kept a cork in his ass all that time.

On the day of the contest, the Greek got in line with the other entries and waited his turn. The first American made five kilos of shit! The second made seven and a half kilos of shit! When the Greek went up to shit on the scale, there was a terrible thunder, an earthquake, and a tidal wave! But on the scale was only three ounces of shit!

"I can't even shit well," thought the poor Greek as he dejectedly left the contest.

The next day the Greek took his last nickel to buy a newspaper to see if he could find some job. And he read the headlines:

RAINING SHIT IN INDIA! ELEPHANT KILLED BY FLYING CORK!

[H1568., Champion test.]

336 A villager went to Piraeus for the first time. He had some business to take care of.

Well, he had to go to the toilet, but he didn't know where to go since he had never been to Pireaus before.

Well, he found a small alley where there were no people, so he went inside and pulled down his pants and did his business.

Just when he was finishing, and putting his pants back on, a policeman walked into the alley!

So the villager grabbed his hat and put it on top of the pile of shit so that the policeman wouldn't see it!

"What are you doing in here?" asked the policeman.

"Oh, er, I just caught a beautiful canary, and so I put my hat on top of it so it wouldn't get away while I go find a bag to put it in!"

"Okay," said the policeman, "I'll watch the hat for you while you go and get the sack."

So the villager left with no intention of returning.

And after a few minutes, the policeman thought:

"To heck with that yokel; I'll take the bird home to my wife!"

So he lifted the hat and stuck his hand inside and grabbed a handful of shit!

[AT1528, Holding Down the Hat.]

337 A villager went to Piraeus for the first time. Well, he had to go to the toilet, but he couldn't find one. So instead he went to a small alley and did his business on top of a piece of newspaper. When he finished, he folded it up like a package,* and went to find somewhere to put it.

Well, a policeman saw him, and, since he was acting nervous, the policeman said:

"Hey, you, what's in that package you've got?"

"Oh, just a kilo of *halváh* [a soft Greek sweet, typically eaten on the first day of Lent]!"

"Let me see," said the policeman. "I'd like to buy it from you!"

After taking the package from the villager, the policeman said:

"But this isn't a kilo, it's less!"

"No," said the villager, "it's a kilo!"

So the policeman took the man and the package to a pastry and sweet ship, and said to the shopkeeper:

"Weigh this package for us!"

So the shopkeeper weighed it, and it was only eight hundred grams!

"Give me two hundred grams of *halváh,* to make it a kilo," said the policeman.

When the shopkeeper opened the package and they saw it was shit, the policeman gave the villager a good beating!

*Greek villagers frequently use newspapers as wrapping paper for the bundles they carry to and from town.

So when the villager returned to his village, he told all the men in the coffeehouse:

"If you can only shit eight hundred grams, don't go to Piraeus or you'll get a beating!"

[Legman II:940.]

338 There was a drunk on a train in Greece, who was being very obnoxious.

"I'm going to shit on everybody, except that man over there in the white suit!"

A while later he repeated the same thing:

"I'm going to shit on everybody, except the guy in the white suit!"

So another man on the train asked him:

"Why not shit on the man wearing the white suit, too?"

"Because, said the drunk, "I'm going to wipe my ass with him!"

339 A man in a village had a problem with his toilet, so he called some plumbers to fix it.

"The cesspool needs to be cleaned out," they told him.

So they started digging out all the muck. One man got down into the hole and filled up a big pail, and the other two men hauled it up and dumped it.

After they had worked for two hours, the owner passed by and saw that they were almost finished. So he counted the number of piles of muck; there were seventeen. Then he went to the coffeehouse.

After he left the workers found it necessary to dig out three more loads.

When they finished they went to the coffeehouse to be paid.

"We want two hundred drachmes for the work. It was twenty loads that we dug out!"

"No," said the man, "I counted it myself; it was only seventeen instead!"

"No, it was twenty," they insisted.

"Stop trying to cheat me," said the man. "It was seventeen!"

"Okay," said one of the plumbers, "pay us one hundred and seventy drachmes and then come to your house and eat the other three piles of shit!"

[AT1035, Clearing Out Manure.]

The next joke deals with the Greek custom of gambling on

New Year's Eve to determine who will have the best luck in the forthcoming year. Many Greeks play a card game called "Thirty-one" on that holiday. The game is similar to "Blackjack," or "Twenty-One," as it is played in America. The object is to reach thirty-one points or below, but not over. Cards count at face value, face cards are worth ten points, and an ace can be worth either one point or eleven points.

340 It was December 31, and the men in Korydallos Prison in Greece wanted to play "Thirty-one" as is the custom all over Greece. But the warden refused to let them have any cards.

So they decided to play the game by farting! The prisoner who could fart the closest to thirty-one times would win the game!

The first prisoner farted twenty-one times; he couldn't do any more.

The second prisoner farted twenty-five times.

The third prisoner farted twenty times; then, when he tried to fart again, he shat instead!

"Thirty-one!" he cried. "Twenty plus the ace!"

[D1273.1.1., Three as magic number; H602., Symbolic meaning of numbers; N99., Gambling.]

341 A very well dressed gentleman went into a Greek restaurant one night. So the waiter went to the table and asked what he wanted for dinner.

"Bring me a plate of shit!" said the gentleman.

"What?" asked the incredulous waiter.

"Shit," repeated the gentleman.

So the waiter went to the kitchen and told the cook:

"I don't know what to do! There's a well-dressed gentleman sitting out there who says he wants a plate of shit for his dinner!"

"Well," said the cook, "that's easy enough! Just take a plate into the toilet and shit on it and give it to him!"

So the waiter went in the toilet and did his business on a plate. Then he put salt and pepper on it, and some olive oil, and served it to the gentleman!

After the man had finished eating, he called for his bill.

"Two hundred drachmes," said the waiter.

The man said nothing; he just paid and left!

Well, the next night the gentleman returned and again ordered shit for his dinner. And the same thing continued for several nights.

One night, as the gentleman was eating, he called the waiter and pointed to the plate.

"What's that?" he asked.

"It looks like a pubic hair to me," said the waiter.

"Then take it back," said the gentleman. "For such expensive food like this, I don't want it getting messed up with dirty pubic hair!"

[Legman II:381.]

342 One time, two friends were walking down the street. Ahead of them was a man who was walking in a very peculiar manner. He had his legs spread wide apart and would shake each leg before stepping.

"Oh, look at that poor man," said one of the friends. "All his life he's suffered from that birth defect!"

"That's not a birth defect," said the other friend. "It's a disease that affects old people!"

Well, they argued back and forth and finally decided to ask the man.

"Excuse me, sir," said one of the men. "We're wondering why it is that you walk that way. I think it's a birth defect, but my friend thinks it's a disease that one gets later in life."

"Neither," said the man, "*I* thought it was air [a fart], but I was mistaken!"

[Legman II:862.]

343 A man went to a restaurant and ordered a bowl of hot soup. But, when the waiter brought him the soup, the man saw that the waiter's thumb was inside the bowl and in the soup!

"Please, take that bowl of soup back and bring me another one," said the customer.

So the waiter took the soup back to the kitchen and returned with another bowl. But again, his thumb was in the soup.

"Please, take that bowl of soup back and bring me another one," said the customer.

So again the waiter returned the soup to the kitchen, and again he brought a bowl of soup in which he had his thumb.

"Please, take that bowl of soup back to the kitchen and bring me another one," said the customer.

Finally, the waiter could take it no more.

"What? Are you crazy? How many times do you think I'm going to go back and forth to the kitchen with your soup?"

"Look," said the customer. "It's your thumb! It's in the soup!"

"What's wrong with my thumb, you dumb idiot?"

"Look," said the customer, "if there weren't so many customers here, I'd tell you *where* to put that thumb!"

"Where to put it?" asked the waiter. "That's where it was before I brought you the soup!"

[Legman II:374.]

344 One time, a man went into a restaurant. When the waiter came he said:

"Bring me a duck soup!"

Well, the waiter brought him a bowl of soup. So the man leaned over and smelled the soup.

"Waiter," he called. "This is *fish* soup. Take it back!"

So he left and went to another restaurant and again ordered a bowl of duck soup. When the waiter brought him the soup, he leaned over and smelled it and said:

"Waiter, this is *meat* soup, not duck soup. Take it back!"

So he went to another restaurant and again ordered duck soup. When the waiter brought him the soup, he leaned over to smell it, and then he called to the waiter:

"Come here! This is *not* duck soup; it's *fish* soup. Take it back!"

So the man got really angry when he left, and he walked around a little. Then he remembered that his friend's restaurant was nearby, so he went there.

When he went inside, the friend, a waiter, asked him:

"What's wrong?"

"I've gone to three restaurants to eat duck soup, but they kept bringing me other soups. I'm really mad!"

"Don't worry!" said the friend. "We'll fix you a duck soup, but it'll take about an hour."

"Never mind, I'll wait," said the man.

So the waiter went into the kitchen and said to the woman who cooked there:

"Maria, take off your drawers and boil them for an hour!"

"What? Are you crazy?" she asked.

"Just do what I told you," he said.

Well, Maria was having her period at the time, so her drawers were bloody! Anyway, she put them in a pot of water and boiled them for an hour like the waiter said.

After an hour the waiter brought the man a bowl of "duck" soup!

So the man leaned over and smelled the soup, and he said:

"Oh, Maria is working here, eh?"

[Legman I:406; X718.1., "Betsy puts a granny-rag (sanitary pad) in the soup, and them old stags can smell it a mile off."]

345 A man went lion hunting in Africa. When he got back he told his friends this story:

"There I was, hiding in the bushes with my rifle loaded, when the biggest lion that I've ever seen came upon me! I tried to fire, but the rifle was jammed. So I started running. Just when the lion was about to catch me, the lion slipped, and I got away. And I ran fast, but the lion caught up with me! Just as it was about to grab me, it slipped again, and I got away. Then I climbed up into a tree and waited for help to come!"

"*Po, po, po!*" said the friend. "If that had been me I'd have been really shitting!"

"So was I!" said the man. "That's why the lion kept slipping and falling down!"

[Legman II:973; X584., Jokes about hunters; X1130., Lie: hunter's unusual experience.]

346 On a crowded bus in Athens, the ticket taker couldn't reach the hand of the man to whom he owed two drachmes change, so he said:

"I'll throw you the money!"

So he threw the two drachmes to the man, but just then the bus hit a bump, and the man missed the coin, and it fell on the floor.

As he reached down to pick up the money, he farted loudly!

A man standing next to him said:

"Terrific! We get music, too!"

And so the man said:

"What do you want for two drachmes? Maria Callas?"

Conclusion

This collection of contemporary Greek jokes, bawdry, and folktales reveals a striking preoccupation with the themes of sex and trickery. Indeed, the combination of those two themes is prevalent in the collection. Stith Thompson (1946:202) observed that the uneducated storyteller or listener always exhibited a greater interest in deceptions connected with sexual conduct than in any other deceptions. Of course, all cultures are not equally concerned with sexual deceptions and with trickster heroes. Cultures that place fewer restrictions on sexual behavior and that permit the two sexes to mingle more freely than is common in the Greek culture probably do not exhibit the same intensity of concern with sexual deceptions. American bawdry does not, for example (see Hoffmann 1973). If its emphasis on sexual deceptions characterizes Greek humor fairly, then Bobos is the star of the collection and probably an ideal role model for young macho Greeks.

An extremely strong emphasis on machismo is present also in the other culture area with which I am familiar: Middle America (Mexico through Panama). In both Greece and Middle America, adult males openly encourage very young males to exhibit masculine traits characteristic of the adult males. Little boys are encouraged to flirt with or to show a sexual interest in girls at a very early age, and when they do they are rewarded with encouragement from their adult male relatives.

Both Greece and Central America (especially Honduras, Nicaragua, and Costa Rica) have in their traditional humor a young, male sexual trickster of great popularity: Bobos in

Greece and Pepito in Central America. I believe that Bobos and Pepito are functional equivalents that serve as outlets for anxieties about sexual behavior. Also, they are useful in socialization processes in both countries, for they typify some of the characteristics that males are expected to possess.

But both Bobos and Pepito are sexual tricksters *and* fools. As tricksters they rebel against parents, teachers, strict sexual standards, and authority in general. As fools they reveal the male anxieties about their masculinity (especially in regard to fulfilling the image of a "Latin Lover" or an "Adonis").

The machismo complex is a widespread, well-developed phenomenon in many parts of the world, including the Mediterranean and Latin American countries. (The historical evidence suggests that the values associated with machismo were transmitted to Latin America by the Spanish and the Portuguese.) The machismo complex is solidly based on a sexual double standard, a tendency to separate the sexes, and rigidly defined sex roles that exaggerate the differences between the sexes. Men are expected to be strong, physically and verbally, active, aggressive, powerful, and independent, and to possess many women. Women are usually characterized as evil by nature and as inferior to men. They are expected to be weak, dependent, passive, and quiet, and to stay in the home to fulfill their duties of marriage and motherhood. The stereotype of women is that they are oversexed and thus constantly encouraging men to seduce them. Such proclivities are "proved" by the fact that women paint their eyes and faces, wear seductive clothes and perfumes, and so on.

Men and women in Greece and in Middle America reinforce the machismo complex by their adherence to the stereotypical roles. Women in both areas expect their husbands (and sometimes even their lovers) to be unfaithful. The infidelity of their men allows many women to play the martyr role and to undergo dramatic suffering, making life anything but dull. The Christian image of the suffering Madonna is a primary role for women in both of those machismo-dominated areas to emulate. Men in both areas worry considerably about the possibility of being cuckolded; thus men also suffer anxiety. Such anxiety is reflected in the jokes that deal with adultery.

Another striking characteristic of the present collection of Greek humor is the dual nature of the primary heroes of the tales. Bobos, Hodjas, the Anogian, and the anonymous villager all possess dual natures: cleverness *and* stupidity. Moreover, their natures are contradictory as well. Thompson has explained that the storyteller does not always make a clear distinction between the fool and the clever man. Thompson's worldwide research revealed that it was not unusual to find that the numbskull had suddenly gained wisdom in order for him to go on a successful career of cheating and deceiving (Thompson 1946:196). I believe that the dual nature of Bobos, of the Anogian, of Hodjas, and of the villager reveals a basic ambivalence that Greeks feel about their lives, their culture, their history, their position in the world today. Outwardly Greeks are strongly ethnocentric, but underneath the overt expression of Greek superiority may lie the nagging doubt.

The material in this collection reveals the sharp urban-rural contrasts and conflicts found in Greek life today: the "dumb" shepherd (the Greek past) versus the clever student (Bobos as a symbol of the new emphasis on formal education); the great achievements of Greece during the Golden Age versus the position of Greece in the modern world. The dual-natured and contradictory-natured characters of the jokes and tales seem to be universally popular in Greek folklore because they serve as mediators between the opposing aspects of the contrasts and conflicts inherent in Greek life today.

A final word about the function of this material in Greek culture. Of the four functions generally served by folklore in society—amusement, validation of culture, education, and maintaining behavioral conformity (see Bascom 1965)—the material in this collection serves two functions equally well. The amusement function is readily apparent, especially in the erotic jokes, which are generally humorous and meant to amuse. Additionally, the jokes in this collection, particularly the *sókin* examples, serve an important educational function in Greek society. The strong taboos on premarital sex in Greece, the close chaperoning of Greek girls, and the lack of sex education in the home or in the schools have resulted in a great deal of ignorance about sexual matters in the population as a whole. Greek children probably learn a great deal about sex from erotic jokes. Unfortunately, they learn a great deal of erroneous information as well, but perhaps even that is better than none.

The foremost function of erotic folklore is that it serves as a safety valve for or release from sexual tension and frustration in a society. Suppressed tensions in the society are released and made manifest in the oral literature (Benedict 1935). Greek culture emphasizes the pleasures of erotic love in folksong and in popular song and denies those same pleasures by customarily arranging marriages between older males and young females on the basis of economic concerns, by enforcing the separation of the sexes, and by emphasizing premarital chastity. The conflicting characteristics of Greek culture are resolved and overcome, temporarily at least, by the transmission of *sókin* jokes and tales.

Appendix A

Index of Tale Types

The following tale-type numbers are from Antti Aarne, *The Types of the Folktale: A Classification and Bibliography*, Folklore Fellows Communications No. 3., translated and enlarged by Stith Thompson (Helsinki: Suomalainen Tiedeakatemia, 1961).

Tale Number	Tale-Type Title	Number, This Collection
AT924	Discussion by Sign Language.	67
AT1035	Clearing Out Manure.	339
AT1176	Catching a Man's Broken Wind.	74
AT1215	The Miller, His Son, and the Ass: Trying to Please Everyone.	121
AT1225A	How Did the Cow Get on the Pole?	112
AT1288A	Numbskull Cannot Find the Ass He Is Sitting On.	108
AT1293*	Learn to Swim.	96
AT1315.3.2.	Seduction Attempted on Promise of Magic Transformation of Woman to Mare.	235
AT1319	Pumpkin Sold As Ass's Egg.	103
AT1324*	The Man Behind the Crucifix.	148
AT1325A	The Fireplace Gives Too Much Heat: Decide to Move It.	122
AT1331*	Learning to Read.	106
AT1331A*	Buying Spectacles.	106
AT1335A	Rescuing the Moon.	90
AT1337	Peasant Visits the City.	91
AT1341B*	Escaped Slave's Talkativeness Brings About His Recapture.	124
AT1363*	The Second Cat.	195
AT1346A*	Guess How Many Eggs I Have and You Shall Get All Seven.	105

229

Tale Number	Tale-Type Title	Number, This Collection
AT1825	The Peasant As Parson.	174
AT1832B	What Kind of Dung?	198
AT1833**	Other Anecdotes of Sermons: Application of the Sermon.	171
AT1842	The Testament of the Dog.	149
AT1920	Contest in Lying.	69, 70
AT1948	Too Much Talk.	139

The following tale-type numbers are from Frank Hoffmann, *An Analytical Survey of Anglo-American Traditional Erotica* (Bowling Green, O.: Bowling Green University Popular Press, 1973).

Type Number	Types of the Erotic Folktale	Number, This Collection
244A**	Sparrow's Courtship of the Mare.	293
1424A	Priest seduces man's wife. Husband, upon returning, serves priest's wife in same manner under pretense of searching for her lost earrings.	143
1563B	Give Him "That." Priest (Peasant) sends servant for an egg (spade). Servant propositions wife (daughter) who shouts to priest, asking if they should give "that." Priest answers affirmatively.	236

Appendix B

Index of Motifs

Motif numbers are from Stith Thompson, *Motif-Index of Folk-Literature*, 6 vols. (Bloomington: Indiana University Press, 1955–58).

Motif Number	A. Mythological Motifs	Number, This Collection
A137.15.	God on throne.	5
A511.1.2.1.	Twins quarrel before birth.	321
A661.0.1.	Gate of heaven.	165–66
A661.0.1.2.	St. Peter as porter of heaven.	165–66
A671.3.1.	Coldness in hell.	163
A1313.3.	Misplaced genitals.	213
A1549.4.	Penance for sins.	167
A1662.	Peculiar smell of body.	332

	B. Animals	
B122.0.3.	Wise owl.	289
B152.2.	Fly indicates successful suitor.	153
B210.	Talking animals.	289, 291–95
B211.2.6.	Speaking hare.	280
B211.3.2.	Speaking cock.	290
B211.3.4.	Speaking parrot.	25, 170, 296–302
B280.	Animal weddings.	291
B562.1.1.	Hogs root up gold treasure.	149

	D. Magic	
D469.	Transformation: Miscellaneous object to other objects.	70

232

Motif Number	D. Magic	Number, This Collection
D480.	Size of object transformed.	70
D1153.	Magic table.	102
D1155.	Magic carpet.	74
D1273.1.1.	Three as magic number.	1, 2, 5, 7, 24, 26, 42, 48, 54, 63, 72, 74–76, 95, 102, 111, 139, 152, 168, 176, 181, 191, 194–95, 202–03, 211, 218, 220–22, 226, 229, 261, 269, 278–79, 287, 299–99a, 303, 315–16, 318, 333, 335, 340
D1420.4.	Helper summoned by calling name.	272
D1610.2.1.	Speaking image.	9
D1620.1.7.	Speaking statue.	16
D1711.	Magician.	259
D1711.0.3.	Means of becoming magician.	259

E. The Dead

E755.2.7.	Devils tormenting sinners in hell.	164

F. Marvels

F513.1.	Person unusual as to his teeth.	216
F547.3.	Extraordinary penis.	228–34
F547.3.1.	Long penis.	228–31, 234
F547.3.4.	Tattoo on penis.	234
F547.3.7.	Man ties penis in knot.	230
F547.5.	Extraordinary vagina.	213, 248, 251

Motif Number	J. The Wise and the Foolish	Number, This Collection
J1341.13.	Servant who receives only one egg for breakfast does half as much work. . . .	128
J1391.6.	Lame excuse: one cannot drink because of no teeth.	215
J1473.1.	999 gold pieces.	123
J1561.	Inhospitality repaid.	114
J1705.1.	Stupid peasant.	109–11
J1744.1.	Ignorance of bridegroom on wedding night.	222, 224–26
J1745.	Ignorance of sex.	223, 226
J1771.3.	Object thought to be turkey.	329
J1772.9.	Excrements eaten by mistake.	198
J1882.	Foolish attempt to educate animals.	292
J2030.	Absurd inability to count.	108
J2133.13.	Fool hanging by hands, claps, then falls.	76a
J2321.	Man made to believe that he is pregnant.	204, 262
J2450.	Literal fool.	42–44, 222
J2470.	Metaphor literally interpreted.	43–44
J2496.2.	Misunderstandings because of ignorance of different language.	209

K. Deceptions

K16.	Diving match won by deception.	254
K115.1.4.	Pseudo-magic charm for engendering offspring.	78
K130.	Sale of worthless animal.	79
K231.3.	Refusal to make sacrifice after need is past.	157
K256.	Deceptive wages.	126–27
K305.3.	Youths clever thieves.	82, 84
K364.	Partner misappropriates common goods.	97
K550.	Escape by false plea.	92
K1273.1.	Priest surprised in intrigue flees in haste.	145
K1315.2.2.	Seduction by alleged retrieving of lost gem.	143

Motif Number	X. Humor	Number, This Collection
X520.	Jokes concerning prostitutes.	244–48, 251
X530.	Jokes concerning beggars.	13
X540.	Jokes on madmen.	184–98
X583.	Jokes about travelers.	176–83
X584.	Jokes about hunters.	276, 345
X650.	Jokes concerning other races or nations.	136–40
X680.	Jokes concerning various cities.	124–28
X681.	Blason populaire.	124–40
X900.	Humor of lies and exaggeration.	70
X904.	The teller reduces the size of his lie.	69
X1014.1.*	Lie: remarkable memory.	51
X1030.1.	Lie: the great building.	69
X1130.	Lie: hunter's unusual experience.	276, 345

The following motif numbers are from D. P. Rotunda, *Motif-Index of the Italian Novella in Prose* (Bloomington: Indiana University Press, 1942).

Motif Number	Description	Number, This Collection
J1578.*	Penniless guest makes an agreement with his host. If he sings a song which the host likes, he must take it as payment. Guest sings: "Put your hand in your money bag and pay the host." Host is forced to admit he likes song.	87
X16.1.*	Mule goes on a rampage and causes melee.	288
X434.4.*	The sermon is misinterpreted.	174
X448.*	Bishop is over-zealous in administering the sacrament. Strikes the parishioner.	156

The following motif numbers are from Frank Hoffmann, *An Analytical Survey of Anglo-American Traditional Erotica* (Bowling Green, O.: Bowling Green University Popular Press, 1973).

Motif Number	Motif-Index of Erotica	Number, This Collection
J1772.4.2.	Child takes mother's pubic hair to be a fur cap.	51
J2136.	Numbskull brings about his own capture.	124
K1339.6.2.	"That and a great deal more." Girl is reluctant to confess, priest progressively holds her breasts, raises her skirts, etc., asking if her lover has done that. After mounting her, he asks what her lover could have done more. Girl: "He has given me the pox."	146
X712.3.2.	Large testicles.	46, 48
X718.1.	"Betsy puts a granny-rag (sanitary pad) in the soup, and them old stags can smell it a mile off." (Why boarding house is so popular.)	344
X721.	Humor concerning birth.	51
X724.1.8.1.	Man disguises himself as girl to effect seduction.	253
X724.10.2.	Seducer receives case of venereal disease.	146
X727.3.	Contraceptives mistaken for something else.	319
X733.1.1.	Man mounts Indian squaw who continually shouts "Wahoo" as he has her. Later he is told that "Wahoo" means wrong hole.	244
X734.3.	Intercourse between male and animal.	274, 276
X734.5.3.	Sparrow has intercourse with elephant; wonders if he is hurting her.	294
X735.1.4.	After first penetration, wife wants husband to put his testicles in as well.	199
X735.2.2.	Bridegroom reads magazines, ignoring bride, who lies in a receptive position. However, he uses her vagina to wet finger to turn magazine page.	226

Motif Number	Motif-Index of Erotica	Number, This Collection
X735.8.1.1.	Man fucks whores to death, then chases heifers in field.	245
X735.9.3.3.	"Do you think my balls are the regimental pot?" Asked by soldier who seeks to seduce woman and then finds her insatiable.	201
X735.9.5.	No more yarn.	55
X749.3.1.	When woman turns up missing, sister holds seance in effort to locate her. Rapping and action of table indicate that missing woman is enjoying intercourse.	102
X749.4.1.	Man with huge member.	228–34
X749.4.3.1.	Man wagers he can mount one hundred women in succession.	245
X749.12.1.1.	Man makes advances to another man who is disguised as woman.	253

Appendix C

Illustrations of Gestures

Photos by Ralph Hogan, Audio-Visual Department, University of New Orleans, New Orleans, Louisiana

Insult gesture: "To my balls!"

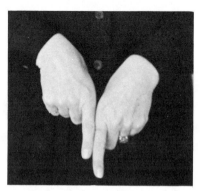

First gesture of copulation: "Together."

Second gesture of copulation: The "Sidewinder."

Third gesture of copulation: "To Jump."

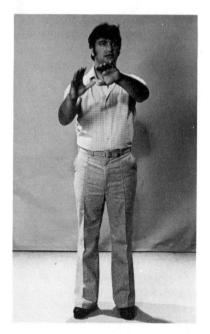

Curse gesture: The *Múntza*

"Balls!"

Notes

Preface

1. Halliday (1927) contends that jokes were very popular among the ancient Greeks (see also Dorson 1970:xxv). Also, Horton (1979) suggests a continuity of the spirit of Aristophanes' form of comedy in the festive folk sense of humor and comedy found in Greece today.

2. Orso (1976). Friedl (1970) also has described her research problems, many of which were quite similar to mine. One of our shared difficulties was adjusting to a widespread Greek tendency to give vehement advice as to what we foreigners should do in every conceivable situation.

3. There are few solitary Greeks, and most Greeks never like to do things alone. (In fact, many Greeks also do not like to see someone else alone, and this was one of my main problems in the first four months of field work when I lived with a family. That I required a certain amount of solitude daily seemed peculiar to many Greeks.) When someone has free time, he or she often looks for company among a group of friends, the *paréa*. Since no equivalent social group seems to exist today in those areas of American society with which I am familiar, the term *paréa* is difficult to translate in one word. Years ago Americans had similar voluntary associations that they called "gangs" or "crowds." The term "gang" has acquired such negative connotations that it no longer seems appropriate in describing the type of social group in question. The word "company" might be used if it is kept in mind that it is a voluntary company in the sense of keeping each other company. The *paréa* may include one's own relatives, either by birth or by baptism, but it may not. It may be all male or all female, or it may be a mixed group. Usually, the *paréa* is a type of age-grade group, but not necessarily. It can be a long-lasting group of friends who regularly get together, or it can be a group of persons who simply get together for one evening to go out together. Economics is one key factor in the Greek *paréa*. A group can go out to dinner to a *tavérna* (a type of popular restaurant that usually features grilled meats, appetizers, barrel wine, and sometimes live entertainment) and eat better and for less money than can a person who is alone. Also, a person who may have no

245

money at all can go out with a *paréa* and still eat and drink but not be expected to pay; he or she can pay the "next" time, when money is available.

Introduction

1. See Lee (1953:70). Many Greeks appear to be rather nervous, perhaps from their diet, which is usually rich in sugar and coffee. Many attempt to keep their hands busy, even when not working, and use such devices as "worry beads" (men) or embroidery and crocheting (women) to "pass the time." Talk and gossip are the most common pastimes, however.

2. Some Greek folklorists were amazed that I was studying Bobos jokes, for example, and clearly did not consider jokes a part of folklore. Their view is probably the result of the early Greek folklorists' (such as Polites' and Kyriakides') concentrated emphasis on relating nineteenth-century Greek folklore to the Golden Age of Greek history and on justifying continuity in Greek culture and folklore. Today Bobos jokes appear to be too "new" for the Greek folklorists to consider them folklore. Bobos may be new, but, as Legman (1968) asserted, jokes do not originate, they evolve.

3. I was surprised to find that ten percent of the material in Randolph's long-suppressed collection of bawdy folktales from the American Ozarks is present in my own collection.

4. See Rayna Green, "Introduction," in Randolph (1976) for a full account of the problems surrounding the publication of the Randolph collection and the situation in the past in regard to bawdy folklore in the United States.

5. Megas (1970:246) states that there are thirty-eight variants of this tale in Greece, but he does not mention whether any of them are bawdy.

6. In classifying the materials according to Thompson's *Motif-Index*, I have used occasionally the concept of the inversion developed by Lévi-Strauss (1971:564). See, for example, joke 329, which involves an inversion of motif number J1771.3., Object thought to be turkey.

Although Thompson's *Motif-Index* is the folklorist's major tool for comparative work, it fails to be of use in regard to most of the bawdy lore contained in this collection because the original edition of the *Motif-Index* (1932–36) and the later revision (1955–58) rigorously omit—or appear to do so—all classification of motifs in erotic and scatalogical humor, allotting to that subject the number X700.–799., Humor concerning sex, but leaving it blank, with the following note:

> Thousands of obscene motifs in which there is no point except the obscenity itself might logically come at this point, but they are entirely beyond the

scope of the present work. They form a literature to themselves, with its own periodicals and collections. In view of the possibility that it might become desirable to classify these motifs and place them within the present index, space has been left . . . for such motifs [Thompson 1955–58:514f].

Thus because of the lack of explicitness involved in Thompson's motif number X700.–X799., Humor concerning sex, the number has not been used in this collection. Since the word "sex" can possibly apply to behavior ranging from autoeroticism, to homosexuality, heterosexual relations, sodomy for revenge, bestiality, and so on, it seems meaningless to attach the number to the many jokes in this collection that deal with sex in one form or another.

Legman (1964:454–93) discusses the obvious deficiency in Thompson's *Motif-Index*, but fails to offer an alternative system for classifying the motifs in erotic and scatological humor. Legman seems to distrust any classification system such as Thompson's *Motif-Index* because of the "arbitrary and subjective approaches" taken by the indexer in evaluating his materials (Legman 1964:454–57). In his own joke collections (1968, 1975), Legman relies on a system of classification based entirely on Freudian psychology, which does not reflect my interpretations of the material in this collection; hence, I do not follow Legman's classification or use his categories.

Because Hoffmann's *Analytical Survey* attempted to fill the gaps in Thompson's X700.–X799. category, it has been used in this collection. Unfortunately, only a few of Hoffmann's designated motif numbers were applicable to the material in this collection.

7. Although much of American culture derived from ancient Greek culture, the passage of time has resulted in the inversion, or turning around, of many elements of culture common to Greece and America. Lévi-Strauss would say that the Greek and the American cultures are in logical but inverted relationships with each other. Thus Greeks and Americans often consider each other "backward" (obviously not in a technological sense). A few examples here will suffice: Greeks traditionally refer to themselves first by the surname (what we call the "last" name) and then by the given name. The Greek order of names shows the primary importance of the family rather than of the individual in Greece. Greeks traditionally do not celebrate their birthdays, which are individual observances. Instead, they mark their name days by communal celebrations. At name-day parties Greeks usually serve sweets first, then offer food and drink. Americans would find it backward to serve a sweet (considered a dessert) at the beginning of a meal. Greeks celebrate carnival, but the first day of Lent, Pure Monday, is the peak of the celebrations. In the United States, in New Orleans and elsewhere along the Gulf Coast where Americans celebrate carnival, the peak of the festivities is the last day prior to the beginning of Lent.

In regard to the socialization of children, American children are trained to be independent and self-sufficient as early as possible (Mead 1975); Greek children, on the other hand, are trained for dependency (Lee 1953). Greeks are impetuous, today as in the ancient world (Slater 1968:221), whereas English-speaking people are generally impulse controlled.

8. Motif number D1273.1.1., Three as magic number, is used in the cases of those jokes in this collection that show obvious three-patterning, but is not used in the cases of those jokes in which the pattern, although present, is very subtle.

9. The Greek army functions as a rite of passage; all Greek young men are required to serve at least two years and endure many hardships, economic ones being the most acute.

1. Political Jokes

1. In 1977 there were thirty-seven drachmes to the dollar. One drachme was .027.

2. The intense seclusion of Greek women dates to the classic period (Slater 1968:24), but present-day customs of chaperoning may derive from the more recent Turkish occupation of Greece, which lasted four hundred years. A Greek woman's place is in the home, today as in ancient Greece.

2. The Bobos Joke Cycle

1. The similarities of the informants' descriptions of Bobos (fat, dumb, large head), suggests that a real type of oversexed, young, male human being is the prototype of the hero of these jokes. Although it is within the range of normal sexual variation for some young boys to engage in adult sex at the age of six or eight (especially when urged on by females), those who do so are typically not unusual as to the size of the head. Young males with large heads, however, may represent several abnormal physiological conditions, all of which result in increased sexual activities, interests, and abilities at an early age: (1) Gilles de la Tourette Syndrome. This apparently rare syndrome involves a lesion of the brain or a biochemical abnormality that results in the child's using dirty words and vile speech and showing sexual precocity. The disease, believed caused by a mutant gene, is found both in isolated cases and in cases of the offspring of marriages of close relatives. Rare in females, it often remits spontaneously in afflicted girls. The syndrome results in both increased sexual impulses and increased sexual behavior. (2) Adrenogenital Syndrome. This syndrome, which is not rare, occurs in the offspring of marriages of close relatives. Improper functioning of the pituitary gland and the adrenal glands produces too

many sex hormones and often, but not necessarily, results in overlarge genitalia. Adrenogenital syndrome is inherited as a simple genetic recessive. (3) Hydrocephaly. In folk speech large-headed children are said to be "water heads" or to have "water on the brain." Actually, the overexpansion of the cranium usually results in increased pressures on the hypothalamus, which can lead to hyperactive libidinal behavior.

Because of historical factors and geography, Greece today contains many pockets of inbred populations. Thus there are above-average levels of illnesses known to be produced by inbreeding such as favism (G6PD) and thalassemia. These blood diseases, widespread throughout the Mediterranean area, bestow a natural resistance to malaria in their mild form. They are inherited by genetically recessive traits, and their high incidence in parts of Greece is due to endogamous marriage customs.

2. John is the standard name of the central character in folktales throughout the European world—for example, Hans in German, Jean in French, Ivan in Russian, and John or Jack in English.

3. Juan Bobo ("Stupid John") is a standard numbskull character in Spanish folklore, both in Spain and in Hispanic America. His name suggests a possible Hispanic origin of the word (name) *Bobos* in Greek folklore, but the tradition of jokes about a clever-dumb young boy is probably indigenous to the entire Mediterranean area. In Honduras, Nicaragua, and Costa Rica, a little boy named Pepito is the exact equivalent of the Greek Bobos, whereas, in those same Central American countries, Juan Bobo is only a simpleton.

4. The shadow theatre evidently diffused from Turkey to Greece, as the hero of the Greek version, Karaghiozis, appears to be a slightly altered version of the Turkish Karagöz (which means "black eyes" in Turkish). In the Turkish plays the hero is equipped with a giant phallus. In the Greek plays Karaghiozis is shown with one very large arm, which he uses in slapstick fashion to beat his children and others. See Myrsiades 1976; and Danforth 1976.

5. Daughters are undesired generally because of the threat (of the girl's sexual misconduct) they pose to the family's honor before they are married and for the expenses incurred in marrying them off (the dowry gifts, and so on). The ancient Greeks held similar sentiments, and the practice of female infanticide was common (Slater 1968:223). The ancient Greek male's immortal happiness depended on leaving a son who would remember the deceased father in the required religious rituals (Slater 1968:238).

Ta paidiá ("children") is a common term of address in the plural, regardless of the age or sex of the individuals in the group being addressed. Venders sell their wares by shouting "Come here, children!" to their prospective clients. Entertainers refer to the members of the audience as "children," even in nightclubs. As Greek society trains the individual for dependency, it is not unusual for even adult Greeks to view themselves as children. That view probably accounts for many other Greek qualities associated with youthfulness such as inquisitiveness, delight in festivities and merrymaking, a preoccupation with courtship and marriage, and the enjoyment in telling *sókin* jokes.

6. The joke is usually set in a university class where a professor's lecture on the large penis size of the aborigines in Africa or Australia shocks two coeds, who get up to leave the classroom. The sarcastic retort at the end is the same as in the version included here. For more on this tale type, see Brunvand (1960).

7. Called *passatémpo* ("time-passers"). The term appears to have been borrowed from Spanish or Italian and is another reinforcement of Lee's (1953) observation that Greeks like to "pass the time." Pumpkin seeds are indeed time-passers since each individual seed cover must be removed by the skillful manipulation of the teeth, and the tongue is then used to remove the inner seed. Although eating *passatémpo* in the movies is the functional equivalent of the American custom of eating popcorn, it is, obviously, much more time consuming.

3. The Clever Greeks: Esoteric Humor

1. See Lee (1946).

2. Many Greeks, however, are very reluctant to admit to any borrowing of Turkish elements in Greek culture. Their narrow-minded attitude is the product of an overzealous nationalism that has been on the rise since 1974. Indeed, since 1974 I have observed in the Greek population at large the steady development of strong anti-Turkish feelings. One incident in particular comes to mind. In August 1974, when I ordered a "Turkish" coffee in the coffee bar of the University of Thessaloniki, the waiter got extremely angry, smashed his fist on the counter, and corrected me: "Greek coffee!"

4. Ethnic-Slur Jokes: Greek Exoteric Humor

1. *Hios*, pronounced "hee-os," is sometimes spelled *Chios* (see also Dorson 1970:xxv). *Hios* contains the Greek letter *Chi* (X, χ), of which there is no comparable phoneme, or sound, in English. The sound has usually been transliterated as *ch* in English. Since *Hios* (also *Vláhos*, *Vláhi*, which occur in some of the jokes in chapter eight) does not contain the English sound *ch* or *k*, I have used the letter *h* to approximate more closely the Greek pronunciation.

2. Almost every country has the equivalent of these jokes. In Mexican folklore, the people of Monterrey are reputed to be so stingy that when somebody dies he or she is buried only to the waist to save the

price of a monument. In the folklore of other countries, people from certain places are reputed to be exceptionally dumb: in Colombia, South America, it is the town of Pasto; in Denmark, it is Aarhus; in France, it is Pontoise. In America jokes about Peoria and Burbank function in a similar manner.

3. I suspect that these ethnic-slur jokes may have been borrowed from foreigners, possibly British and American, living in Greece.

5. Humor Directed at the Church and the Clergy

1. Kazantzakis (1965:74–75) described a Cretan folk-belief that had currency during the Greek struggle against the Turkish occupation of Crete. Saint Minas, the patron saint of Heraklion, is in ikons depicted seated astride a gray horse and holding a red lance pointed at the sky. According to Kazantzakis, the Cretans believed that the saint, remaining motionless during the day, only pretended to be a picture; at night he pushed aside paints and silver ex-voto offerings, spurred his horse, and rode out on patrol to protect his Greek charges and to strike terror into the hearts of the Turks.

6. Transportation Jokes

1. Although cars are extremely expensive by American standards, and although gasoline is over a dollar a gallon, everybody seems to have a car. Salaries are appreciably lower than they are in the United States, but the prices of all basics such as houses and clothes are extremely high by our standards. Even food is practically as costly as it is in the United States.

2. S. Obolensky, P. Sapountis, and A. Sapountis, *Greek: Basic Course*, vol. 1 (Washington, D.C.: Foreign Services Institute, 1967), p. 43.

3. Lee's observations (1953:70–72) about Greek attitudes toward time seem relevant twenty-five years later. In Greece today to be late for an appointment is acceptable, and performances of various types may be late getting started without upsetting people in the audience (unless they are foreigners). Being on time is not a positive virtue in itself, as it is in America or in West Germany.

7. Lunatic Jokes

1. Dafni has other attractions, including an eleventh-century Byzantine monastery and church that contain some of the best mosaics in Greece. In summer the Dafni wine festival, held in a wooded grove nearby, offers an endless variety of Greek wines free of charge, plus fun and revelry in the true Greek style.

2. Jokes about lunatics seem to be the functional equivalent of traditional jokes and tales about fools and numbskulls.

3. In the version that I heard in America several years ago, the folklorists get up, one at a time, to read papers at a convention, but they read only tale-type numbers such as "1528" from the Aarne-Thompson system (see appendix A).

4. See Nilsson (1940). Dionysus was connected with drunkenness and sexual orgies. A phallus made of fig wood was used in Dionysian processions (Slater 1968:233).

8. Very *Sókin* Jokes

1. Lesbianism seems to be a taboo theme in Greece, for with the exception of one well-known woman entertainer who is widely considered to be gay, very few women are described as lesbians. The spring of 1977 witnessed the first public rally in support of the gay liberation movement in Greece, but attitudes toward female homosexuality are still very negative.

2. The Greek home typically has a special room, the *salóni* (parlor) that is reserved for the entertaining of guests. The *salóni* is usually perceived as the male part of the house. In many villages in Greece, women remain in the kitchen when their husbands or male relatives entertain male guests.

3. The mistrust of women in general and wives in particular, common to Greece and the Middle East since ancient times, is described and thoroughly analyzed in Slater (1968). The mistrust in part derives from the concept of male vulnerability through feminine betrayal.

4. See DuBoulay (1974, particularly the chapter titled "Men and Women: Their Divine Natures"). The negative attitude toward women in Greek society may ultimately be derived from ideas of ritual pollution associated with menstruation. Those ideas were widespread in the Old World, especially in the Mediterranean region. In Greece, for example, a special ceremony must be performed in the home by an Orthodox priest forty days after childbirth so that the new mother may enter the church once again. Many other taboos are placed on menstruating women (see DuBoulay 1974:102). In ancient Greece women were excluded from the sanctuary for forty days after miscarriage (Slater 1968:223). The controversial documentary film, *Kypseli: Women and Men Apart*, filmed on the island of Thira, emphasized the inequalities of the sexes in traditional Greek culture. See Allen (1978) for a complete list of available documentary films pertaining to Greece.

5. Although today the values and customs of the Sarakatsani (such as the custom in regard to the disgrace of a female family member) are in conflict with other values of urban and alien origins, they still reflect what Greek villagers describe as "the old customs," those moral atti-

tudes in family and community that one hundred years ago were general throughout Greek mountain communities (Campbell 1974:6).

6. *Paiderastia* (the spelling is from the ancient Greek and is used by Vanggaard [1972:23f] to avoid the meanings and connotations of the latinized modern term "pederasty") for the ancient Greeks was neither inverted homosexuality nor a substitute for normal heterosexual sex. Instead, especially among the Dorians, it was the means by which an older man bestowed his *areté* (manly qualities and heroism) on a younger male; the Dorian boy attained manhood through his submission (Vanggaard 1972).

7. The classical Greeks also seem to have centered their erotic interest in the buttocks (Slater 1968:47). In Greece today young men often howl with delight during movies when the camera focuses on the derriere of a woman. Their reactions are much less vocal when the camera focuses on the breasts or on other regions of the female anatomy.

According to Dover (1968:228) a favored posture in heterosexual intercourse in ancient Greece was penetration from the rear. Dover sees much of Greek sexual behavior as the result of a relationship between a dominant person and a subordinate person. The dominant male mounts the subordinate (male or female) from behind. Anthropologists, especially those who study the behavior of nonhuman primates, have observed this pattern in the sexual behavior of many of the higher primates, particularly baboons. Mounting from the rear is often only a signal of dominance, without actual sexual penetration.

8. Ancient Greek art depicted several different males as being endowed with enormous penises—for example, the gods Priapus, Pan, Hermes, and the Satyrs (see Dover 1978, illustrations). Today many statues depicting those figures, missing the phallus, can be seen in museums. The statues were defaced in some cases by early Christians, in other cases by native doctors who ground up the stone phallus and gave the powder to barren women in a potion to "impregnate" them. Frazer (1958) describes that type of imitative-magic custom.

9. The association of the fig with homosexuality is also probably of ancient origin in Greek culture, if scholars are correct in asserting that castration was also a part of Dionysian rituals. At any rate, Dionysus was associated with the fig and was effeminate (Slater 1968:268).

9. Light *Sókin* Jokes

1. See Miner (1956) for a description of the characteristic American aversion to natural bodily functions.

Glossary

Listed below are most of the Greek words used in the text. Although the words are defined in the text when they are first used, they are often used again without definition. The transliteration of the words into the Roman alphabet has been done phonetically, according to standards designed by the author, who is solely responsible for the spelling. Every Greek word of more than one syllable must have a stress mark to indicate where stress is to be placed in correct pronunciation; stress marks have been retained in the transliteration here. Beside the transliterations are the words in the Greek alphabet, with correct articles and diacritics. The definitions given are those deemed correct by usage in the jokes, according to the author.

akatália	ανατάλληλα	unfit, unsuitable
anáthema	τό ἀνάθεμα	curse, anathema
anékdota	τά ἀνέκδοτα	jokes
areté	ἡ ἀρετή	manly qualities, heroism
arhídia	τά ἀρχίδια	testicles, balls
arkoudítsa	ἡ ἀρκουδίτσα	little bear
astéia	τά ἀστεῖα	funny, humorous, or jokes
athivolés	οἱ ἀθιβολές	anecdotes (funny stories about real persons and real events); the word is most often used in Crete)
babáki	τό μπαμπάκι	cotton
bakaláos	ὁ μπακαλάος	dried codfish
baklavás	ὁ μπακλαβάς	pastry with cracked nuts and honey
bazáari	τό παζάρι	open-air market
bóbos	ὁ μπόμπος	a surname, a hairstyle, a bogeyman, the stomach of a bird
bouzoúki	τό μπουζούκι	a long mandolin; in the plural (bouzoúkia) a nightclub featuring bouzoúkia music.
brávo!	μπράβο!	Cheers! Congratulations!
bríki	τό μπρίκι	small coffee pot
cafeníon	τό καφενεῖον	coffeehouse

Glossary

dhimotikí	ἡ δημοτική	informal, popular Greek
dífranco	τό δίφραγκο	coin. worth two drachmes
dolmádes	οἱ ντολμάδες	vine leaves stuffed with rice
éklase	ἔκλασε	to break, to fart
elefrá	τά ἐλαφρά	light (in terms of weight)
éronta	ὁ ἔρωντας	wild plant from the high mountains of Crete that is brewed to make a tea
érota	ὁ ἔρωτας	love, sex
eskrá	τά αἰσχρά	dirty, nasty
éthnos	τό ἔθνος	nation or tribe, a people
fránco	τό φράγκο	coin worth one drachme
gamísi	τό γαμύσι	to fuck, to screw, to fornicate
gámos	ὁ γάμος	wedding
gígantes	οἱ γίγαντες	giant beans such as lima beans
ginéka	ἡ γυναῖκα	woman, wife
gómena	ἡ γκόμενα	sexy woman, woman used as a sex object
halváh	ὁ χαλβᾶς	sweet made of sesame and honey
Hanióporta	ἡ Χανιόπορτα	the western gate of Heraklion, Crete, that leads to the town of Hania
hazós	ὁ χαζός	dull, stupid, absentminded
heliotherapía	ἡ ἡλιοθεραπεία	sunbath
Híos (Chios)	ἡ Χίος	island of Hios, near the coast of Turkey in the eastern Aegean Sea
historía	ἡ ἱστορία	story, or funny story
hondrós	ὁ χονδρός	fat
ipokámiso	τό ὑποκάμισον	shirt
ispráktoras	ὁ εἰσπράκτορας	the money-collector and ticket-giver who accompanies the driver on the buses in Greece
kalapódi	τό καλαπόδι	shoe last
káno	(ἐγώ) κάνω	to do, to make (or first-person singular of the verb to do or to make)
kápote	κάποτε	sometime
kataífi	τό καταΐφι	oriental pastry that resembles shredded wheat
katharévusa	ἡ καθαρεύουσα	formal, educated Greek
kéntron	τό κέντρον	center
keratás	ὁ κερατάς	cuckold

kiría	ή κυρία	madam or Mrs. (married woman's title)
kólos	ὁ κῶλος	behind, backside, ass
koukiá	τά κουκιά	fava bean, broad bean, or horse bean
koutós	ὁ κουτός	stupid, foolish, silly
kséreis	(ἐσύ) ζεύρεις	second-person singular of the verb to know
kumbáre	κουμπάρε	term of address used when speaking to the kumbáros
kumbároi	οἱ κουμπάροι	plural of kumbáros
kumbáros	ὁ κουμπάρος	co-parent (godparent), wedding sponsor (best man)
líres	οἱ λίρες	gold coins (British sovereigns), worth nine hundred drachmes in 1977
loukoúmia	τά λουκούμια	Turkish delight, a sweet and sticky candy
Mágos éisai?	Μάγος εῖσαι;	So, you're a magician? (when someone has observed the obvious)
malákas	ὁ μαλάκας	man who constantly masturbates, does not properly protect his women, or is foolish and inefficient
mallí	τό μαλλί	wool, fleece
manávis	ὁ μανάβης	fruit and vegetable vendor
mandinádes	οἱ μαντινάδες	song-poems from Crete
mángas	ὁ μάγκας	tough guy, with macho qualities and very "heavy"
mánges	οἱ μάγκες	plural of mángas
mia forá,	μία φορά,	one time (standard opening phrase of many jokes)
mialó	τό μυαλό	mind, brain, intelligence
Mi hirótera!	Μή χειρότερα!	No worse! (Be careful! Watch out!)
miló	(ἐγώ) μιλῶ	to speak, to talk (or first-person singular of the verb to speak)
mizíthra	ή μιζήθρα	soft (cream) cheese
moré (re, vre)	μωρέ, ρέ, βρέ	terms of address implying that addressee is stupid or childish
mouní	τό μουνί	vagina, pussy
múntza	ή μοῦντζα	curse of great intensity delivered by gesture in which the open palm of the hand is thrust

		at the face of the person being cursed
nános	ὁ νάνος	dwarf
nay	ναί	yes
ópos to léne	ὅπως τό λένε	as they say (standard phrase, which sometimes follows "one time" as the beginning of a joke)
óra	ἡ ὥρα	hour, time
oúzo	τό οὖζο	Greek liquor served as an aperitif before meals with hors d'oeuvres
paidí	τό παιδί	child, male child
panaghía	ἡ Παναγία	Virgin Mary
papadiá	ἡ παπαδιά	priestwife
paréa	ἡ παρέα	informal friendship group, peer group, gang, company
passatémpo	τό πασατέμπο	pumpkin seeds
pénde	τό πέντε	five
períptero	τό περίπτερον	kiosk where cigarettes, newspapers, and other sundry items are sold
philótimo	τό φιλότιμον	honor, pride, self-esteem
piátsa	ἡ πιάτσα	plaza, used in Athens to refer to taxi stands, from the Italian word for plaza (piazza)
pidów	(ἐγώ) πηδῶ	to jump, to fuck, to screw
pígen-e-élla	πηγαινέλα	go-and-come, round trip
piláfi	τό πιλάφι	cooked rice pilaf
pinélo	τό πινέλο	paint brush, shaving brush, or sexual "delicacies"
po! po! po!	πώ! πώ! πώ!	exclamation (similar to "Wow!")
poneriá	ἡ πονηριά	cleverness, craftiness
pouláki	τό πουλάκι	little bird, penis, loved one
poularomána	ἡ πουλαρομάννα	mare's offspring, pregnant mare
poústis	ὁ πούστης	homosexual who takes woman's role
poutána	ἡ πουτάνα	whore, prostitute
poutánes	οἱ πουτάνες	plural of poutána
praktikós	ὁ πρακτικός	native doctor, empirical healer
psolí	ἡ ψωλή	penis, prick
psomí	τό ψωμί	bread
rakí (or tsikoudiá)	τό ρακί, ἡ τσικουδιά	liquor made from distilled grape squeezings (very popular in Crete)

retsína	ἡ ρετσίνα	resinated white wine
rizógala	τα ριζόγαλα	rice pudding
saríki	τό σαρίκι	black scarf with fringe worn in Crete by older men, a modified turban
skatá	τά σκατά	shit, feces
sókin	τά σόκιν	shocking, "dirty" (jokes)
soúvla	ἡ σούβλα	spit, skewer
sóvrako	τό σώβρακον	man's undergarment, underpants
stavrós	ὁ σταυρός	cross
stoupí	τό στουπί	flax, wadding
táliro	τό τάληρο	coin worth five drachmes
tavérna	ἡ ταβέρνα	restaurant featuring grilled meats, appetizers, barrel wine, and ouzo
timí	ἡ τιμή	honor, price, value
trahanás	ὁ τραχανάς	soup made with coarse flour and sour milk
tsiftetéle	τό τσιφτετέλι	belly dance (of Turkish import)
tsimboúki	τό τσιμπούκι	long-stemmed pipe, fellatio
veránda	ἡ βεράντα	open-air porch, veranda
Vláhos	ὁ βλάχος	hick, hillbilly, shepherd
vrákes	οἱ βράκες	baggy trousers worn principally in Crete and in Skiros by older, traditional men
vrómika	τά βρώμικα	dirty
Zíto!	Ζήτω!	Cheers! Hurrah!
Zo kai vasilévo!	Ζῶ καί βασιλεύω!	I'm on top of the world!

References

Aarne, Antti Amatus
  1961 *The Types of the Folktale: A Classification and Bibliography.*
       Folklore Fellows Communications No. 3. Translated and
       enlarged by Stith Thompson. Helsinki: Suomalainen
       Tiedeakatemia.
Allen, Peter S.
  1978 "Visual Anthropology in Greece: An Annotated Filmography."
       Modern Greek Society Newsletter 5, no. 2: 15–22.
Bascom, William R.
  1965 "Four Functions of Folklore." In *The Study of Folklore*, ed. A.
       Dundes. Englewood Cliffs, N.J.: Prentice-Hall.
Beckman, Petr
  1969 *Whispered Anecdotes: Humor from Behind the Iron Curtain.*
       Boulder, Colo.: Golem Press.
Benedict, Ruth
  1935 *Zuni Mythology.* 2 vols. New York: Columbia University Con-
       tributions to Anthropology, 21.
Brunvand, Jan Harold
  1960 "Sex in the Classroom." *Journal of American Folklore* 73:
       250–51.
  1968 *The Study of American Folklore.* New York: W. W. Norton.
Campbell, J. K.
  1974 *Honor, Family, and Patronage: A Study of Institutional and
       Moral Values in a Greek Mountain Community.* New York:
       Oxford University Press.
Danforth, Loring
  1976 "Humor and Status Reversal in Greek Shadow Theatre."
       Byzantine and Modern Greek Studies 2: 99–111.
Dawkins, Richard M.
  1950 *Forty-Five Stories from the Dodekanese.* Cambridge: Cam-
       bridge University Press.
  1955 *Modern Greek Folktales.* Oxford: Clarendon Press.
Dorson, Richard M.
  1970 "Foreward." In Georgios A Megas, *Folktales of Greece.*
       Chicago: University of Chicago Press.

1972   *Folklore and Folklife: An Introduction.* Chicago: University of Chicago Press.

Dover, K. J.
1978   *Greek Homosexuality.* Cambridge, Mass.: Harvard University Press.

DuBoulay, Juliette
1974   *Portrait of a Greek Mountain Village.* Oxford: Clarendon Press.

Dundes, Alan
1965   *The Study of Folklore.* Englewood Cliffs, N.J.: Prentice-Hall.
1968   "The Number Three in American Culture." In *Everyman His Way,* ed. A. Dundes. Englewood Cliffs, N.J.: Prentice-Hall.
1971   "Laughter Behind the Iron Curtain: A Sample of Rumanian Political Jokes." *Ukranian Quarterly* 27, no. 1: 50–59.

Frazer, Sir James
1958   *The Golden Bough.* New York: Macmillan.

Friedl, Ernestine
1962   *Vasilika: A Village in Modern Greece.* New York: Holt, Rinehart and Winston.
1970   "Field Work in a Greek Village." In *Women in the Field,* ed. Peggy Golde. Chicago: Aldine.

Frye, Ellen
1973   *The Marble Threshing Floor: A Collection of Greek Folksongs.* Austin: University of Texas Press.

Hall, Edward
1966   *The Hidden Dimension.* Garden City, N.Y.: Doubleday.

Halliday, William R.
1927   *Greek and Roman Folklore.* New York: Longmans, Green.

Hoffmann, Frank A.
1973   *An Analytical Survey of Anglo-American Traditional Erotica.* Bowling Green, O.: Bowling Green University Popular Press.

Hollander, Xaviera
1972   *The Happy Hooker.* New York: Dell.

Horton, Andrew
1979   "The Aristophanic Spirit in Greece Today." *The Classical Outlook* 56:54–56.

Jansen, William H.
1965   "The Esoteric-Exoteric Factor in Folklore." In *The Study of Folklore,* ed. A. Dundes. Englewood Cliffs, N.J.: Prentice-Hall.

Kazantzakis, Nikos
1958   *Zorba the Greek.* London: Faber and Faber.
1965   *Report to Greco.* New York: Simon and Schuster.

Kyriakides, Stilpon P.
1968   "The Language and Folk Culture of Modern Greece." In *Two*

Studies on Modern Greek Folklore, trans. Robert Georges and A. A. Katranides. Thessaloniki, Greece: Institute for Balkan Studies.

Lawson, John C.
1964   *Modern Greek Folklore and Ancient Greek Religion*. New York: University Books.

Lee, Dorothy D.
1946   "Greek Tales of Nastrade Hodjas." *Folklore* 52–58: 188–95.
1947   "Greek Tales of the Priest and the Priestwife." *Journal of American Folklore* 60: 163–67.
1953   "Greece." In *Cultural Patterns and Technical Change*, ed. M. Mead. Paris: UNESCO.

Legman, Gershon
1964   *The Horn Book; Studies in Erotic Folklore and Bibliography*. New Hyde Park, N.Y.: University Books.
1968   *Rationale of the Dirty Joke*. New York: Grove Press.
1975   *Rationale of the Dirty Joke: Second Series*. Wharton, N.J.: Breaking Point Press.

Lévi-Strauss, Claude
1963   *Structural Anthropology*. New York: Basic Books.
1971   *Mythologiques: L'Homme nu*. Paris: Plon.

Mead, Margaret
1975   *And Keep Your Powder Dry*. New York: William Morrow.

Megas, Georgios A.
1970   *Folktales of Greece*. Chicago: University of Chicago Press.

Miner, Horace
1956   "Body Ritual of the Nacirema." *American Anthropologist* 58: 503–07.

Myrsiades, Linda S.
1976   "The Karaghiozis Performance in Nineteenth-Century Greece." *Byzantine and Modern Greek Studies* 2: 83–97.

Nilsson, Martin
1940   *Greek Folk Religion*. Philadelphia: University of Pennsylvania Press.

Orso, Ethelyn
1976   "Current Research in Greece." *Human Mosaic* 10: 35–37.

Papas, William
1972   *Instant Greek*. Athens, Greece: Athens Publishing Center.

Polites, N. G.
1871–
   74 *Studies of the Life of the Modern Greeks.** 2 vols. Athens, Greece.
1899– *Studies on the Life and Language of the Greek People: The*
1902   *Proverbs.** 4 vols. Athens, Greece.

*Translated titles of works in modern Greek.

Randolph, Vance
1976 *Pissing in the Snow and Other Ozark Folktales.* Urbana: University of Illinois Press.
Rotunda, D. P.
1942 *Motif-Index of the Italian Novella in Prose.* Bloomington: Indiana University Press.
Slater, Philip E.
1968 *The Glory of Hera.* Boston: Beacon Press.
Thompson, Stith
1946 *The Folktale.* New York: Holt, Rinehart and Winston.
1955–
58 *Motif-Index of Folk Literature.* 6 vols. Copenhagen and Bloomington: Indiana University Press.
Vanggaard, Thorkil
1972 *Phallós.* New York: International Universities Press.

Suggested Readings

Blum, Richard, and Blum, Eva
1970 *The Dangerous Hour: The Lore and Culture of Crisis and Mystery in Rural Greece.* New York: Charles Scribner's Sons.
Campbell, J. K.
1974 *Honor, Family, and Patronage: A Study of Institutional and Moral Values in a Greek Mountain Community.* New York: Oxford University Press.
Durell, Lawrence
1951 *Bitter Lemons.* London: Faber and Faber.
Kazantzakis, Nikos.
1956 *Freedom and Death.* London: Faber and Faber.
1958 *Zorba the Greek.* London: Faber and Faber.
1965 *Report to Greco.* New York: Simon and Schuster.
Lee, C. P.
1957 *Athenian Adventure.* New York: Alfred A. Knopf.
Miller, Henry
1941 *The Colossus of Maroussi.* New York: New Directions.
Sanders, Irwin T.
1964 *Rainbow in the Rock.* Cambridge, Mass.: Harvard University Press.